Communication

Communication

An Introduction

Karl Erik Rosengren

SAGE Publications
London • Thousand Oaks • New Delhi

First published 2000

SAGE Publications Ltd
6 Bonhill Street
London EC2A 4PU

SAGE Publications Inc.
2455 Teller Road
Thousand Oaks, California 91320

SAGE Publications India Pvt Ltd
32, M-Block Market
Greater Kailash – I
New Delhi 110 048

British Library Cataloguing in Publication data

A catalogue record for this book is available
from the British Library

ISBN 0 8039 7836 7
ISBN 0 8039 7837 5 (pbk)

Library of Congress catalog card number 99–072931

Typeset by Keystroke, Jacaranda Lodge, Wolverhampton
Printed in Great Britain by The Cromwell Press, Trowbridge, Wiltshire

Contents

List of Figures   ix
Preface   xi

PART ONE: INTRODUCTION   1

1 Communication: Elusive Phenomenon, Emergent Discipline   1

   1.1   On communication   1
   1.2   On science and scholarship   2
       1.2.1 Concepts and terms, types and typologies   2
       1.2.2 Typologies of science and scholarship   3
   1.3   On society and individuals   5
   1.4   Four basic approaches in the humanities and social
        sciences   8
   1.5   The cube of humanities and social sciences   10
   1.6   Communication studies located   16
   1.7   Three different perspectives on communication studies   17
   1.8   Theories, models and data   18
   1.9   Theories and models in three traditions of communication
        research   20
       1.9.1 Uses and gratifications research   21
       1.9.2 Lifestyle research   21
       1.9.3 Reception analysis   22
  1.10   The study of communication: an historical perspective   23
  1.11   On the rest of the book   25

**PART TWO: FORMS AND FUNCTIONS OF
COMMUNICATION**   27

2 Forms and Levels of Communication: Some Elementary
   Distinctions   27

   2.1   A communicating animal   27
       2.1.1 On our history   27
       2.1.2 On signs, symptoms and symbols   29
       2.1.3 On codes and languages   30
       2.1.4 On human language   33
   2.2   Interaction and communication   35

2.3   Forms of communication   38
       2.3.1   Verbal and non-verbal communication   38
       2.3.2   Mediated communication   40
       2.3.3   On the number of human languages   41
       2.3.4   From writing to printing to computing   42
2.4   Functions and acts of human communication   44
2.5   Levels of communication   46
2.6   Patterns of communication   48
2.7   Communication between levels   51

3 Culture and Society, Media and Communication   53

3.1   The human group regarded as a system of three systems   53
3.2   The value system of society   54
3.3   Socialization   58
       3.3.1   Introduction   58
       3.3.2   The meaning of meaning   59
       3.3.3   Agents of socialization   60
3.4   Agency and structure   61
3.5   Continuity and change   65
       3.5.1   The rate of societal change   65
       3.5.2   Indicators of societal change and continuity   66

PART THREE: LEVELS OF COMMUNICATION   70

4 Individual Communication: Intrapersonal, Interpersonal
   and Group Communication   70

4.1   Individuals in groups and societies   70
       4.1.1   Introduction   70
       4.1.2   Factors influencing individual communication   71
4.2   Intrapersonal and interpersonal communication:
       some preliminaries   74
4.3   Interpersonal communication   78
       4.3.1   Introduction   78
       4.3.2   Individual communication differentiated   80
       4.3.3   Variation and stability in individual communication 82
       4.3.4   Taking turns and other norms of reciprocity   85
       4.3.5   Does the exception prove the rule?   86
4.4   Group communication   86
       4.4.1   Introduction   86
       4.4.2   Group structure   88
       4.4.3   Societally institutionalized groups   89
       4.4.4   Group leadership   91
       4.4.5   Socialization and the family communication climate 91
4.5   Functions of group communication   93
4.6   The strength of the weak tie   95

	4.6.1 The concept of the weak tie	95
	4.6.2 Some functions of the weak tie	96
4.7	Mediated individual and group communication	98
	4.7.1 Introduction	98
	4.7.2 Telephone communication	99
	4.7.3 Individual communication by computer	101

5 Organizational Communication — 105

5.1	Organizations, groups and networks: an introduction	105
5.2	Some historical examples of organization and organizational communication	109
5.3	Theories and models of organization and organizational communication	112
5.4	Formal and informal organizational communication	116
5.5	Models of organization	118
	5.5.1 Introduction	118
	5.5.2 Three models of organization	119
	5.5.3 'Adhocracy'	121
	5.5.4 Academic adhocracies	124
	5.5.5 Organizations in time and space	125
5.6	The climate of organizational communication	125
5.7	Organizations especially designed for communication	129
5.8	Research on innovation and diffusion	131
5.9	Organizations for furthering adoption and diffusion	135
	5.9.1 The general pattern	135
	5.9.2 Lobbying	135

6 Societal Communication, Mass Communication — 138

6.1	Types of societies, types of communication	138
6.2	A necessary precondition	140
6.3	Media of sounds and pictures	141
6.4	From society to individual and back again	143
	6.4.1 Different perspectives of time	143
	6.4.2 Gate-keeping and access	146
6.5	Homogeneity and heterogeneity	149
6.6	Individual use made of mass media: quantity and quality, causes and consequences	152
	6.6.1 The study of individual media use	152
	6.6.2 Media use among young people – how much?	153
	6.6.3 Relations between viewers and the content viewed	158
	6.6.4 Effects of television viewing	163

7 International and Intercultural Communication — 170

7.1	International and intercultural communication: an introduction	170

7.2   Ways and means of international communication   173
        7.2.1   The origins   173
        7.2.2   Migration in an historical perspective   173
7.3   High politics and international communication: a brave
        new world?   175
        7.3.1   Peace and conflict   175
        7.3.2   International propaganda   176
7.4   Levels of international and intercultural communication 178
        7.4.1   On time, space and personality   178
        7.4.2   International communication at the interpersonal level   179
        7.4.3   International communication at the organizational level 182
        7.4.4   International communication at the mass media level   184
7.5   International news: intra and extra media data   190
7.6   International popular culture   191
        7.6.1   Popular culture as innovation   191
        7.6.2   Popular music   192
7.7   Computerized international communication: the global
        village green?   196

PART FOUR: THE FUTURE OF COMMUNICATION   199

8   The Future of Communication and Communication Research   199

    8.1   Some general tendencies   199
    8.2   Scholarship and research in the area of computerized
            communication   201

References   206
Name Index   212
Subject Index   214

List of Figures

1.1	A typology of paradigms	8
1.2	A three-dimensional typology of academic disciplines	14
2.1	A communicatively-oriented typology of action and behaviour	37
2.2	Four types of basic communication patterns	49
2.3	A model of mediated communication	50
2.4	A typology of intra-level and inter-level communication	51
3.1	The Great Wheel of Culture in Society	55
3.2	A typology of relations between culture and other societal systems	57
3.3	Forms of life, ways of life and lifestyles	62
3.4	Four approaches in socialization research	64
3.5	A typology of relations between culture and other societal systems	65
3.6	The values of freedom and equality as upheld in Swedish editorials 1945–75	67
4.1	Four types of personality	77
4.2	Degrees of social distance affecting interpersonal communication	82
4.3	The Johari Window	83
4.4	A target sociogram	89
4.5	Family communication patterns	92
4.6	Robert Bales's Categories for Interaction Process Analysis	94
5.1	Three simplified models of organization	120
5.2	A realistic model of organization	122
5.3	Organizational communication climates in 50 countries	128
5.4	Processes of diffusion and adoption	132
5.5	A typology for innovators' reward systems	134
6.1	The growth and decline of literary traditions	147
6.2	Relationships between the use of various media – simultaneously and over time	155
6.3	Television viewing and listening to music among children and adolescents, 1976–81	157
6.4	Amount of TV plus VCR viewing and listening to music, 1976–90	158
6.5	TV viewing and TV relations, ages 11–21	160
6.6	Long-term stability in media preferences (beta coefficients)	162

6.7   Self-esteem and TV viewing, boys aged 11–21
          (beta coefficients)   164
6.8   Self-esteem and TV viewing, girls aged 11–21
          (beta coefficients)   165
6.9a/b   TV and VCR, violence and restlessness   167
7.1   Levels and arenas of communication   171
7.2   International diffusion of news: the assassination of
          Swedish Prime Minister Olof Palme in 1986   185
7.3a   Media maps, mental maps and real maps: girls, low TV   187
7.3b   Media maps, mental maps and real maps: boys, high TV   188
7.3c   Media maps, mental maps and real maps: media map
          of Swedish TV   189

Preface

When writing this book, I have tried to use all the good knowledge on communication I could find and remember. My debt of gratitude is therefore so large that it is impossible to acknowledge all cases of direct or indirect influence.

I have also spent four enjoyable decades in the company of leading scholars and researchers (too many to name in fact), who are active in a number of academic disciplines and are geographically located in different parts of the world. In particular, I have had the good fortune to be involved in two Swedish research programs, the *Cultural Indicators Program* and the *Media Panel Program*. In the former program, Kjell Nowak was an especially resourceful colleague. In the latter, Sven Windahl was an initiating co-director, Ulla Johnsson-Smaragdi and Inga Sonesson headed various sub-panels, and Bertil Flodin, Elias Hedinsson, Ingrid Höjerback, Gunilla Jarlbro, Thomas Johansson, Ulla Johnsson-Smaragdi, Annelis Jönsson, Fredrik Miegel and Keith Roe were graduate students who became colleagues and co-authors. I am very pleased that the MPP is now in the experienced hands of Ulla Johnsson-Smaragdi.

During the years spent with Jay Blumler and Denis McQuail as a founding co-editor of *European Journal of Communication* I learned a lot about the study of communication – and about communication between scholars.

Over the years, my family, friends, colleagues and students have taught me new things about communication, especially Peter Arvidson, Adam Babocsay, Karin Franzén, Denis McQuail, Edison Otero-Bello, Ulla Johnsson-Smaragdi, Anna Rosengren, Jörgen Rosengren, Inga Sonesson, Yvonne Waern, Lennart Weibull and Sven Windahl who read preliminary versions of parts of the manuscript, and some of them read all of it. They offered valuable comments, criticism and advice. I have tried to use it all, as best I could and as much as circumstances allowed.

Johan Albertén very patiently and efficiently turned my rough sketches and copies into computerized figures.

Special thanks go to the two editors of the book – Stephen Barr, who asked me to start writing the book and also discussed early drafts of the first chapters with me, and Julia Hall who kindly and professionally saw to it that it was finally delivered. Sarah Bury took care of the copy editing and Claire Cohen very professionally saw the book through each stage of production.

The Allmänna barnhuset, The Bank of Sweden Tercentenary Foundation, The Swedish Council for Research into the Humanities and the Social

Sciences, The Swedish Council for Social Research, The Swedish National Board of Education, the Wahlgrenska stiftelsen, as well as the Universities of Lund, Växjö, Göteborg and Wisconsin-Madison provided the economic means and the infrastructural support necessary for long-term scholarship and research.

Finally, more than four decades spent with a certain professor of the German language at the University of Lund have no doubt left their traces – in this book also.

Thank you.

Karl Erik Rosengren
Lund, April 1999

PART ONE
INTRODUCTION

1
Communication: Elusive Phenomenon, Emergent Discipline

1.1 On communication

The word 'communicate' is historically related to the word 'common'. It stems from the Latin verb *communicare*, which means 'to share', 'to make common', and which in turn is related to the Latin word for common: *communis*. When we communicate, we make things common. We thus increase our shared knowledge, our 'common sense' – the basic precondition for all community.

Shared knowledge, of course, may sometimes also include knowledge about conflicting views and interests. It may thus lead to conflict rather than to community. In addition, conflicting parties also need to communicate with each other. Sometimes continued communication may make them agree to disagree – an often very productive outcome, characterizing, for instance, all democracies.

Communication may take place between units of very different size and complexity. It may occur between and within individuals, groups, organizations, social classes, nations, countries and regions of the world. Obviously, the character of communication varies with the size and complexity of the communicating units (see section 4.1 below). The distance in space and time between the communicating units is also very important.

Over the millennia, human beings have used various media to communicate in space and time: wood and stone, parchment and paper; fire, smoke, flags and semaphors; electricity and electro-magnetic waves. As new media for communication have been created, the old ones have become specialized, but none have been completely abandoned. We still write in both wood and stone. Nor did radio disappear when television was invented. Instead, it became a specialized medium: light music, noisy commercials and fast information in commercially-oriented radio; in public service-oriented radio, classical music and serious fiction, as well as political, economic and cultural analyses.

Although communication media have changed drastically as centuries have passed by, communication shows some basic characteristics common to all times, regardless of the size and complexity of the communicating units, and regardless of the distance in time and space between them. Communication is thus a phenomenon basic to all human beings and to all things human. Indeed, in a sense it is common to all living beings.

All animals communicate in one way or another, within their own species and with animals of different species, sometimes including *homo sapiens*, the only species of man extant today (see section 2.1.1). Plants may also be said to communicate. Think, for instance, of the way flowers attract bees and other insects. Plants may even be said to communicate with other plants; they may produce stuff attracting other plants, which in their turn have something valuable to offer to the first type of plant. Most of us would hesitate, however, to regard this as communication in the sense in which human beings communicate with each other.

Later on, we will define the concept of communication more precisely, in a way which will allow us to differentiate between various kinds of communication (see sections 2.2 and 2.3). For the time being we will stay with the common-sense meaning of the term, realizing that communication is a very basic phenomenon indeed. It should be mentioned, however, that this is a book about communication by means of signs and symbols. It is not a book about communications in the sense of the transportation of goods or people, although both the production and transportation of goods tend to be accompanied by communication by means of signs and symbols – as does, of course, the transportation of people.

This book is about the systematic, scholarly and scientific study of *communication by means of signs and symbols* in general, and of human communication in particular. Before turning to the study of communication, however, we will briefly discuss the following:

* the general character of science and scholarship (section 1.2);
* the general relations between society and the individual (section 1.3);
* four approaches in the humanities and social science (section 1.4); and
* the general relations between communication studies and other academic disciplines (section 1.5).

1.2 On science and scholarship

1.2.1 Concepts and terms, types and typologies

Human beings are learning beings. In many different ways we are learning all the time – any number of skills, capacities and knowledge. The process of learning is often haphazard, and as a rule is not very systematic, but in order to result in really new knowledge for other individuals, the learning process has to be systematic. There are only two basic instruments for gaining new knowledge – reason and experience – and both science and scholarship have to use these instruments in combination.

In order to understand and explain a given aspect of the world surrounding us, the *world of phenomena* – all those buzzing, blooming, overwhelming things out there which we call reality and which all the time we experience with our senses and try to understand by our reason – we need *concepts*. To understand any phenomenon of the world we must first conceptualize it.

To conceptualize is to make distinctions, and distinctions have to be made along some dimension or other: some important aspect of an otherwise bewildering world of phenomena. We must be able to make distinctions between light and darkness, earth and water, man and woman and so on, in never-ending processes of conceptualization which all of us must engage in. Then we also need names for our concepts. That is, we need a great number of (more or less technical) *terms*.

In everyday parlance, we do not always distinguish between *phenomena*, *concepts* and *terms*. Sometimes, it may be quite difficult to do so. In scientific and scholarly activities, however, it is absolutely mandatory.

When we have made distinctions along a number of dimensions, as a rule, another problem will announce itself. One way or another we need to combine the various dimensions so that a given phenomenon can be characterized along more than one dimension at a time. We must be able to distinguish not only between men and women, young and old, but also between young men and old women etc. What we need is a *typology*, and the corresponding *terminology*.

A typology is an instrument for classification. All typologies build on a number of basic dimensions which, when combined, result in a space of ideas and concepts, a 'conceptual space' in terms of which the phenomena under study may be located – classified – in a meaningful way, so that they can be better understood. This process is facilitated if we also manage to create a good terminology, corresponding to the basic dimensions of the typology at hand.

To create good typologies and corresponding terminologies is no easy thing to do. Human beings have been busy with the task since the beginning of humankind, in various ways ordering plants, animals, minerals, diseases and so on (see Box 1.1). In Antiquity, Aristotle (384–322 BC) presented the basic principles for classification. But it was only some 2,000 years later that Linnaeus (1707–78) presented the typologies for plants and animals which still form the basis for the generally accepted terminology in those areas.

1.2.2 Typologies of science and scholarship

During the last century, a number of typologies for scientific and scholarly activities have been presented by philosophers, scholars and scientists from

---

BOX 1.1 'LET THERE BE LIGHT'

'In the beginning God created the heavens and the earth. The earth was a vast waste, darkness covered the deep, and the spirit of God hovered over the surface of the water. God said, "Let there be light", and there was light; and God saw the light was good, and he separated light from darkness. He called the light day, and the darkness night. So evening came; it was the first day. . . .

'Then God said, "Let us make human beings in our image, after our likeness, to have dominion over the fish in the sea, the birds of the air, the cattle, all wild animals on land, and everything that creeps on the earth."

God created human beings in his own image: in the image of God he created them.

God blessed them and said to them, "Be fruitful and increase, fill the earth and subdue it, have dominion over the fish in the sea, the birds of the air, and every living thing that moves on the earth." . . .

'So it was, and God saw all that he had made, and it was very good. Evening came, and morning came, the sixth day.

'Thus the heavens and the earth and everything in them were completed.'

From: *The Revised English Bible* (1990) Cambridge: Cambridge University Press.

---

various disciplines. What is the difference between science and scholarship, then?

One difference, of course, is based on the *subject matter of study*. Classical science is the study of *nature* in the widest sense of the word – all forms of dead and living matter. In a number of natural sciences, human beings are studied primarily from biological, bio-chemical, medical etc. perspectives, much as all other living beings are studied. Scholarship, on the other hand, is the study of specifically *human matters*: human ideas, human action, human artefacts, human history.

Another difference is the *general approach* used by science and scholarship. In simple terms, it could be said that scholarship tends to be particularizing (or idiographic); science, generalizing (or nomothetic). Both approaches use specific hypotheses and general theories, but in rather different ways. Generalizing science is interested in testing hypotheses and theories by means of empirical data, with a view to arriving at evermore general hypotheses and theories *explaining* the phenomena under study in terms of causes and effects. Classic, particularizing scholarship, on the other hand, is less interested in testing hypotheses and theories, but rather in using them as tools, interpretative devices for *understanding* the concrete case under study in terms of intentions and goals – intentions and goals fulfilled and achieved or failed and missed.

Related to these basic differences between the two ways of gaining knowledge is their way of looking at human beings. Particularizing scholarship tends to look at the individual as a willing and acting *subject*. Generalizing science tends to look at individuals as *objects* of strong forces which – from within and from outside – determine their behaviour. Particularizing scholarship may thus be said to focus *intentions and consequences*; generalizing science, *causes and effects*.

During the last 150 years or so, there has been a tendency in the study of human beings and all things human to develop approaches that are strongly influenced by natural science. Psychology is perhaps the best example of this tendency, but also in sociology there have been strong tendencies towards approaches used in natural sciences. As so often happens, such tendencies have been met with counter-tendencies, various types of reaction. Thus during the last few decades, there has been a strong reaction towards regarding the natural sciences as ideal models when it comes to the study of human phenomena. More humanistically oriented types of psychology and sociology have appeared or re-appeared. (At the same time, however, linguistics has become a highly formalized science, using logical models as basic tools of analysis.)

Ultimate truth – complete explanation and full understanding – will never be reached. New theories and hypotheses always have to be tested, and in the long run, many theories will be forsaken for lack of empirical support. But meanwhile, surviving hypotheses and theories may be used – by generalizing science and particularizing scholarship, by political leaders and social critics alike – to explain the world in which we live, to try to understand and interpret specific phenomena at the individual and societal level. (In the special case, of course, we often complement available scholarly and scientific knowledge with our own, personal knowledge about particular circumstances pertaining to the case at hand.)

In the process of creating new knowledge, be it scholarly or scientific, it is absolutely mandatory to have good and easy access to previous knowledge in the area of study. We thus need to store our knowledge in ways which make it accessable to ourselves, and to colleagues in different disciplines, all over the world. This is a problem which has been with human beings from the very beginning, but over the last 50 years or so computerization has offered increasingly powerful ways of storing knowledge, be it scholarly or scientific (see Box 1.2).

1.3 On society and individuals

Beside the distinctions between scholarship and science mentioned above, there is another important distinction to be made: that between different ways of regarding society. In the humanities as well as in the behavioural and social sciences there are two main ways of regarding society: as characterized primarily by *conflict*, or primarily by *consensus*. Adherents of the former view hold that all societies are at bottom characterized by conflict, often between classes of people located at different positions within the overall societal

BOX 1.2 FROM SCROLLS TO SEARCH ENGINES – ON THE STORAGE OF KNOWLEDGE

There are a number of ways of storing knowledge:

- in your own brain;
- in other people's brains;
- on wood and stones, by way of tombs, monuments, etc.;
- on walls and hoardings (bills, posters, placards, graffiti) etc.;
- on a scrap of paper;
- in a notebook;
- in a newspaper;
- in a magazine;
- in a journal;
- in a book;
- in a library;
- on a computer.

All of them are good ways, but good for different purposes, for different people, in different situations. There are different criteria for evaluating ways of storing knowledge. Two very important criteria are the *accessability of the knowledge stored* and the *permanence of storage*.

On the whole, the best way of storing knowledge is in a well-organized library of books, journals and newspapers. For scholarly purposes, of course, what is needed is a good university library, backed up by a good national library. Already, thousands of years ago, the empires of Babylon and Mesopotamia had their national libraries of parchment book rolls, so-called *scrolls*. The first large university library was in Alexandria in Egypt, which is said to have housed hundreds of thousands of scrolls. Unfortunately, it was destroyed in a great fire during the first century AD.

Today, most countries have a more or less well developed, more or less nation-wide library system, including the 'national library' of each country. For example:

- the *Library of Congress* in Washington (some 25 million books);
- the *British Library* in London (more than 20 million books);
- *Le Bibliothèque National* in Paris (more than 10 million books).

The catalogues of most good libraries are now computerized, and so are many *bibliographies*, listings of books, journals and newspapers in different fields of knowledge, from different parts of the world. All good libraries offer a number of bibliographies, and also service desks which, as a rule, are staffed by very knowledgeable and friendly librarians.

Increasingly often, however, new knowledge is stored directly on computers, and only later does this knowledge reach the print media of newspapers, journals, books, etc. In addition, many old, classical texts have now been transferred to computers. Many computerized bibliographies and library catalogues can also be accessed on the Internet (see sections 2.3.4, 4.7.3, 7.7).

continued

To find knowledge on the web, one needs what is called a *search engine*. There are a number of such search engines, often having rather fancy names. Some powerful ones are *Altavisa, Excite, Hotbot, Infoseek, Lycos, Yahoo*. A recent guide to the use of such search engines is: A. and E. Glossbrenner (1999) *Search Engines for the World Wide Web*. Berkeley, CA: Peachpit Press.

structure. Adherents of the latter view do not deny the existence of societal conflicts, of course, but maintain that in order to exist, in spite of sometimes very serious conflicts, all societies must be characterized by an overriding consensus about at least some basic values and what may be called a fair distribution of those values within the population.

These two basic ways of regarding society may be combined with each one of the two basic ways of regarding human beings: the scientific perspective and the scholarly perspective. We thus get a typology for humanistic scholarship and social science in general, expressed in terms of a fourfold table (see Figure 1.1).

BOX 1.3 ON THE TWO WORDS, 'SOCIAL' AND 'SOCIETAL'

The two words 'social' and 'societal' are often used vaguely and somewhat indiscriminately, but in this book the word 'social' will be used primarily to denote 'phenomena governed by mutual expectations between at least two individuals or groups of individuals', and the word 'societal' will be used primarily to denote 'phenomena pertaining to some aspect of (human) societies and/or existing at the level of society, as distinct from phenomena existing at the individual, group or organizational levels'.

A point of discussion is whether and to what extent, when used in connection with animals and animal phenomena, plants and plant phenomena, the terms 'social' and 'societal' have a meaning basically different from the one used in connection with human phenomena.

The typology was first presented about two decades ago by an Anglo-American team of sociologists, Gibson Burrell and Gareth Morgan, in a book about sociological 'paradigms' (roughly: traditions of scholarship and science). Discussing a number of more specific dimensions, Burrell and Morgan found that those specific dimensions may quite efficiently be summarized in terms of two very basic and general dimensions: assumptions about society, and assumptions about science and scholarship. Their typology (hereafter B&M typology) is presented in Figure 1.1 in somewhat revised form. It is highly relevant when trying to understand different traditions within the study of communication. In terms of the two concepts discussed in Box 1.3 – *social* and *societal* – the left hand side of the typology represents a *social* perspective; the right hand side a *societal* perspective.

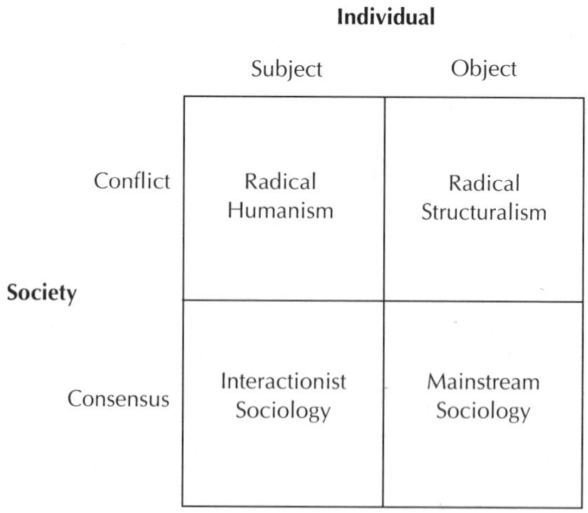

Individual

	Subject	Object

FIGURE 1.1   A typology of paradigms (*source*: Burrell and Morgan, 1979)

In the following chapters with a slight revision of Burrell and Morgan's original terminology, the two orientations towards science and scholarship will be called 'Subjectivistic' and 'Objectivistic' respectively (roughly corresponding to, but not entirely coinciding with, the distinction between scholarship and science discussed above). The two orientations towards society are called 'radical change' and 'regulation', respectively. With another slight change in terminology, the four approaches defined by the typology have here been named 'radical structuralism', 'radical humanism', 'functionalism' and the 'interpretative approach', respectively.

1.4 Four basic approaches in the humanities and social sciences

What we see depends on where we stand. Our perspective varies with our location. Obviously, our ways of regarding any society and its communicative systems will be strongly dependent upon where in the typology we are located when creating or using new knowledge in order to better describe, understand and/or explain some communicative phenomenon or other. There is considerable disagreement in both humanistic scholarship and social science as to which approach is considered to be the most preferable one. Also, the relative strength of the four different orientations as represented among scholars and scientists varies considerably over time. With some simplification it could be said that when in the 1950s, after the disruption of the Second World War, modern communication research was established, 'functionalism' clearly dominated the humanities and the social sciences. The other three orientations were rather weakly represented (although by no means non-existent). 'Functionalism' – the consensus-oriented, objectivistic perspective – was thus leading the field.

In the late 1960s and early 1970s, the divide between conflict and consensus orientation gradually emerged as an important dimension. A Marx-inspired, conflict-oriented perspective grew in strength, and for some 15 or 20 years the two perspectives of 'radical structuralism' and 'radical humanism' were topical. Today, it is rather the subjectivistic/objectivistic dimension which characterizes the scientific and scholarly debates – in the humanities and the social sciences at large, and also in communication studies. It is easy to understand why. There are both push and pull reasons.

Because of long-term, global political and intellectual change, the radical schools in the upper half of the typology find themselves in a somewhat awkward situation. In 1989, Marxist socialism proved politically inviable. Intellectually, that giant of a thinker, Karl Marx (1818–83), returned to his niche among other niches in the mausoleum of the classics. In other words, during the last decade or so the horizontal divide of the typology has become less important – or, at least, less visible. Representatives of schools originally located in the upper half of the typology are less eager to bring up for discussion the dimension which once defined their very existence. Vague terms such as 'critical', 'radical' and 'left', therefore, have recently become increasingly more popular, while more precise terms such as 'Marxism' or 'Socialism' – not to mention 'Leninism' or 'Stalinism', of course – are on the wane.

Instead, interest has focused on the vertical divide, differentiating between subjectivistically and objectivistically-oriented scholarship and research. Humanistically-oriented communication scholarship – always an important tradition – has grown stronger, vitalizing the debate in a way which was beginning in the 1980s. This general development has two articulations. In the first place, the acting and willing subject, the human individual *qua* human individual, is in focus much more than previously. Secondly, a humanistic, historical, 'scholarly' perspective has grown ever stronger, a useful complement to the sometimes rather one-sided, ahistorical perspective of the behavioural and social science approaches of yesterday.

With some simplification, then, we may say that while between 1945 and 1965 the lower, right-hand corner of the B&M typology had the upper hand, between 1965 and 1985 the two upper perspectives of the B&M typology showed strong growth and vitality. During the last 10 or 15 years, however, it is rather the vertical divide of the typology which has been dominating discussion and debate. Thus the vital debates are carried on between adherents of subjectivistically and objectivistically-oriented studies (located in the left-hand and right-hand side of the typology, respectively). In somewhat vaguer and more general terms, the debates seem to be going on between, on the one hand, humanistically-oriented scholarship, on the other, behaviourally or social science-oriented research.

For the time being, no one camp may be said to have carried the day. Also, because of the growth of the whole field of communication studies and research, each one of the four main perspectives seems to be strong enough to stand out as more or less self-contained. As a result, there may well be a risk that the stimulating debates between representatives of the four main perspectives will gradually peter out, to be replaced, perhaps, by complacent self-sufficiency. A more positive outcome might be that representatives of the four different perspectives come to realize that in the final analysis, these are not mutually exclusive categories. No society is characterized by conflict or consensus alone. On the contrary. Most – not to say all – societies are characterized by both conflict and consensus. Similarly, all individuals are both subjects and objects.

Actually, the really interesting problems are often to be found when we combine the seemingly contrary alternatives of the typology. How may people who are now regarded and misused as powerless objects raise themselves, claiming the status of full subjects with corresponding rights and duties? How may a measure of consensus be created between individuals, groups and factions in conflict? How may we articulate existing conflicting interests between groups and factions for the time being characterized by superficial consensus? How may subjectively strong subjects come to realize that they may sometimes be objects of biological and societal forces far too strong for them to resist?

From both theoretical and practical perspectives, these are the really interesting and vital problems – not least to an expanding discipline of communication. In order to solve them, we must learn to apply both a con-flictual and a consensual perspective on society, at the same time regarding the individual both as an object and a subject. In the terms of Figure 1.1, when striving to understand and explain both conflict and consensus, we must try to combine a scholarly and a scientific perspective in communication studies. That is no easy thing to do. A practical solution may well be to apply different perspectives during different phases of our studies. Here one suggestion may be as good as another. There is no doubt, however, that these are stimulating days for those interested in the study of communication.

In the following section, we shall widen the argument from the study of communication to a general overview of scholarly and scientific research in both the humanities and the social sciences.

1.5 The cube of humanities and social sciences

A basic dimension when trying to grasp the intricate relationships existing between academic disciplines is the degree of complexity or organization of the phenomena under study, from the level of atoms to molecules, to cells and organs, organisms and individuals, groups and societies. All empirical disciplines may be ordered along this dimension, with physics at one end, followed by chemistry, biology, psychology and sociology. The number of levels is arbitrary, but five levels probably represent a minimum, thus:

* sociology;
* psychology;

- biology;
- chemistry;
- physics.

The list may be extended downwards and upwards, of course, to include the sub-atomic world, as well as a level sometimes called the 'World System Level' (see Box 1.4, and also Chapter 7, on international communication). In addition, a number of intermediary levels could be inserted, for instance, social psychology between sociology and psychology (remembering that there are two rather different traditions of social psychology: the psychologically-oriented social psychology, and the sociologically-oriented social psychology).

BOX 1.4 WHAT IS A SYSTEM?

A system is composed of a number of different units or elements. These elements are related to each other within a more or less permanent structure. This structure governs a number of processes going on within the system. In turn, the processes are continually affecting the structure. As the processes change, the structure tends to change gradually. The 'World System' is a very complex system, and so is the human body. A small group of human beings may turn out to be a quite complex system too (see section 4.4).

The number of levels, then, is a matter of convention, and the names of the five levels must be understood in a very general sense. And yet the dimension itself is almost self-evident. At each level of the dimension, important 'emergent phenomena' appear – phenomena which are not to be found at the level below and which make each level different from the ones below and above. Molecules are phenomena of a different order from atoms, just as cells are different from molecules, organs from cells, and so on.

Our next dimension is much less self-evident. Indeed, it is not even a dimension in the sense of the former one. It applies primarily to some humanistic and social science disciplines, and it builds on a small number of basic values: truth and beauty, righteousness and holiness, utility and efficiency (see section 3.2). These are values which have followed man from the very beginning. They were discussed by the philosophers of Antiquity in terms such as *Logos* and *Ethos*, *Pathos* and *Praxis*. Over the centuries, they were celebrated by philosophers and poets from Plato and Aristotle to Goethe and Schiller, Keats and Shelley and their latter-day colleagues. They are also carefully heeded in present-day public relations campaigns. Around these few basic values have grown a small number of very basic societal institutions found in all human societies. (Institutions in this sense of the word are more or less standardized, more or less accepted, or even prescribed, ways of solving general problems facing individuals, groups, organizations and societies when trying to honour one or more of the basic values mentioned above.)

As our societies have become ever more complex, such basic societal institutions have gradually become ever more *differentiated from each other*: religion and law, politics and economy, art and literature, science and scholarship, etc., each one developing its own set of norms and mores, telling us (sometimes in a very detailed way) how to feel, think and act in order to realize the basic values defining the specific institution. And as time has passed by, each one of these basic institutions has also become more *internally differentiated*, more institutionally developed (think of the many institutions within the economic sector, for instance) ranging from, say, small local shops to world-wide conglomerates. Each one of the sectors also has an academic superstructure of its own: theology, political science, economics, law, aesthetics, etc. It is therefore obvious that the institutional dimension is basic indeed when we wish to build a typology for scholarship and science. For our present purposes, let the typology comprise five large institutions: economics, religion, law, politics, culture (in the sense of art, literature, etc.).

Combining the institutional dimension with the levels dimension, we might produce a two-dimensional typology for scholarly and scientific disciplines. As a rule, since it admits simultaneously noting two different types of distinction, a two-dimensional typology is much to be preferred to a one-dimensional one. But two dimensions do not always suffice when trying properly to order and understand some aspect of reality – in this case the various disciplines to be found within the humanities and the social sciences. A moment's reflection is enough to realize that we cannot meaningfully differentiate between all humanistic and social science disciplines within our emerging typology. We need at least one more dimension.

A third basic dimension builds on a number of only apparently disparate societal phenomena, all of which have something to do with control and communication: language, education, mass communication, etc. Social and societal phenomena, to be understood in terms of this dimension, are closely related to a very basic control function which in sociologese is called 'socialization' and in ordinary parlance is known as upbringing, training or education. (This is a basic phenomenon indeed, and we shall have occasion to return to it in sections 3.3 and 4.4.5).

What socialization, in this sense of the word, is all about is transferring society's basic ideas – its total culture in the most general sense – from the level of society to that of the individual, and from one generation to the next. Socialization makes us all social, makes us human. All things human pre-suppose socialization, as well as more or less legitimate rebellion against socialization. Directly or indirectly, all socialization is carried out by means of communication. Individuals, groups and organizations responsible for this special kind of communication are often called *agents of socialization*.

In modern societies there are at least eight main agents of socialization:

- the family, the peer group, the working group;
- schools, churches and law agencies;
- popular movements and the mass media.

All of them have their specific tasks. Also, all of them are informally and/or formally located within more or less hierarchically-organized groups and organizations: sometimes very large networks of relatives, business organizations, educational systems, dioceses, county government boards, courts of appeal, media conglomerates and so on.

More important in this connection, however, is that besides their specific tasks – such as working, supervising, educating, entertaining, etc. – all of them are busy with the never-ending task of socialization. As agents of socialization, all of them, of course, have to work by means of various instruments of communication and control. Another group of social phenomena along this dimension, therefore, has to do, not with control and socialization as such, but with *communicative instruments for control and socialization*: natural and artificial languages (that is, communication in its most general form) as well as all corresponding societal institutions.

One group of cognitively-oriented disciplines – for instance, philology, linguistics, cybernetics, computer science – primarily study the more or less formal characteristics of basic instruments for processes of communication and control. Another group of disciplines are oriented primarily towards the substantive and institutional aspects of processes of control and communication: pedagogy, journalistics, media and communication studies. For various reasons, the studies of some other agents of socialization, say, the family, the working group, the peer group, and large social movements and organizations, although often quite active, have not (yet) become institutionalized as academic disciplines of their own. They are thus not represented in our emerging typology (although they are often visible as specialties within various disciplines: sociology of family, psychology of organization, political communication, etc.). Some primeval instruments of socialization, on the other hand, were institutionalized very early, and so were the disciplines studying them: law and religion. They have therefore been included in the institutional dimension of our typology.

Combining the control-and-communication dimension with our two previous ones, we get a three-dimensional typology within which many (but by no means all) disciplines within the humanities and the social sciences may be located in a meaningful way (Figure 1.2). Theological disciplines, for instance, are to be found as a horizontal beam, number two from the right, within the two uppermost layers.

Simplified, the three dimensions may be regarded as representing:

• the five levels given by nature and humanity in interaction;
• the institutions created by man when building a human society;
• the institutions created to ensure the continued existence of society over time.

This three-dimensional typology represents an attempt to provide a provisional overview of the kaleidoscopic intellectual world within which the emerging discipline of communication is located. The typology as such must

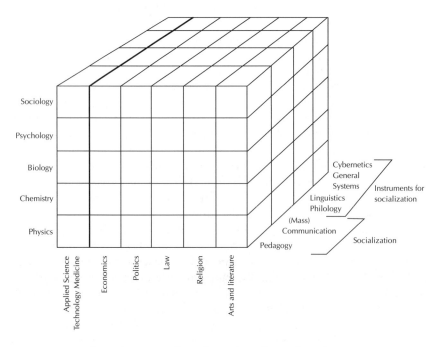

FIGURE 1.2   A three-dimensional typology of academic disciplines
(*source*: Rosengren, 1995)

be presented only with a number of reservations. The levels dimension, for instance, is much more clearly defined than are the institutional and communication-related dimensions. The most important reservation, however, concerns the fact that two basic dimensions are not included in the typology: those of time and space. (In schools and universities, of course, these dimensions are covered by a number of historically and geographically-oriented disciplines and sub-disciplines such as, say, economic history, social geography.)

In its way, this limitation is the most serious one – but also the one most easily remedied – in principle, that is. We 'only' have to add two more dimensions to our three-dimensional space. It is not easy graphically to present a five-dimensional space on a two-dimensional surface, but in logic, mathematics and statistics it is by no means unusual, of course, to deal with multi-dimensional space. The simplest way to do it in our case is to divide our cube into four new cubes, combining the two simplest possible options offered by the two new dimensions:

• Is time an integrative dimension of the phenomena under study: yes or no?
• Is space an integrative dimension of the phenomena under study: yes or no?

Yet another, different distinction to be mentioned is the one between formal and empirical disciplines. There are three large groups of formal disciplines: logic, mathematics and statistics, characterized by qualitative, quantitative and probabilistic operations, respectively. Although, explicitly or implicitly, all empirical disciplines draw on one or more of these formal disciplines, they need not concern us much here and now. See, however, section 1.8 below.

Such as it is, our three-dimensional cube is interesting enough. It does raise some intriguing questions. How many disciplines may be classified on the basis of our present typology, for instance? Disregarding science, technology and medicine (that is, the three lowest levels and the left-most vertical disk of the cube) quite a number of humanistic and social science disciplines are covered by the cube, more specifically $5 \times 4 \times 2 = 40$ disciplines. Heeding also the dimensions of time and space, we arrive at $40 \times 2 \times 2 = 160$ as a minimum. Including one intermediary level between sociology and psychology, and one level above sociology, the number is further increased, of course (224 to be more precise).

Not all of these combinations stand out as meaningful today, but on the other hand our typology does not cover all conceivable variations. The vertical slice called 'arts and literature' in Figure 1.2, for instance, covers a number of time-honoured humanistic disciplines, remaining unspecified in the figure but focusing culture in the sense of 'the fine arts': the history and theory of art, music, literature, etc. And if all languages in the communication and control dimension should have their own vertical slice (situated at right angles relative to the culture slice) the number would be much greater. In the long run, finally, the two uppermost levels of the cube – psychology and sociology – will not suffice for the study of human beings and their society.

In future societies, or perhaps one should say in another world, the level of biology will become much more central. Already today it is becoming increasingly important, both politically and economically – and, therefore, also academically. We seem to be on our way towards getting a biologically-founded politics for the whole globe taken as one ecological system. This is a phenomenon which has already drawn the interest of various classical and more recent disciplines, initiating a slow process gradually resulting in new fields of research, a number of scientific and scholarly specialties often referred to as *ecology*, an important specialty of which is human ecology (see Box 1.5).

Society is always changing, and with society, so are its scholarly and scientific disciplines, not least in the humanities and the social sciences. Our typology does not picture a static system, then, but a dynamic one. Inside the lattice-work formed by the typology we have a number of organically growing disciplines, a whole jungle of creepers, climbers and runners finding their way as best they can, in directions where they can grow – and where they are needed, perhaps. For more than a century, for instance, the modern mass media system has been establishing itself in societies of our type, and in parallel with this process there has emerged a field of research which, during the last few decades, has become an academic discipline in its own right: *communication*.

BOX 1.5 ON ECOLOGY

'The term *ecology* comes from the Greek word *oikos* (house). Significantly, it has the same Greek root as the word *economics*, from *oikonomos* (household manager). Ernst Haeckel, the German biologist who in 1868 coined the word "ecology", viewed ecology as a body of knowledge concerning the economy of nature, highlighting its roots in economics and evolutionary theory. He defined ecology as the study of all those complex interrelations referred to by Darwin as the conditions of the struggle for existence.

'Ecologists like to look at the environment as an eco-system of interlocking relationships and exchanges constituting the web of life. Populations of organisms occupying the same environment (habitat) are said to constitute a community. Together, the communities and their abiotic environments constitute an eco-system. The various eco-systems taken together constitute the eco-sphere, the largest ecological unit. Living organisms exist in the much narrower range of the biosphere, which is said to extend a few hundred feet above the land or under the sea. On its fragile film of air, water, and soil, all life is said to depend.'

From: E.F. Borgatta and M.L. Borgatta (eds) (1992) *Encyclopedia of Sociology* New York: Macmillan. p. 848.

1.6 Communication studies located

In terms of our three-dimensional typology, we find the emerging discipline of communication

- at the levels of psychology and sociology (levels dimension);
- next to disciplines dealing with other great agents of socialization and/or the basic processes of control and communication (communicative dimension);
- crossing classical, institutionally-oriented disciplines such as economics, political science, theology, etc. (institutional dimension);
- covering the dimensions of time and space, since obviously, any study of communication must heed both a temporal and a spatial perspective.

Visualized in this way, the emerging discipline of communication seems to be situated in a rather precarious position. Indeed all disciplines are – always. A certain amount of diplomacy is always needed, therefore, in inter-disciplinary relations, especially from a recent, still emerging discipline. Especially within an established or emerging discipline, however, some diplomacy is no doubt called for. One way to demonstrate this obvious truth is to point to the simple fact that in terms of our typology, not only communication but virtually all humanistic and social science disciplines may be defined in terms of at least three different perspectives:

- the levels perspective;
- the institutional perspective; and
- the communication/control perspective.

Indeed, every single cell in the large cube may be approached from each one of these three perspectives. If such an approach were to be consistently applied, the figures given above for humanistic and social science disciplines have to be trebled, of course. For instance, the little cube defined as politics–sociology–communication may be approached and understood in terms of an institutional perspective, a levels perspective and a communicative perspective. It may be defined, that is,

- as *political science*;
- as the *sociology or psychology of politics*; and
- as the *study of political communication*.

In addition, we must not forget the temporal and the spatial perspectives (political history and geo-political studies). All of these five variants of politically-oriented academic studies have their disciplines, sub-disciplines, specialties, international organizations, etc. And so it is with many or most of the little cubes in that large cube of humanities and sciences.

Three institutionally-oriented perspectives have been especially successful in their efforts at institutionalization, already reaching the status of Faculty in the medieval European university system: Theology, Law and Medicine. Other classical subjects – levels-oriented and institutionally-oriented alike – were originally lumped together within the Faculty of Philosophy, later on to be divided into new faculties, sections etc. according to levels, institutional, temporal and spatial perspectives. In more recently-founded universities, many such faculties, divisions and sub-divisions have appeared in various institutional forms, under a number of different names: schools, colleges, institutes, departments, etc. of communication. It may well be that as time goes by, the communicative perspective may grow so strong as to necessitate a communication faculty of its own within the European university system, and similar institutional status in other types of university system.

1.7 Three different perspectives on communication studies

Now, looking at the emerging discipline of communication in the light of the three perspectives discussed above – a levels perspective, an institutional perspective, and a communicative perspective – what do we see?

We have already seen that the humanities and the social sciences were first established in the light of an institutional perspective (left–right perspective of our typology). The temporal and spatial perspectives – history, geography and related subjects – were also important right from the beginning. Only

much later, in the eighteenth and nineteenth centuries, did the levels
perspective (primarily, chemistry and biology, later on psychology and
sociology) make itself increasingly strongly felt. And only during the last few
decades has the third, communicative dimension emerged as a defining factor
in its own right. As to our special case – communication – the actual
institutionalization has proceeded very differently in different countries.
Indeed, even within one and the same country very different approaches may
be found (see section 1.10).

Taking a bird's-eye view, it is obvious that communication studies
have been institutionalized in terms of all three dimensions of our typology.
Communication studies are right now being carried out as a number of
specialties within both institutionally and levels-oriented disciplines. There
are institutionally-defined chairs of Media Economy and Political Communication at some universities, and there are at least two types of levels-
oriented specialties: not only a well-established psychology of communication,
but also a well-established sociology of communication. (Sometimes one may
even find a social psychology of communication.) And first and last, but not
least, we have an increasing number of chairs, units, departments and schools
of communication and mass communication defining themselves in terms,
not of a *levels* perspective, not of an *institutional* perspective, but in terms of
a *communicative* perspective.

There is a huge process of institutionalization going on, then. This process
of institutionalization has proceeded at a different pace in different parts of
the world. In addition, the institutionalization may show quite different
characteristics in different countries and in different regions of the world.
Students in the broad fields of humanities and social science thus often have
quite interesting choices to make, choices which will indeed exert powerful
influence on their future professional lives. This book is written to help
students of communication in the broadest sense, regardless of the degree of
institutionalization of the academic subject of communication in the country
or university at hand. It will also help students of communication whose
academic backgrounds are located in either the humanities, the behavioural
sciences or the social sciences.

Our three-dimensional figure represents a special case of what is often
called a 'model'. It thus also serves to illustrate the theme of the next section
of this chapter: the role of formal models in conceptualization and theory-
building. (Another attempt at representing societal insitutions in terms of a
typology is represented by the 'Great Wheel of Culture in Society' discussed
in section 3.2 below.)

1.8 Theories, models and data

In modern behavioural and social science, and also in the humanities
(especially, perhaps in linguistics), there is a growing consensus that it is
important to make a sharp distinction between, on one hand, the *substantive*

theories of the discipline, and on the other, the *formal models* in terms of which these substantive theories are explicated and analyzed.

Substantive theory is often expressed in ordinary verbal language, using, of course, the special terminology which is always necessary to express sophisticated thought. By definition, however, the formal models are substantively empty, since they are expressed in terms of logical, mathematical or statistical language (often visualized in terms of graphic models). Two plus two makes four, whether we are adding apples or people. The same statistical model may be used to explain both the frequency of TV viewing among youngsters and crime frequency among different strata of a population.

It is considered important to let substantive theory, formal models and empirical data interact in a cumulative, spiralling process of knowledge-building. In this chapter, a simplified substantive theory of science and scholarship is being presented: a number of verbally formulated basic concepts and their interrelationships, visualized in graphic models such as a fourfold table or a three-dimensional space. As such, these graphic models, of course, are as substantively empty as are the mathematical or statistical models, and just like these, they may be used for any classificatory or causally-oriented theoretical purpose. A graphical model such as the fourfold table, for instance, is often used not only as a classificatory device, but also as a formal model for a hypothesis about a causal relationship, say, the relationship between social class and media habits.

The world of phenomena will always be that 'buzzing, blooming thing out there', and theory is at best only a dim mirror image of that blooming richness. In their clarity and unambiguity, on the other hand, the formal models call for maximum explicitness in the processes of translation between theory and model, model and data. In so doing, they create increased clarity also with respect to the process of translation between theory and reality as represented by data. It is this demand for explicitness in the process of translation which initiates the spiralling process of knowledge-building between substantive theory, formal models and empirical data. It also makes confrontation and co-operation between different traditions of research possible and meaningful.

Actually, it is precisely because of such an interplay between empirical data, substantive theory and formal models – be they logical, mathematical or statistical, be they visualized in graphical models or not – that the modern behavioural, cognitive and social sciences have developed at the pace they have during the last 50 years. The insistence on translation between theory and model, model and data – established in order to make possible theoretically relevant analysis of empirical data in terms of theoretically derived formal models – has brought about an enormous growth in highly general knowledge. Translation between theory, model and data has thus made strong generalization possible.

Now, this essential interplay between substantive theory, formal models and empirical data sometimes seems to be lacking in some emerging traditions of communication research, both in the humanities and the social sciences. More specifically, substantive theories in verbal form are directly used to interpret and explain empirical reality and data derived from that reality, without relating either theory or data to explicit, formal models. As time goes by, however, the formal models are gradually being introduced to clarify things, and this initiates a positive spiral of development, in which substantive theory, formal models and empirical data are combined to produce certified and precise knowledge. Typical examples of such a development may be found in a number of traditions as different as, say, 'diffusion of news', 'agenda-setting', 'spiral of silence', 'uses and gratifications' (see sections 1.9 and 6.4).

It would seem, then, that the challenge facing any emerging tradition of communication research in the humanities and the social sciences is precisely this: to carefully heed the distinction between substantive theory and formal models, and to start a productive interplay between empirical data and those two vehicles of scientific analysis.

If such an interplay should not come about, it is highly probable that even the initially most promising tradition of communication research will be stuck at the basically descriptive, narrative and, in the technical sense of the word, of course, anecdotal level which seems to mark the beginning of most new traditions of communication research. The absence of translation between substantive theory and formal model and, between formal model and empirical data, will prevent strong generalization. Consequently, such a tradition will remain a fad among other fads, and it will ultimately, just like all other fads, disappear. Lacking that indispensable interplay between substantive theory, formal models and empirical data, those productive processes of confrontation and co-operation between various schools of research will also be lacking. Consequently, no cumulative growth will take place. (A good start when trying to formalize so-called qualitative research might be to use the technique of 'ideal models' originally developed by the path-breaking German sociologist, Max Weber (1864–1920), and successfully applied in his innovative studies of organizations (see section 5.3).)

Some concrete examples of differential development in three different traditions of communication research will now be presented with a view to illustrate and support this line of argumentation.

1.9 Theories and models in three traditions of communication research

In this section, three examples will be given, with a view to illustrate the way in which an interplay between substantive theories, formal models and empirical data may further the intellectual development in a given tradition of communication research, while the absence of such an interplay will delay development, or even prevent it completely. The three traditions are

- uses and gratifications research;
- lifestyle-oriented research on media use; and
- reception analysis.

In order to facilitate comparison, all three examples have been drawn from mass communication research. More specifically, they concern the individual use made of mass media. Similar examples could have been chosen, of course, also from the study of individual, organizational or international communication.

Research is a very time-consuming business. The uses and gratifications tradition, which is interested in the way individuals use mass media for more or less conscious purposes, has been around for at least half a century. The roots of lifestyle-oriented mass communication research, which is interested in the way media use an integrated and integrating part of a more or less consciously chosen lifestyle, may be traced back at least to the turn of the century. The study of developments within old traditions such as these may be used to understand the situation of new traditions of research whose history covers only a decade or so, for instance, the emerging tradition of reception analysis – a recent, special development, it might be said, of the uses and gratifications tradition (see also section 6.4).

1.9.1 Uses and gratifications research

Uses and gratifications (U&G) research deals with the individual uses made of mass media, and with the gratifications derived from that use (see section 6.6.1). On the whole, it is characterized by a productive interplay between substantive theory, formal models and empirical data. Empirical data have been collected in a number of ways ranging from informal interviews, focused interviews, survey schedules and questionnaires, to laboratory experiments. These data have been analyzed in terms of formal models ranging in complexity from simple cross tabulations to advanced multivariate statistical modelling. As a result, the tradition has developed from an initial stage characterized by descriptive studies, to a typological phase, to an explanatory phase characterized by a fully-fledged interplay between substantive theory, formal models and sophisticated designs of data collection. It has now reached a stage in which detailed and precise comparative studies, over both time and space, have become possible. Altogether, this development took half a century.

1.9.2 Lifestyle research

The term 'lifestyle' was originally introduced into science and scholarship in the early twentieth century by the well-known Austrian psychologist and psychiatrist, Alfred Adler, one of the founders of modern individual psychology. Lifestyle-oriented mass communication research has its roots in classical social science as carried out in the early twentieth century by, among others, the American/Norwegian economist Thorstein Veblen and German sociologists Georg Simmel and Max Weber. Looking back on its long history, it is striking to observe how, after the first insightful, sometimes brilliant observations made by the classical scholars, communicatively-oriented lifestyle research illuminated by striking examples never really left the stage of verbal description and verbal theories. Studies based on fully-fledged combinations of substantive theories, formal models and empirical data seem to have been few and far between. This is probably one reason why lifestyle research, in spite of having a history more than twice as long as that of U&G research, needed such a long time to reach its take-off point. Only in the last two decades or so have any signs of such a development turned up, primarily in the USA, Britain, France and Germany, and also in the Scandinavian countries. Typically, this new international wave of lifestyle studies is interested in communicative phenomena – music, for instance – as an integrating element of any lifestyle. It has also managed to combine typological and other theoretical work with formal models and empirical data in terms of both quantitative and qualitative research. Once substantive theory, formal models and empirical data were combined, representatives of this kind of research were able to move relatively quickly from the original descriptive level to the explanative level (see sections 3.5, 6.6).

1.9.3 Reception analysis

Reception analysis is a relatively new tradition of audience research, focusing on the ways in which media audiences 'receive' media content of different types. It has a number of roots in the humanities and the social sciences. Two of these roots are located in disciplines which for decades have systematically applied a continuous interplay between substantive theory, formal models and empirical data: linguistics and cognitive psychology. More often than not, however, in reception analysis these formal models and substantive theories have been used primarily as rhetorical devices and/or analogies. The systematic interplay between substantive theory, formal models and empirical data seems to have been only sparingly used so far.

Instead, this specific tradition is dominated by what is called qualitative studies, based on anecdotal data and defined as unformalized, interpretative studies of the meaning of individual experience. *Understanding* communicative experiences in terms of verbal theories, rather than *explaining* them by way of new hypotheses to be tested in empirical studies based on formalized data has been the rule of the day (see section 1.2 above). Such studies tend to neglect otherwise generally accepted tests of reliability, validity and representativeness as presented in elementary methodological textbooks. What has been produced, on the other hand, is an impressive number of ingenious and insightful case studies of what is often – rather loosely – called 'interpretative communities' (see section 6.6.4).

Against the above background, it does not seem far-fetched to predict that in the near future an enterprising group of communication scholars will concentrate on the highly strategic variables to be found in the substantive theories of so-called qualitative reception analysis. Aiming at empirical and theoretical generalization, they will start the laborious work of

- *relating* the substantive theories to relevant formal models;
- *translating* the variables into empirical measurements, applicable in studies of representative samples drawn from carefully defined populations under carefully defined circumstances and
- *analyzing* the empirical data in terms of both substantive theories and formal models.

As a matter of fact, that is precisely what happened half a century ago, in the early phases of the U&G tradition. In that way, a wealth of new knowledge about media use, its causes and consequences was produced within the U&G tradition, even if it took more than half a century. In that way, U&G was saved from the fate of being just a fad among so many other, now long forgotten fads in communication studies. In principle, the same thing happened to lifestyle-oriented communication research during the last two or three decades, albeit on a much broader scene, and only after half a century of backwardness. Very probably, much the same development will take place with respect to the many interesting results currently being achieved within qualitative reception analysis. The question is who will do it, and when. Whoever does it, though, it will take time. We can only hope that it will not take half a century.

1.10 The study of communication: an historical perspective

The systematic study of communication is very old, and it started as the study of the most basic form of human communication: oral communication. Right from the beginning, the art of communication and persuasion was vital to those in power. During Antiquity, therefore, rhetorics – the study and art of eloquence – flourished in the Greek and Roman empires, in centres of learning such as Athens, Rome, Constantinople and Alexandria. In the European university system, the rhetoric tradition lived on through the Middle Ages and into the Renaissance and the Baroque periods of the sixteenth and seventeenth centuries.

When in the sixteenth century the first printed newspapers appeared, they soon attracted the interest of university scholars. In France and Germany for instance, communication studies became predominantly historical, producing learned treatises about this or that publishing house, its books, journals and newspapers, its authors, journalists and directors. In the early twentieth century there were special chairs and institutes for *Zeitungs-wissenschaft* ('newspaper studies') in Germany, and studies of mass media were also carried out within departments of history, literature, etc. Similar developments were to be found in other countries.

These early examples of communication studies were often carried out within the humanities. In the terms previously discussed in this chapter, they thus applied scholarly rather than scientific perspectives. Similar tendencies may be found in the USA, where departments of speech, originally created within the rhetorical tradition, gradually added a scientific perspective to their originally humanistic, scholarly orientation. In other cases, perspectives from the behavioural and social sciences were applied relatively early. A US pioneer of a sociological perspective was Robert Park, who in 1904 took his doctorate in Germany, with a thesis on *Masse und Publikum* ('Mass and Public'), and later on was a professor of sociology at the University of Chicago. Other efforts followed, sometimes in the wake of so-called 'moral panics' which tend to appear in connection with societal change, for instance, when new media or new kinds of media content are being introduced (such as film, television, video, jazz, punk, etc.). During and after the Second World War, the behavioural and social science perspective was strengthened in some countries, partly as a result of war efforts to resist enemy propaganda and partly to create successful propaganda for its own side.

Especially in the USA, these efforts were carried over to the university system by *political scientists* such as Harold D. Lasswell, *psychologists* such as Carl Hovland and Hadley Cantril, and *sociologists* such as Vienna-born Paul F. Lazarsfeld. At the same time, a critical, more humanistic perspective was advocated by other European *émigré* scholars in the USA, with Theodor W. Adorno, founder of the 'Frankfurt School', as a leading name. There was thus a strong European theoretical and methodological influence behind the establishment of special institutes and departments of communication which started in the USA after the Second World War, often joining forces with vocationally-oriented schools of journalism which had a somewhat longer history. These tendencies were then re-exported to Europe during the following decades, as departments or institutes of communication were established or re-established especially in north-western Europe, sometimes as follow-ups to efforts that were partly interrupted by the War. Also in other parts of the world – for instance, in Japan, Latin America and Australia – similar tendencies may be found.

As the new discipline of communication spread over the world, two large international organizations appeared (see section 7.4.3). An International Communication Association (ICA) was founded on the basis of an American Communication Association, and the International Association for Media and Communication Research (IAMCR) was founded under the auspices of the UNESCO. While today ICA does have many non-American members, its membership is still dominated by US academics. The IAMCR has a more balanced international character. It is strongly represented, for instance, in Asia, Africa and Latin America, but also in Europe and North America. Both organizations hold large international conferences, rotating between countries and continents. The ICA publishes three scholarly journals: *Journal of Communication*, *Human Communication Research*, and *Communication Theory*. For some time, the IAMCR has been planning a journal of its own.

In parallel with the establishment of international organizations for communication research and studies, a number of national organizations have been founded in countries around the globe, often with their own national publications, conferences, etc. Efforts have also been made to create a federation of such national organizations.

In terms of the cube of humanities and social sciences presented in section 1.5 above, the developments just outlined exemplify the growing importance of the third, communicative dimension of the cube. For hundreds of years, studies of communication were defined primarily in terms of a temporal perspective (as in newspaper histories), an institutional perspective (as in political communication), or a levels perspective (as in the psychology or sociology of communication). Since the Second World War, however, they are increasingly carried on within a *communicatively*-defined perspective, that is, within a discipline in its own right. Within this communicative perspective, of course, a number of different tendencies may be found, as discussed above.

1.11 On the rest of the book

The second part of the book (Chapters 2 and 3) is dedicated to the study of the form and functions of communication. Basic elements and functions of the act of communication will be introduced, as will the main relationships between the main levels at which communication may take place (the individual, group, organizational, societal and/or international levels) and the general character of the communication taking place at those different levels. Also, a brief outline of the history of communication will be given, a history which to a large extent coincides with the history of humankind and its societies. One reason why this is so is because culture, a constitutive element of human societies, is created and maintained by communication. In a similar vein, socialization, the upbringing of young humans, as well as the twin processes of *individualization* of humankind over the millennia and the *individuation* of the single individual over just a score of years, are only understandable as communicative processes (see sections 2.5 and 3.3).

Building upon the previous parts of the book, the four chapters in part three will discuss in somewhat greater detail communication at each one of the four main levels: the individual, organizational, societal and international levels. Just as in previous parts of the book, emphasis will be put on both the specificities of communication as it takes place at the different levels, and the general characteristics common to communication regardless of the level at which it takes place.

Finally, in the fourth part of the book, the future of human communication, as a general phenomenon and as a field of study, will be briefly discussed against the background of the ongoing, world-wide processes of change in various sectors of modernizing, modern and postmodern societies: the so-called 'communications revolution'.

A short bibliography of classic and contemporary books on communication science and scholarship will also be offered.

PART TWO

FORMS AND FUNCTIONS OF COMMUNICATION

2

Forms and Levels of Communication: Some Elementary Distinctions

2.1 A communicating animal

2.1.1 On our history

Biologists sort animals into a complex typology (see section 1.2.1 above), a hierarchical system of

- *phyla*, e.g., insects and *vertebrates*;
- *classes*, e.g., among vertebrates, fishes, birds and *mammals*;
- *orders*, e.g., among mammals, whales, rodents and *primates*;
- *families*, e.g., among primates, *hominids* and monkeys;
- *genera*, e.g., among hominids, *homo* and apes;
- *species*, e.g., among homo, *homo neanderthalensis* and *homo sapiens*.

The *genus* of man (*homo*), as we know ourselves today, has a history covering about two million years, an immense evolutionary process starting even two million years earlier, when a group of now extinct *hominids* rose for good on their hind legs, so that the front paws could be used for other tasks than walking around. At much the same time the brain started to grow considerably: from about 400 cm^3 to three of four times as much, craving ever-more energy. (Today, our brain accounts for 2% of our bodily weight, but consumes more than 10% of our energy intake.) In parallel with this development, our palate and tongue gradually acquired the shape it now has. We also learned to use natural tools, and, much later, to *make* tools.

(Elephants and some apes do use tools, but they do not seem to make them, although individual chimpanzees may have a 'tool-kit' of different stones, sticks, etc., the use of which they may also demonstrate to their cubs.)

The hand, the brain and tools produced for a purpose, were important steps in our development, but only with language did we become really human. Four or five million years after the first *hominids*, approximately two million years after the genus of *homo*, the species of *homo sapiens* stepped forward. That was probably about 200,000 years ago – that is, approximately 5% of the huge time-span that has passed by since the first hominids appeared (Box 2.1).

BOX 2.1 ON OUR PEDIGREE

'Descended from monkeys? My dear, let us hope that it isn't true! But if it is true, let us hope that it doesn't become widely known!'

Possibly apocryphical exlamation, sometimes ascribed to the wife of a nineteenth-century bishop of Worcester. Quoted from Jo Liska, 'Bee Dances', *Western Journal of Communication*, 57 (1953): 1–26.

'As ape mothers became more highly evolved and more capable of solicitous parental care, the survival rate of their infants *vis-à-vis* the infants of less solicitous mothers was bound to be better. . . .

'If parental care is a good thing, it will be selected for by the likelihood that the better mothers will be more apt to bring up children, and thus intensify any genetic tendency that exists in the population toward being better mothers. But increased parental care requires . . . a great IQ on the part of the mother; she cannot increase parental care if she is not intellectually up to it. . . . To express this in reverse: if one is going to have fewer offspring, one had better have a larger brain to take better care of them. That is the feedback principle in action. Each tendency works with, depends on and reinforces the other.

'In the case of primate evolution, the feedback is not just a simple A–B stimulus forward and backward between two poles. It is multipoled and circular, with many features to it instead of only two – all of them mutually reinforcing. For example, if an infant is to have a large brain, it must be given time to learn to use that brain before it has to face the world on its own. That means a long childhood. The best way to learn during childhood is to play. That means playmates, which in turn, means a group social system that provides them. But if one is to function in such a group, one must learn acceptable social behaviour. One can learn that properly only if one is intelligent. Therefore social behaviour ends up being linked with IQ (a loop back), with extended childhood (another loop), and finally with the energy investment and the parental care system which provide a brain capable of that IQ, and the entire feedback loop is complete.'

From: D.C. Johanson and M.A. Edey (1982) *Lucy. The Beginnings of Humankind*. London: Granada Publishing. pp. 329–30.

The chronology outlined above is still under discussion among the experts in the field. Also, the relationships between the various *genera* of *hominids* and between the various *species* of *homo* have by no means been definitely established, and there is still room for different classifications at these levels. In addition, the experts sometimes use more levels of classification than two, thus distinguishing, for instance, between *homo sapiens sapiens* and *homo sapiens neanderthalensis*. Furthermore, the terminology varies between different schools. In terms of the terminology used here, however, there seems to be agreement about the fact that since 30,000 to 40,000 years ago, when the species of *homo neanderthalensis* for so far unknown reasons disappeared, man (*homo sapiens*) is the only extant *species* of the *genus* of *homo*.

It is also quite clear that, genetically speaking, the differences between all human so-called 'races' represent only relatively marginal adaptations to the surroundings, produced by gradual natural selection, not by developmental leaps. That variation has been estimated to cover only about 15% of the total genetic variation within *homo sapiens*, and it has been governed mainly by spatial variation of climatic conditions. Thus about 85% of the genetic variation is common to all human so-called races. A better name for race, therefore, would perhaps be *geographical variants*. No variant has ever been absolutely pure, but there seem to be three main geographical variants: the Indo-European, African and Asian variants. International transportation and communication, of course, long ago created innumerable combinations of these three main variants. From a biological perspective, however, these processes are but short and rather insignificant moments in the very long history of humankind.

Our genetic heritage does still play an important role. But it is always tempered by the environment. The so-called *phenotype* of a given individual (the way he or she actually is at a given moment) is determined by interaction between biological heritage and environmental influences. It cannot deviate very much from its *genotype*, defined at the moment of conception. Unfavourable surroundings may prevent it from reaching its full potential, however.

2.1.2   On signs, symptoms and symbols

With *homo sapiens* a strange animal had arrived, characterized by a basic innovation in communication potential – the capacity to develop and use a very special type of sign: *symbols*.

All communication takes place by means of *signs*: phenomena signifying something other than the phenomenon itself. The science of signs is called *semiotics*. Emerging in the early twentieth century, one of the founding fathers being the American philosopher Charles S. Peirce (1839–1914), semiotics is principally associated with the disciplines of philosophy and linguistics. Although there is some disagreement on the terminology of semiotics, there is certainly agreement about the basic characteristics. A fundamental characteristic is the relation between the sign and that which it signifies. A sign which is *similar* to what it signifies is often called an *icon*. In this sense of the word traffic signs are icons. A sign which, directly or indirectly, is closely related to a different phenomenon is often called a *symptom* – yawning may be a symptom of sleepiness or boredom, while a feigned yawn is an icon imitating a symptom. If the sign is not only closely related but directly *caused* by what it signifies, it is often called an *index* or a *signal*. Signals can act as commands. For example, the warning signals of smoke or heat will make you run away from a fire. A signal thus often equals an order of sorts.

Signs such as icons, symptoms, indices and signals have a narrow relation between the sign and that which is signified: a relation of similarity or causality. When the relation between a sign and what is signified is more or less arbitrary (a convention more or less explicitly agreed upon) signs are often called *symbols*.

In relation to what they signify, animal signals may sometimes seem arbitrary or even conventional. Many animals have the capacity to signal over large distances in space, a capacity which bears witness to a well developed sense of space extending far beyond the immediate surroundings. Elephants, for instance, can signal over large distances by way of infrasound calls, and so can whales. Apes can also learn how to use a number of signals at will, (for example chimpanzees, especially the pygmy chimpanzees called *bonobos* which appear to be more closely related to humans than are other apes). *Bonobos* apes have been trained to understand and use a relatively large number of signs reproduced on cards etc., applying their meaning in various, fairly complex ways.

Animals are also able to signal *over time*, often in order to mark spatial characteristics. They mark their territory in various ways, thereby warning potential rivals for food or sexual partners that they are entering private territory.

In spite of all this however, there is widespread agreement that only human beings have brains able to produce symbols. As a rule, animal signals are caused in a standardized way by perceptions of that which they signal. Their system of symbols is closed. A perceived threat causes a signal of fear or warning.

2.1.3 On codes and languages

Signs, and especially symbols, tend to be organized in systems called *codes* or *languages*. These are systems of signs and rules for their use, relating signs (icons, indices, signals and/or symbols) to each other and to various aspects of reality. By way of codes or languages reality may be represented, understood, evaluated, explained and, sometimes, changed.

Language is man's most important tool of communication – a fantastic instrument for transferring cognitive, affective and conative (action-oriented) *information*. The concept of information is a difficult one. It is dealt with in a relatively new and rapidly developing branch of science, *information science*, the results of which – in the shape of what is commonly called Information Technology (IT) – have indeed revolutionized human communication. For our present purposes, however, we may define the concept of 'information' simply as 'knowledge'. When talking of information we also often mean 'new knowledge'.

We have an inborn capacity for language, and all human languages have some basic characteristics in common. Yet human language is always learnt; it builds primarily on conventionalized symbols organized by way of a specific grammar. There are a small number of *onomatopoeic* words (words which imitate the sound of the thing meant, for instance (Bang!, sizzle, etc.). However, the same sound is conveyed differently by different languages, and these words too are learnt by children. The cockerel's cry is rendered as 'cock-a-doodle-do' in English, as 'kikeriki' in German, as 'kukuriku' in Hungarian, as 'kakaryku' in Latvian and as 'kuckeliku' in Swedish.

Human language also has another unique characteristic. It is doubly articulated: at the level of sounds (*'phonemes'*, linguistically relevant sounds) and at the level of *morphemes* (minimal meaningful units). Words are composed of conventional combinations of phonemes building conventional morphemes.

All human languages are closely governed by intricate systems of rules, which are unknown to most users of the language and yet immediately observed when broken down. All human languages thus have a fully developed

- *phonology* (a system of rules for aspects of pronounciation: pitch etc.);
- *syntax* (a system of rules for relating the verbal symbols to each other);
- *semantics* (a system of rules for relating the verbal symbols to aspects of reality); and
- *pragmatics* (a system of rules for relating the verbal symbols to the actions of the communicants).

The rules of language are *recursive*: they may be applied to themselves, thus being able to produce a virtually infinite number of different utterances.

Over the millions of years, when some *hominids* were gradually superseded by different variants of *homo*, human language, as just described, slowly developed. Most of the time, this was a gradual process, but sometimes development took great leaps. A truly decisive phase was the change *from* a primitive code mainly built of icons, signals and indices, probably having only rudimentary semantics and syntax but a relatively well developed pragmatics, *to* a fully developed language predominantly building on verbal symbols and characterized by double articulation and highly developed semantics, syntax and pragmatics. We know that the Neanderthals buried their dead, used magic, and made stone tools. They thus seem to have had an advanced system of communication. A crucial difference between the now extinct *homo neanderthalensis* and *homo sapiens*, however, may have been that while our language builds mainly on symbols, theirs probably did not, or not to the same extent, in spite of the fact that their brain was larger than ours. The difference, then, seems to have been located in *brain structure* or *brain functions*, not in *brain size*. (Less relevant may have been the fact that the Neanderthal vocal tract seems to have been different from ours, so that their speech may well have sounded different from ours.) These are fascinating problems that are often discussed outside as well as within science and scholarship. For example, Neanderthals have been the subject of fiction (see Box 2.2).

BOX 2.2   A SCENE FROM THE DAYS OF THE NEANDERTHALS

Nil came in sight along the trail. She was moaning gently as was her habit when tired and hungry. She glanced at the little one as he clung to Fa's hair, saw that he was asleep, then went to Ha and touched him on the arm.

'Why did you leave me? You have more pictures in your head than Lok.'

Ha pointed to the water.

'I came quickly to see the log.'

'But the log has gone away.'

The three of them stood and looked at each other. . . . Now they could hear the last of the people coming along the trail. It was Mal, coming slowly and coughing every now and then. . . . He looked at the water, then at each of the people in turn, and they waited.

'I have a picture.'

He freed a hand and put it flat on his head as if confining the images that flickered there. 'Mal is not old but climbing to his mother's back. There is more water not only here but along the trail where we came. A man is wise. He makes men take a tree that has fallen and –.'

His eyes deep in their hollows turned to the people imploring them to share a picture with him. He coughed again, softly. The old woman carefully lifted her burden.

At last Ha spoke.

'I do not see this picture.'

The old man sighed and took his hand away from his head.

'Find a tree that has fallen.'

Obediently the people spread out along the water side.

From: William Golding (1955) *The Inheritors*. London: Faber & Faber Chapter 1.

The key word summarizing the difference between human communication on the one hand and communication between animals and/or plants on the other is probably *meaning*. Human communication is meaningful – it is full of meaning. Not so animal communication, and much less so plant communication, both of which are better characterized as physiological interaction with the environment. What is meaning, then? That is a big question indeed, and we shall return to it in section 3.3.2.

2.1.4   On human language

Human language as we know it today is a mainly symbolic language, accompanied by bodily icons, indices and signals (visual and aural mimicry, physiological indices or signals such as laughing, blushing or crying). Human beings can learn or be taught how to consciously produce bodily indices or signals (of, say, joy or sorrow). Conversely, few animals can be taught to behave *as if* they can understand rather complex symbolic codes, sometimes seeming to use them in quite amazing ways. It is a fact that, just as with other animal calls and cries, the beautiful songs of certain bird species are partly innate, partly learned and partly *ad hoc* original variations. But it is generally agreed that the codes or languages of animals are basically built on signals, and that those codes or languages are by and large innate and, as a rule, only to a relatively small extent learnt. This is not to deny, of course, that many animal codes are quite complicated and very efficient, for instance, the code or 'language' used by bees.

The human *voice* is shaped by the larynx, the palate, the tongue and the lips. Human *speech* is produced by the brain. It alone is capable of using the symbolic functions, by which we interpret signals from our surroundings, analyze them in spatial, temporal, causal and finalistic (intentional) terms, and evaluate them in moral and aesthetic terms of good and bad, beautiful and ugly, thus producing *meaning*.

All animals must analyze signals from the surroundings, of course, and we have already mentioned that a number of non-human animals also have very complex systems for communication: dolphins, whales, elephants and many insects, for instance. (The language of whales is even reported to show different dialects.) But only *homo sapiens* have languages based on symbols: conventionally defined signs. Only *homo sapiens* have languages based on double articulation (see above).

Yet another communicative characteristic of the human animal is that it, more than any other animal, knows and sometimes, more or less successfully, practises the art of sending out false signals or of lying. Indeed, many animals send out false messages. A mated male great tit may sometimes signal 'I'm not mated', much as certain flowers may falsely signal to insects that there is juicy nectar inside them. But downright lying presupposes consciousness. You know when you do not tell the truth – unless, of course, you are successfully practising the noble art of self-deception (see Box 2.3).

The act of lying comes naturally to all of us, from time to time. Most of us have told well-prepared lies. And then there is the socially acceptable lie. We feign pleasure at an unexpected visit although we may not actually like the visitor. When a friend becomes ill or grows old, we feel we need not always tell him how ill or old he really looks.

There is considerable variation in this way of communicating. One variant is to tell the truth by way of exaggerating its opposite. You say 'Oh, grand!' when you mean 'What a disaster!'. This is *irony*, of course. *Concealment* may be regarded as a way of passive lying, a sometimes very successful type of

BOX 2.3 ON LIARS AND LYING

On Moral Choice

'Individuals, without a doubt, have the power to influence the amount of duplicity in their lives and to shape their speech and action. They can decide to rule out deception wherever honest alternatives exist, and become much more adept at thinking up honest ways to deal with problems. They can learn to look with much greater care at the remaining choices where deception seems the only way out. . . . Finally, they can learn to beware of efforts to dupe them, and make clear their preference for honesty even in small things.

'But individuals differ greatly in their ability to carry through such changes. They differ in their knowledge of deception and its alternatives; in their desire to bring about changes; and in their understanding of what lying can do to them, either as deceiver or as deceived. Many who might be able to change the patterns of duplicity in their own lives lack any awareness of the presence of a moral problem in the first place, and thus feel no need to examine their behavior and explore the alternatives carefully. Others are beyond caring.'

From: Sissela Bok (1978) *Lying: Moral Choice in Public and Private Life*. New York: Pantheon Books. Chapter XVI, p. 243.

Some Truths about Lies and Liars

'If sender and receiver know and like each other, the way of lying becomes different from when they do not know and like each other.

Compared with truth tellers, deceivers . . . engage in greater strategic activity designed to manage information, behaviour and image.

Receiver suspicion is manifested through a combination of strategic and nonstrategic behaviour.

Liars tend to perceive suspicion when it is present.

Perceived and/or actual suspicion increases the liar's strategic behaviour.'

Adapted from: D.B. Buller and J.K. Burgoon (1996) 'Interpersonal deception theory', *Communication Theory*, 6 (3): 203–42.

Is That True?

'There are three types of lies: lies, damned lies, and statistics.'

From: Mark Twain and Charles Neider (ed.) (1959) *Autobiography*. New York: HarperPerennial Library. Part V, Chapter 1.

deception. Lying on a really grand scale, as boards and governments sometimes feel they have to do, may appear to be something else, but basically it is just lying, even if undertaken with the best of intentions. Company *advertising* and *publicity*, as well as international *propaganda*, have to be true in details but at the same time often show a rosier picture than actual reality (see sections 5.7 and 7.3.2 below). In Marxist theory, what has been called 'false consciousness' is another name for society's way of lying to itself (or, rather, for one part of society to lie to another part, thus creating 'false consciousness' among parts of the population).

There are many excuses for lying, of course:

- No harm is done.
- They have no right to know.
- It's none of their business.
- We have to lie this time, in the best interest of everybody.

There are ways and means of finding out lies, even if those ways and means are not always all that successful. Systematic inquiry undertaken by a skilled interrogator sometimes makes even the best of liars tell the truth. The lie detector, based on measurements of biological processes supposedly impossible to control, may be useful at the individual level. At the societal level, what is sometimes called 'ideological critique' aims at unmasking otherwise generally accepted societal ideology, with a view to prevent – or at least, to reduce – supposedly generally widespread 'false consciousness'.

Twenty years ago, H. Paul Grice, an English philosopher interested in communication, suggested some basic principles for human communication. When communicating, we should be *co-operative, rational* and *efficient*. More specifically, what we say should be *true, informative, relevant* and *clear*. These are good principles. Human life, however, is such that sometimes being co-operative, rational and efficient are not very good principles to follow. In war, business and love, for instance, it can be useful to lie – for both rational and emotional reasons. The sad truth is that sometimes the best solution is to be co-operative, rational and efficient by way of lying and obfuscating, talking of irrelevant things, or just muddling up the whole story.

Finally, man seems to be the only animal able to use language as an instrument for self-reflection, including also reflection on self-reflection, and reflection on the language used for self-reflection – a so-called *infinite regress*. In addition, we also know the both useful and dangerous art of self-deception, the art of combining self-reflection with lying. Human language is a unique instrument for interaction, communication and control.

2.2 Interaction and communication

Let us return for a moment to the discussion above, about plants 'communicating' with animals and with other plants. Obviously, that kind of communication is rather different from the kind of communication called human communication. What is it, more precisely, that characterizes the difference? This is an important question, because the difference tells us something about what makes human beings human.

One way to understand the difference is to reduce the definition of communication to an absolute minimum, in order later on to add elements which preferably should be included when defining something called, say, 'full human communication'. What would such a 'minimalistic' definition look like? Perhaps it should refer to the notion of 'interaction' in the narrow sense of 'mutual influence':

> some of A's processes (including behaviour) change as a result of some of B's processes (including behaviour), and *vice versa*, in at least one – and often more than one – full cycle.

This is the way plants interact with plants, plants with animals, and animals with animals. But is it communication? Most people would probably reply 'No' to that question. What, then, is the difference between interaction in the sense of 'mutual influence' and 'communication'? There are several differences and all of them stem from the basic characteristics of man. Perhaps the most important difference relates to the notion of *consciousness* or *awareness* (see section 4.2). (We disregard for the moment the fact that the degree of consciousness may vary considerably over time and between individuals.)

When human beings communicate, we know that we do so. Each one of two communicating participants is aware of the (sometimes potential) presence of the other, and of the fact that communication is occurring (or may occur). What is more, we also know that our partner in communication knows. Actually, we know that they know that we know, and so on – again in an infinite regress (luckily seldom followed up). A prime characteristic of human communication is thus *intersubjectivity*. Communication between plants is not intersubjective in that sense. Communication between animals tends to lack intersubjectivity in this sense (although many pet-owners would not agree at all, thus demonstrating a case of the so-called *'pathetic fallacy'*, the mistake of ascribing human characteristics to nature).

Another difference is the fact that human communication is basically *intentional*. When communicating, we do so more or less intentionally, with a purpose. (Even when consciously communicating against our will, we prefer to do so rather than risk the consequences of not communicating.) Communication is thus not just unintentional, more or less reflexive *behaviour*. It is conscious, willed *action* by at least two parties.

Combining the two distinctions between intentional and non-intentional, conscious and unconscious we may further differentiate our argument. This is done in Figure 2.1. The typology actually applies to all types of action and behavioural reaction, but our interest is focused, of course, on that basic type of action, individual communication.

Individual communication in the full sense of the word preferred here is found in cell 1 of the typology. The other cells offer three variants of communicative action and/or behaviour ranging from

- completely non-communicative behaviour which may, however, offer valuable information to the individual's surroundings (cell 4), to
- signals providing potentially valuable information to the surroundings (cell 2), to
- subconscious or unconscious communicative action indirectly betraying circumstances which would otherwise have been secret, and sometimes remain unnoticed by both sender and potential receivers (cell 3).

Now, granted that there are at least two parties to an act of communication, in each one of the four cells of Figure 2.1, each party to the act of communication may or may not

(a) perceive the co-communicant's communicative behaviour/action correctly;

(b) be behaving/acting in terms of one or more of the four cells of the figure.

Individual is conscious of action/behaviour

	Yes	No
Action/behaviour is intentional Yes	Communication as action 1	Communication as subconscious action 2
No	3 Bodily behaviour such as blushing, stuttering, sweating, trembling	4 Unconscious bodily behaviour such as, for instance, small facial changes

Figure 2.1 A communicative-oriented typology of action and behaviour (*source*: Rosengren, 1984)

For each single potential communicative act there are thus 2 x 2 x 4 x 4 = 64 alternatives. Communication is a phenomenon both complex and brittle, composed of several series of sometimes very subtle actions and behaviours, which as a rule are felicitous but quite often less than completely successful.

The difference between behaviour and action is basic indeed. It is related to the difference between subject and object discussed in section 1.2.2 above. As *subjects*, we are willing and acting individuals. As *objects* we are passive receivers of strong forces acting from within and from outside ourselves. A human paradox is that we are always both objects and subjects, also when we communicate. Individually willed actions by a number of knowing subjects, including acts of communication, thus tend to show sometimes quite surprising regularities, as if they were patterns otherwise found among passive objects of strong regulatory forces – say, patterns of tidal waves. Such 'tidal waves' can be seen, especially at the level of societal mass communication (see Box 6.1 on pp. 147–8).

Conversely, we communicate also when, as helpless prisoners of our physiology, we blush for shame or sweat for nervousness. That is why it has been maintained that as human beings we 'cannot not communicate'. That is why the full study of man and of human society must always include both an objectivistic and a subjectivistic perspective, and must always include both science and scholarship. That is also why the study of human communication is such a fascinating subject.

Now, let us summarize our attempts at defining the concept of communication. We have discussed the concept in terms of what might be called a *hierarchical* or *stepwise* definition of communication. Starting with a broad definition of communication as interaction, we gradually added the conditions that are necessary to establish full human communication, thus:

- *interaction* (i.e., mutual influence), which is both
- *intersubjective* (i.e., mutually conscious), and
- *intentional, purposive*, and which is carried out by means of
- *a system of signs*, mostly building on
- *a system of verbal symbols*, characterized by
- *double articulation*, and in its turn building on fully developed systems of
- *phonology, syntax, semantics* and *pragmatics*.

This gradualistic or hierarchical definition of human communication may be used to differentiate between a number of different forms and types of communication. However, since in this connection we are using the most specific sense of the word, communication is *intersubjective, purposive interaction by means of doubly articulated human language based on symbols*.

In the following section we shall discuss various basic forms of communication thus understood. We shall also discuss communicative processes which do not satisfy all seven conditions included in the above definition.

2.3 Forms of communication

2.3.1 *Verbal and non-verbal communication*

As already mentioned, human communication occurs in a variety of different forms, differentiated from each other along a number of dimensions. The most basic among these dimensions is no doubt *verbal* versus *non-verbal* communication (see section 2.1 above). As the capacity to use symbols developed among the first human beings, so did verbal language. Out of signals and icons made up of gestures, facial expressions, grunts and cries, there gradually grew a language of verbal symbols, building on words and simple sentences based on double articulation – an immense feat which no doubt took many millennia. The process did not imply, however, that non-verbal communication was reduced in absolute terms. In parallel with verbal communication, non-verbal communication remained, and it is still an important part of human communication.

There are several types of non-verbal communication, the oldest being the bodily signals of affects (emotions, feelings, moods) which very probably formed an important part in the genesis of human language. Joy and anger, fear, surprise, disappointment etc., are still signalled by all of us – sometimes even without our being aware of the fact – in ways which probably have much in common with the ways our early forefathers signalled them (see Box 2.4; note the high confidence in verbal communication expressed by the scholar!).

Other forms of non-verbal communication include dance and music, as well as more directly representing and imitative arts such as miming, drawing, painting, sculpture and architecture. All of these arts seem to be about as old

---

BOX 2.4 PROFESSOR ROGER BROWN ON NONVERBAL COMMUNICATION

'Nonverbal communication is communication by facial expression, hands, feet, body, and vocal quality. Without doubt, the nonverbal channels are continuously attended to and do communicate information – primarily affective in quality and connected with personal relationships. An inappropriate interpretation of results that combine verbal messages and nonverbal cues in various ways has led some investigators to assert that the nonverbal channel is more informative than the verbal either in general or with respect to affect. That cannot be the case, because language is a universal medium able to express anything that can be thought or felt. However, nonverbal channels do have a special relationship with affect or feeling, because they are likely to "leak" information deliberately concealed in the controllable verbal channel. Channels of communication can be ranked in a hierarchy from high controllability (verbal) to low controllability or highly leaky (vocal quality). In general, when channels are congruent . . . the more controllable the channel, the more informative it is. But when messages are incongruent, because of a deception effort, the leakier, or less controllable channels are the more informative.

'It is an ancient question whether the expressions of emotions in the face is entirely culturally determined or is, as Charles Darwin thought, to some extent universal. Ekman and Friesen and their associates found the key to an answer in distinguishing display rules (cultural) from the natural expressions the face shows when unobserved. For six emotions – happiness, fear, anger, sadness, disgust, and surprise – universality of facial expression has been established by showing that members of cultures having no visual contact can correctly recognize one another's expressions.'

From: R. Brown (1986) *Social Psychology* (2nd edn). New York and London: The Free Press. pp. 521f.

as man. Actually, their elementary forms must be even older, since the imitative, representing function of gesture and mimics must have been used for tens of millennia before human symbolic language with highly specific articulation developed. Indeed, the most ancient musical instrument (a flute) to be discovered to date is estimated to be between 40,000 and 70,000 years old, which is older than the estimated age of human speech. (Such estimates vary quite a lot, however.) The art of *conserving* the mimetic, representative function in lasting material must be younger, of course. However, as early as some 30,000 years ago, tools of bone carried simple, representative carvings (icons and/or symbols), and it is probable that similar, even older findings will turn up. Also, small statues of animals and human beings have been found from about the same time. The function of such artefacts may have been decorative, expressive or magical, or a mix of all these, but in order to fulfil these functions, they must first have fulfilled the representative function. They must have been communicating some important meaning. In a similar way, non-verbal arts such as dance, painting and music are still used to communicate meaning – sometimes, perhaps, in more powerful ways than is possible by verbal communication.

Another special case of very powerful non-verbal communication is represented by the three formal languages developed by man: *logic, mathematics* and *statistics*, used to represent and analyze *qualitative, quantitative* and *probabilistic* phenomena and relationships, respectively. These are formidable communicative instruments, deriving their strength from the fact that they are substantively empty and thus not subject to undue influence from concerns other than the purely logical, mathematical or statistical ones. They are often used in combination with verbal explanations, as well as pictorial representations, for example graphical models, which represent another important form of non-verbal communication of course (see section 1.8 above).

2.3.2 Mediated communication

The three formal languages represent very special cases of formalized communication. In a sense, all communication must be formalized to some extent of course: by definition, all codes are at least somewhat formalized. Various kinds of non-verbal, more or less formalized communication have probably been with humanity right from the beginning, possibly as remnants or developments of instinctive signals of domination and supremacy, subjection and submission, sorrow and happiness, etc. Formal communication in this sense is especially liable to appear in connection with relations of power. In its purest form it may be found, perhaps, in large bureaucracies, manifesting itself in any number of ceremonies and rites – and also in all those innumerable forms to be filled in by the applicant, supplicant and subordinate.

Formal language may be oral or written. Primitive forms of oral language, of course, were with us from the earliest times, and right from the beginning oral language was supplemented with other forms of bodily and material signs and symbols. Very early the most important signs were reproduced in one form or the other: carved into wood, bone or stone; drawn with charcoal on whatever suitable material was at hand; pressed into clay. Out of *direct* communication, *mediated* communication was thus emerging from early on. This meant that an articulate 'external memory' was being created among humankind.

After millennia, several advanced written languages developed, starting with Sumerian cuneiforms, the hieroglyphs of ancient Egypt and the pictograms of ancient China (about 3,000 BC), taking a great leap forward with the Phoenician alphabet (about 1,000 years BC), which was the first to build on the only seemingly simple principle of one sound (phoneme), one letter. This alphabet originated in the Middle East, by and large in the areas now called Lebanon and Syria, and it was fully developed in ancient Greece. Communication over virtually unlimited distances in time and space had thus become possible.

Why did all this happen, one may well ask.

It is no coincidence that the emergence of written – pictographic, hieroglyphic or alphabetic – language occurred in areas where agriculture produced a surplus of food. Powerful societal units – states and empires based on systematic taxes administered by formal bureaucracies – formed where trade flourished. For their very existence, these centres of power, these formal bureaucracies *needed* the art of writing. So it was created, although in rather different ways, in a small number of powerful empires around the globe. Later on, formal bureaucracy and trade continued to call for ever more advanced forms of written language. Thus, it was the change from the many small hunter-gatherer societies to a much smaller number of larger agricultural societies that created the use of written language.

2.3.3   On the number of human languages

In parallel with the dramatic change discussed in the previous section, there was another, at least equally basic process of change going on: the number of languages was drastically reduced. Societies of hunters-gatherers tend to be rather small: a few thousands of people, often composed of between, say, five and ten clans of some 150 people each, in their turn operating in bands of about a score of people, and the bands, in their turn, being composed of small groups of between five and ten people (cf. the traditional structure of today's large organizations – say, a national army, with its groups, platoons, companies, battalions, brigades, divisions, army corps etc.). Such pristine, small societies often have a language of their own. Back in the days when the whole human population consisted of just a few million people living in such societies, Mother Earth must have been listening to quite a number of different languages, certainly many thousands of them, an overwhelming majority of which never developed any written language.

Today, in spite of the fact that the total human population has multiplied more than a thousandfold (in 1998, it was between five and six thousand millions of people), it is usually estimated that there are 'only' about 5,000 languages left. In addition, it is generally assumed that about 50% of them will disappear within less than a century, since no children are speaking them any more. In the long perspective, it is also noteworthy that only about 70 different languages are recognized as state languages.

New Guinea offers a good example of this development. It is a large island – 775,000 square kilometres – but has only approximately five million inhabitants, mainly living as hunter-gatherers (cf. the 240,000 square kilometres and about 60 million people of Great Britain). In spite of its small population, however, New Guinea is said to boast about 1,000 languages. That is so because rugged terrain and the form of life of the inhabitants create a large number of small societies ranging from a few hundred members to a few thousand ones. This structure of population and communication very probably mirrors a pristine stage of humanity. As modern civilization takes over, it is doomed to disappear, however – a development which is foreshadowed by the two Americas.

The total population of this double continent when discovered by the Europeans has been estimated at *70 million people, using about 1,000 different languages*. Parts of the indigenous population were killed by violent means, but many more died from the diseases brought to the Americas by the Europeans and their domestic animals. Today, the two Americas have about *700 million inhabitants, using three main languages* (English, Spanish and Portuguese) and a comparatively small number of indigenous languages, many of which are doomed to disappear within the not too distant future. This pattern is repeated in other parts of the world. On the other hand, the proportion of people who are able to speak more than one language is rapidly increasing, and very probably it will continue to do so.

An important element in the global developments just described was the invention of writing.

2.3.4   From writing to printing to computing

Once human thought could be captured, repeated and retrospectively analyzed in writing, human thinking started to develop in ways which up till that moment in history had been impossible. That was a tremendous feat. Small wonder that writing was sometimes regarded as a holy and secret art, jealously guarded by its masters. A basic aspect of human thought was changed, and one of the greatest thinkers of all times, Socrates (470?–399 BC), did not like it. He did read, but he never put his own teachings into writing. His disciple Plato (427?–347? BC), on the other hand, took great pains to reproduce (and/or reformulate) Socrates' thinking in his written *Dialogues*.

In parallel with, but somewhat later than, this development was the development of written symbols representing numbers which ultimately resulted in the decimal system. A decisive moment in this development was the creation of the concept and symbol of *zero*. This feat was accomplished in India about AD 500, gradually spreading by way of the Arabic world to Europe, and from there, to other parts of the world.

These two parallel developments having taken place, human thought was freed from the fetters of time and space. The stage was set for a seemingly never-ending communicative revolution, a new decisive phase of which started with the invention of printing, traditionally ascribed to Johannes Gutenberg (in Mainz, Germany, *c.* 1450; see section 6.1) a millennium later.

Another 500 years later, this stepwise and accelerating development took a new giant leap forward with the development of the computer, the 'electronic brain' as it was often called. When mechanical machines for handling symbols were superseded by electronic ones, not only the *repro-duction* of ideas, but the very *production* of new ideas was immensely facilitated (see section 6.1). This happened during and immediately after the Second World War. Since then, of course, the development of the computer has been going on for half a century, with seemingly ever-increasing speed.

The impact of the computer on individuals, organizations and society has been immense, and so has the influence of the theorizing which preceded and has followed the creation of the computer. A basic need in this field of knowledge is, of course, a precise definition of the concept of information. Such a definition must necessarily be dependent upon the language or 'alphabet' in which it is expressed, not least on the number of symbols in that alphabet. A binary alphabet has just two symbols – 0 and 1. In such an alphabet, every symbol is said to have an informational value of *1 bit* (short for *binary digit*). That is just a tiny bit of information, of course. But these tiny bits form the basis for the concept of information as formally defined and measured in the theory of information. A string of 8 bits is thus usually called a byte (B) and can have $2^8 = 256$ different values. A kilobyte (kB) consists of $2^{10} = 1024$ B. A megabyte (MB) consists of 1,024 kB, representing quite a lot of formally defined information – more precisely, $8 \times 1,024 \times 1,024$, i.e. some 8.4 million bits of information.

Such formalized measures of amounts of information are the basic units out of which computer science and related disciplines build their theories. As such they are indispensable. It should be remembered, however, that information thus defined is related to, but not identical with, the common-sense term 'information'. The common-sense term has more to do with semantically-defined information, which is, of course, an entirely different matter. When stored in the memory of a computer, the running text of a chapter in this book builds on between 50 and 150 kB of information as defined in this formal way. The whole book thus represents some 850 kB of information – about four-fifths of a Megabyte. But the quantity and quality of information which its author has tried to put into the book – and the quantity and quality of information which its readers may get out of it – must be estimated in terms other than those of information theory.

Be that as it may, one thing is clear, however. The combined effects of the computer and new reproduction technologies have been immense during the last 50 years or so. While previous technological developments tended to lead human communication towards group and mass communication, the most recent technological developments have actually offered immensely increased opportunities for communication between individuals separated by large physical distance, and also for communication

- *within* small and large groups of individuals,
- *between* individuals and large masses of easily available knowledge, and
- *between* powerful centres of communication, such as large organizations, companies and authorities.

During the last few years, these tendencies have been further strengthened by continuing developments in recent information techniques (IT), combining mass and individual communication. On the 'World Wide Web' (WWW), large chunks of information are electronically stored in a form which makes them available for individual search, use and exchange at times and locations suitable to the individual communicator (see sections 4.7.3 and 7.7). IT thus offers new possibilities for overcoming spatial and temporal distance. As always, these possibilities are available at a cost. Every new technique of communication, therefore, inevitably opens up what has been called 'information gaps', or 'knowledge gaps' (see section 6.2). Not everybody has a computer at home – not to mention the other technological facilities necessary for electronic communication over large distances, for instance, a modem. Those who have the technology, however, will tend to increase their store of knowledge in various ways, while those who do not have the technology will tend not to do so, or to do so to a much smaller extent. Hopefully, however, these gaps of information and communication between the 'haves' and the 'have nots' will gradually close, just as many similar gaps have done before. Such processes may actually take a century or two – just a short period in the history of man, but a very long period in the history of a developing country.

2.4 Functions and acts of human communication

The art of communication as developed by *homo sapiens* represents an immense developmental advantage, the consequences of which are still unfolding and will, perhaps, be doing so for millennia to come. One aspect of this development is that it is so multifaceted. That is so because the functions of human communication are many and important indeed.

When a large number of important phenomena have to be understood and explained, they have to be grouped into a small number of more general phenomena, in ways which have already been demonstrated a couple of times in earlier sections of this book. We thus often distinguish between four general *functions of communication*, as follows:

- the *informative* function of communication;
- the *control* function of communication;
- the *social* function of communication; and
- the *expressive* function of communication.

These general functions may be said to correspond to a small number of large societal institutions (law and art, religion, science and scholarship, etc.), which will be discussed at some length in the next chapter (section 3.2; see also section 1.5 above). What we shall discuss in this chapter, however, is the fact that the various functions of communication relate to elementary so-called *speech acts* (also called *illocutions*), which time and again have been identified in various ways by philosophers, philologists and linguists. A speech act is something you perform when you communicate, regardless of whether you communicate by talking, writing, gesticulating or whatever.

There are several different lists of such speech acts. A somewhat simplified list featuring five speech acts is as follows:

- a statement: 'He is leaving';
- a question: 'Will he leave?';
- an order: 'Come! Don't leave!';
- a declaration: 'I promise to leave';
- an exclamation: 'Wow!'.

It is obvious that there is a relationship of sorts between functions of communication and speech acts. The *informative* function thus corresponds to statements and questions; the *control* function, to orders; the *expressive* function, to exclamations, whereas declarations may have a number of different functions. The social function may be fulfilled by any speech act, or any combination of speech acts. Conversely, the speech act of declaration may be used in more than one function. Actually, the speech act of declaration represents a rather special case. In a declaration *you do what you say you are doing*. When saying, 'I promise to leave', you do just that: you promise to leave. When saying, 'I hereby resign', you resign.

Successful speech acts are called *felicitous*. Obviously, for a speech act to be felicitous, the conditions necessary for that specific speech act must be present. For instance, for orders to be obeyed, they must be issued by a person or some other communicative agency possessing authority.

Speech acts may be evaluated by some very basic criteria (see Grice's maxims in section 2.1.4):

- They should be *true* in relation to actual conditions.
- They should be *sincere* in relation to the speaker.
- They should be *correct* in relation to generally accepted norms.

These criteria are quite natural, and indeed, rather modest. Yet it is a tragic fact that much successful communication is successful precisely because it does not honour these basic criteria – liars and hypocrites, swindlers and other scoundrels are often all too successful. Some speech acts can fail, that is they are not perceived, understood and/or responded to. They just do not work. Your statements are not believed; your questions are left unanswered; your orders are disobeyed; your promises are laughed at; your declarations are ignored; and your exclamations are found to be improper.

The problematics of speech acts has been discussed primarily at the level of interpersonal communication. But in various shapes, speech acts may also appear at other levels of communication – say, the group level, or the societal level (see section 4.3.4). In the next section of this chapter, we shall briefly discuss communication at various levels, ranging from interpersonal communication to mass communication and international communication.

2.5   Levels of communication

Human communication may occur within and between units of different size and complexity. Here is a list of some formal and informal human units whose very existence depends on communication:

- individuals and small groups;
- local, regional, national and international communities and networks;
- formal organizations;
- municipalities such as villages, towns, cities and districts;
- societies, nations, states;
- coalitions and other international organizations of sovereign states.

These units are not always precisely defined. In particular, the term 'community' may be used to designate quite different phenomena. But by and large, there is agreement about the rough meaning of these terms. Also, this meaning may be explicated in terms of communication. Thus:

In order to become an *individual* (see sections 1.3, 3.4 and 4.2 on the twin processes of *individuation* and *individualization*) you must be able to communicate with other individuals. You must master the art of interpersonal communication, and in order to do so, you must also possess a capacity for communication with yourself – indeed, also *on* yourself: *intra-individual* communication, including self-reflection. You must be able not only to think and feel, but also to think and feel about your own thoughts and feelings – a capacity only gradually mastered during childhood and adolescence.

Groups may be defined as a number of individuals with some reciprocal communication. A special case of groups are *networks*, often characterized by mediated, partly formalized but more or less sporadic communication over distance in time and space. (The development of email and other forms of electronic communication have greatly facilitated communication within and between groups and networks; see section 4.7.3, 7.7).

Formal organizations are groups which have a formalized, more or less hierarchical structure of communication, and a fairly well-defined goal, as a rule laid down in a founding charter; as well as a system of standardized procedures for recruitment and exclusion, for decision-making, communication with the surroundings of the organization, etc. (see section 5.1). Formal organizations may transcend boundaries between other social units mentioned in this list, be they small or large (groups, societies, nations, etc.).

Municipality is a general term sometimes used to denote villages, towns and districts having a measure of self-governance.

Communities are fairly large groups of groups of individuals characterized by a relatively loose hierarchy and a relatively high intra-community communication, in combination with a relatively low extra-community communication. They often have a stable spatial location, but recent facilities of communication and transportation have helped, shaping geographically widely dispersed communities, including so-called *virtual communities* built on electronic communication.

Towns and *cities* are communities with a relatively large population concentrated in a relatively small geographical area and having a more or less formalized system of local laws and rules regulating the social interaction between inhabitants and also the physical structure of the town or city. Towns tend to be smaller than cities and to have a less formalized organization, but in both respects there is a large gray zone between the two categories.

Societies are large, complex groups which in turn are composed of other groups, networks, organizations, communities, etc. Societal communication as a rule takes place within a structure of basic laws, more or less formalized rules, conventions, mores and habits. (Obviously, we are not talking about 'society' in the sense of a club or an association here.)

Nations are groups of societies with a common history, often a common language, common culture, etc.

States are nations, or coalitions of nations, organized with a common political body, a common jurisdiction and currency, a common police force and army, sometimes also having a state church, a politically dominating state party, etc. States communicate in various ways with their citizens, as a rule in more or less formalized terms (announcements, acts of parliament, governmental decisions, etc.). Heads of states communicate with their citizens in various, more or less formal ways: speeches from the throne, mass rallies, etc., sometimes making conscious efforts to personalize the otherwise somewhat abstract relations to their citizens (see section 4.1.1). Within their territories, states also have a legal monopoly on a very crude form of communication: systematically organized physical violence (a monopoly which in reality, of course, is far from being watertight).

Some states are federations of states, only the federation and not its component state is internationally acknowledged as the sovereign state. The USA and Germany are such federations of states; Germany's 'Länder' including, for instance, Bavaria and Hesse.

States communicate with other states. They often build international alliances, etc., sometimes to enable them to communicate by way of physical violence outside their own territories. They also form, join and communicate with and within international organizations such as the United Nations, which in its way is the most important international organization there is (for other examples of international organizations, see sections 5.1 and 5.2).

Obviously, there is a certain overlap between the categories just listed, and the terminology is rather loose and far from completely agreed upon. Nevertheless, the list of social units may have an heuristic value, which will be discussed in section 7.1.

It will be seen, for instance, that this only semi-formalized typology of increasingly complex human groups is defined to a large extent by communicative criteria. *Communication may thus be regarded as a defining factor of human groups and organizations of all degrees of size and complexity.* Communication may indeed sometimes stand out as *the* defining factor. In any case, it certainly is one of the most important factors when it comes to defining all sorts of human groups, the basic rule being that within-group communication is more frequent than between-group communication. (Note that between-group information flows are often carried by human individuals, although the subjects formally communicating are units at the group level or higher.)

All units above the individual level may be regarded as groups (and in theoretical sociology and social psychology even very large units may indeed be called groups). Individuals acting as representatives – agents of communication – for groups may be characterized by their level of independence of, and power over the group which they represent. This degree of independence may range from full capacity to take a decision on behalf of the group to practically no capacity at all to do so (for example, a dictator as compared to a queen or king in a constitutional monarchy). Obviously both within-group communication and between-group communication are strongly influenced by the communicative capacity of the group leader. It is also strongly affected by the communicative development of the surrounding society, as briefly described above – as well as by its overall culture, communicated to the individuals by the so-called agents of socialization (see sections 1.3, 3.3.3 and 4.4.5).

In the following chapters we shall have the opportunity to return to these basic questions more than once (see sections 7.1 and 7.2). Before ending this chapter, however, we shall discuss perhaps the most important characteristics of communication: initiative and direction.

2.6 Patterns of communication[1]

When two units (let's call them A and B) communicate, their communication may be described in terms of two characteristics basic to all communication: *direction* and *initiative*. Information may flow from A to B, and/or from B to A. Information may flow from A to B either by way of A *sending* something to B, or by way of B *extracting* something from A, and the same distinction applies, of course, to information flowing from B to A. By combining the concepts of direction and initiative, and applying them to the flow of information between the two units of A and B, we obtain four types of simple communication patterns. These are visualized in Figure 2.2.

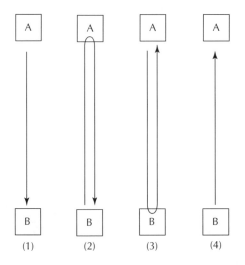

Figure 2.2 Four types of basic communication patterns
(*source*: Rosengren, 1997)

In order to make the abstract patterns more concrete, we may assume that A has an advantage over B (say, more power, or more knowledge, symbolized in the model by the fact that A is situated above B). We may then call the four types of communication:

1 Order
2 Consultation
3 Registration
4 Report.

Consultation and registration may be regarded as concrete examples of various combinations of the three basic speech acts presented and discussed in section 2.4 above: *order* (1), *statement* (4), and *question* (2, 3).

Assuming instead that A and B are *on a par* with each other, the four types taken all together can be said to represent a *conversation* between A and B. This conversation may then be assumed to consist primarily of the two speech acts of *questions* and *statements* (some of which may be replies to questions), from time to time also including, perhaps, an *order*, a *declaration* and even a stray *exclamation* or two.

Heeding the fact that communication between two units often has to go by way of a mediating agency of one kind or other, we have to complicate the model with one more step. This situation is presented in Figure 2.3.

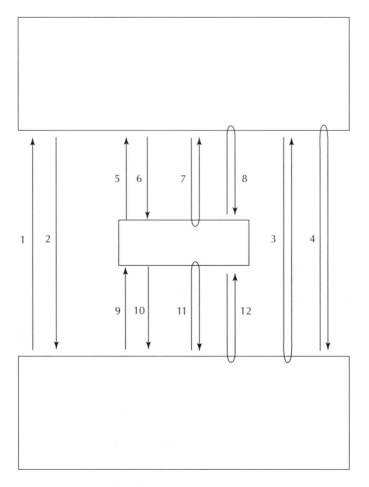

Figure 2.3 A model of mediated communication
(*source*: Rosengren, 1997)

Contemplating Figure 2.3, we realize that communication between two units by way of a mediating unit is a quite complicated affair – in spite of the obvious fact that the figure represents a strong simplification of real-world communication between two units by way of a mediating unit. Communication is a complicated phenomenon indeed. In order to understand that complicated affair at all, we have to build simplified models along the lines exemplified by Figure 2.3.

As a matter of fact, Figure 2.3, precisely because of its simplicity and abstractness, may be used as a model of many, rather different kinds of mediated inter-level communication, for instance, communication between authorities and citizens (by way of a more or less bureaucratic organization), mass communication by way of various more or less advanced forms of media, and so on. That is exactly the strength of formal models. As we mentioned in section 1.4 above, it is by way of a systematic interplay between substantive theories, formal models and empirical data that science and scholarship make their advances. We shall have occasion to return, therefore, from time to time to the models presented in Figures 2.2 and 2.3 for continued discussion of direct and mediated communication between different organizational and societal levels (see, for instance, the notions of 'gate-keeping' and 'access' in sections 5.7, 5.8 and 6.4.2). In the next section we shall indeed return to Figure 2.3 for a discussion of communication between units located at different levels of society and social life (see also section 5.9.1).

2.7 Communication between levels

A large part of all human communication takes place at one and the same specific level. Individuals communicate with individuals, organizations with organizations, etc. This is what might be called 'within-level communication' or 'intra-level communication'. In modern societies, however, communication *between* levels – 'inter-level communication' – probably represents an increasing portion of all human communication. Figure 2.4 offers a schematic picture, a typology of the various types of intra-level and inter-level

	To:				
From:	Individual	Group	Organization	Community	Society
Individual	o	y	y	y	y
Group	x	o	y	y	y
Organization	x	x	o	y	y
Community	x	x	x	o	y
Society	x	x	x	y	o

Figure 2.4 A typology of intra-level and inter-level communication
(*source*: Rosengren, 1997)

communication theoretically possible, given the various levels of communication discussed in section 2.5 above. (Note that in the figure, for the sake of simplicity, the three levels that we distinguished between on p. 47 ('nations', 'societies', 'states') have been collapsed into one, roughly corresponding to what is sometimes called a nation-state (e.g., Denmark, the USA, etc.).

Intra-level communication will be found in the diagonal running from the upper left-hand corner to the lower right-hand corner of the figure. By definition, there are five such types of communication in the figure (denoted by o). There are many more off-diagonal cells, of course – 20, to be exact. Ten such off-diagonal, inter-level types of communication (denoted by x) go from higher levels to lower levels, say, from the societal level to the group or individual levels. Ten off-diagonal types of communication (denoted by y) go from lower levels to higher levels – say, from an organization to the surrounding society.

Intra-level communication at the individual level, of course, includes also what is sometimes called our 'inner life': all our feelings, moods, thoughts, etc. Intra-level communication is carried out by units of lower complexity than the unit within which it is going on. Thus, intra-group communication is carried out by individuals; intra-organization communication, by individuals and groups, etc.

Although there certainly are exceptions, intra-level communication above the individual, group and organizational levels is as a rule mediated one way or the other, and so as a rule is inter-level communication, having at least one communicating part at a level higher than the group level. Also intra-organizational communication is often mediated. By definition, such mediated communication must be carried out by way of a medium.

There are two basically different kinds of mediated communication. Mediated communication may be carried out by individual representatives, who are often more or less formally appointed or elected: lawyers, diplomats, ombudsmen and other examples of what is sometimes called 'professional intermediaries'. For an example, think of an individual communicating with an organization, say, an employee communicating through the union (as represented by an 'ombudsman') with the company (as represented by the employee's boss). In modern societies, however, large portions of both intra-level and inter-level communication take place in the mass media, or in various media specializing in communication at one level or the other – an organizational newsletter, for instance (see Chapters 4–6). It is not for all of us to have access to such media.

Both intra- and inter-level communication thus mirror the power relations existing between individuals and between groups, organizations and societies. From time to time, we shall have occasion to return to this problematic.

Note

1 This section draws heavily on Rosengren (1997).

3

Culture and Society, Media and Communication

3.1 The human group regarded as a system of three systems

When trying to understand communication in society from a general point of view, the notion of *system* is very useful. We have already noted that a system may be defined as a number of units or *elements* (see Box 1.4 above). These elements are related to each other within a more or less permanent *structure*. This structure governs a number of *processes* going on within the system. In their turn, the processes are continually affecting the structure; as the processes change, the structure tends gradually to change too.

A group of friends is a good example of a system. Just like all other groups, even a small, completely informal group of friends has a certain structure, although that structure is by definition informal. In general sociology, however, the concept of group is defined in very general terms. It may thus include the type of large groups called organizations – indeed, even those very large groups called societies. Special theories and methodologies have been developed to study the informal structure of small groups in terms of formalized models. The formalized study communication in small groups – called *sociometry* – will be presented in section 4.4 below.

Much like human beings, groups are born, live and die. Most groups are rather short-lived. But if, one way or the other, the structure of the group is formalized, it tends to live longer. Good examples of such, more or less highly formalized groups are clubs, organizations and, indeed, all nation-states. An example of a very long-lived, highly formalized group is the Roman Catholic Church. As a rule, however, the term 'group' is used to designate a relatively small, informal group, while large, formalized groups are called organizations (see Chapter 5). The human family is, perhaps, the most important group of all (see sections 4.4.3 and 4.4.5).

At bottom, the actions of group members are governed by the *value system* which is more or less common to the members of the group: what the group members find good and true, useful and beautiful, etc. This system of values is basic to all groups, small and large. Indeed, the whole of society may be regarded as a gigantic group, and in the final analysis this group, just like all other groups, is characterized by its value system.

In its turn, the value system is part of one of three closely related systems found in all human groups, be they large or small, for example a boys' street gang or a whole nation. The three main systems common to any human group or society are:

- a *cultural* system of ideas;
- a *social* system of actions; and
- a *material* system of physical artefacts.

In empirical reality, of course, ideas, actions and artefacts are closely intertwined, so that it may be extremely difficult to untangle the ideational, actional and material aspects from each other. The *cultural* system of ideas, for instance, is expressed – 'materialized', if you will – in terms of the *social* system of actions, and also in terms of the *material* system of physical artefacts. The social system of actions and the material system of physical artefacts thus may be said to express the ideational system of culture. This makes empirical analyses difficult, especially since there is a large number of other societal sub-systems, all of which, in all societies, necessarily encompass elements of these three basic systems: the cultural system of ideas, the social system of action, and the material system of physical artefacts. The fact that this is so is no argument against the analytical distinction, however. *All human systems may be understood in terms of an ideational, an actional and an artefactual perspective.*

All three systems are absolutely necessary for any human group or society to survive. For theoretical purposes, each of these three systems may be used, therefore, to characterize any society (and from either the structural or the processual side of the system, or from both sides). It is often practical, however, to regard societies and other human groups as being structured primarily by a central element in the ideational, cultural system: its value system.

3.2 The value system of society

Actually, all societal structures may be understood in terms of two pairs of value orientations:

- cognitive value orientation versus normative value orientation; and
- expressive value orientation versus instrumental value orientation.

In the final analysis, the two pairs of value orientations are defined by the four values of truth and righteousness, beauty and usefulness, respectively. These value orientations are very basic. Indeed, they seem to be virtually timeless. They may be expressed in terms of four Indo-European verbs – in Latin, *sapere/debere, esse/facere*; in French, *savoir/devoir, être/faire* – having their functional counterparts in other families of languages. These basic value orientations were discussed by early Greek philosophers, in terms of *logos* and *ethos*, *pathos* and *praxis*. In the eighteenth century, the German poet Friedrich Schiller (1759–1805) wrote poetry about them, as did many of his predecessors and followers. Recent students of modern advertising and public relations also use them, and we shall meet these basic value orientations again in various sections of this book. Indeed, all societal institutions may be said to have emerged out of these two pairs of value orientations, and they are still gradually developing around them.

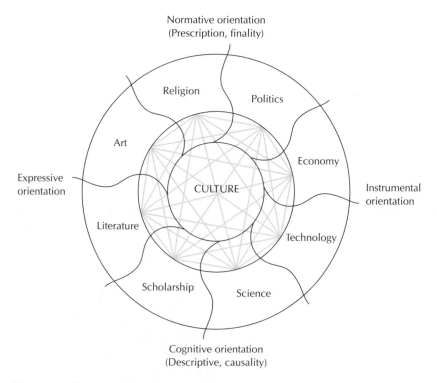

Figure 3.1   The Great Wheel of Culture in Society
(*source*: Rosengren, 1994b)

Figure 3.1, representing the 'Great Wheel of Culture in Society', offers a typology of basic societal institutions grouped around the two pairs of fundamental value orientations: expressive versus instrumental value orientation, and cognitive versus normative value orientation (see sections 1.2 and 1.3). The typology is shaped as a so-called *circumplex*. The circumplex locates the main societal sub-systems in a two-dimensional space in a way which suggests their closest 'neighbours' in society: the system of economy is located between the political and technological systems; literature, between art and scholarship, etc.

The figure represents the three basic systems of ideas, actions and artefacts by means of concentrical circles. At the centre of the circumplex – the 'hub of the wheel' – we find *culture*, the ideational system of society. Culture, then, is both cognitively and normatively oriented, both expressive and instrumental. It unites and relates, one to the other, the four basic value orientations and their various sub-systems. The dashed network relating the eight societal sub-systems to each other tells us something about the complexity of the overall system, and about the immense communicative and co-ordinating functions fulfilled by culture: 8 (8–1)/2 = 28 first order interdependencies, hundreds of secondary ones, thousands of tertiary ones etc. (On the general importance of size and complexity in communication, see section 4.4.)

These relations connect society's institutional sub-systems to each other: religion and politics; politics and science; science and technology; technology and religion, religion and scholarship, and so on, in never-ending chains of mutual interaction. Small wonder, then, that we shall have occasion from time to time to return to the idea of the 'Great Wheel of Culture in Society' (see sections 4.4.5, 5.2, 5.5.1, 6.4.1 and 7.2.2). Note, finally, that such inter-institutional relations may affect ideas, actions and artefacts of the sub-systems, while for pictorial convenience, the lines have been drawn only as going from the system of action within one institutional sub-system to that of another.

This way of pictorial representation signals that all these relations have to be established by means of action, often by means of that special type of action called *communication*. In all societies, these relations are established, maintained and carried out by means of interpersonal, face-to-face communication. In modern societies, they also are often established, maintained and carried out by means of mediated interpersonal communication, as well as by organizational and mass communication, national and international communication. As these relations continue, a never-ending process of *differentiation* between the various societal institutions continues. The institutions thus become increasingly differentiated and yet remain mutually interdependent. All of them have to keep some part of the general societal culture incorporated within their own sub-structures, continually balancing their specific type of culture ('political culture', 'economic culture', etc.) against general societal culture – and also against the specific cultures of other institutions. In this precarious balance, it is often the case that one sector dominates, the sectors of religion, politics and economy primarily being the ones which from time to time have dominated different societal systems. (According to Marxist theory, however, the economic sector tends to have the upper hand, constituting what Karl Marx (1818–83) called 'the last instance'.)

It is a fact, however, that culture is not only a huge switchboard for society, connecting different societal systems to each other or an immense exchange, converting values of one type into values of another type. It is also an important societal system in its own right. As such, culture itself has to relate to other large societal systems, including the two basic systems of action and artefacts, as well as to virtually all institutionalized sub-systems, although, paradoxically, and unlike other large societal systems, culture has no clear-cut, well-established institution of its own. The institutions of art and literature, of course, deal primarily with *high culture*, certainly an important component of societal culture, but even more certainly not to be mistaken for societal culture – not even when taken together with those close relatives, popular art and popular culture (see sections 6.5 and 7.6). What culture actually *does* have, however, is a set of institutions handling its relationship with the rest of society, primarily the so-called agents of socialization (see sections 1.3, 3.3, 4.4.5, 6.4 and 6.6.2).

The relations between culture and other societal systems is a classic problem of social science. Within any given society, there are four main types of such relations. Figure 3.2 orders these four types in a typology. On one hand, this is a typology of the *relations* between the ideational system of culture and the systems of actions and artefact; on the other hand, it is also a typology of *theories* concerning these relations.

For centuries, heated philosophical debates raged along the Materialism/ Idealism axis, debates which were rekindled by the wave of Marxist revivalism in the 1960s and 1970s. Gradually, however, the scientific and scholarly

Other societal systems influence culture

	Yes	No
Yes	Interdependence	Idealism
No	Materialism	Autonomy

Culture influences other societal systems

Figure 3.2 A typology of relations between culture and other societal systems (*source*: Rosengren, 1994a)

discussions moved over to the ideologically less flammable, but perhaps more realistic, Interdepedence/Autonomy axis. It must be added, though, that the answer to these classical debates to a high degree is related to the time perspective applied. Values and value systems may change on a time scale ranging from millennia, over centuries and decades, to years and parts of a year. It would be strange indeed if the relationship between culture and other societal structures was the same within those different time scales. More often than not, however, *interdependence* seems to be the best answer. The three systems of ideas, actions and artefacts mutually affect each other, in never-ending processes of interaction. They are mutually interdependent.

These processes of interaction between large societal systems include practically everything that happens in our daily, individual lives. We spend our lives in an environment saturated with our society's culture. Our daily labours reproduce societal culture and in a few cases actually change it. Our daily lives are also interrupted by festival days and commemoration days, marking not only the great events of our personal lives but also those of our society. All of us are immersed in our society's culture, and in that culture's relationships with other societal systems.

3.3 Socialization

3.3.1 Introduction

The horizontal relations between culture and other societal systems are important, but there is also another kind of relation to be noted, the 'vertical' relations linking units at the macro, mezzo and micro levels of society to each other. In these vertical relations, society's culture flows from the level of society down to the individual level and back again, in modern societies often by way of the organizational, 'mezzanine' level. Society speaks to the individual, as it were, and the individual sometimes tries to talk back. In this ever-continuing process relating the macro to the micro level by way of the mezzo level, *societal culture* is transformed into an *individually internalized culture*.

The vertical flow between the macro and the micro levels may also be conceived as a flow between one societal generation and the next, an immensely important process, as a rule conceptualized in terms of upbringing, training, education, etc. A general term for these closely related phenomena is *socialization* (a process radically different from 'socialization' in the sense of 'nationalizing').

Are there processes of socialization among animals, other than human beings? Among some animal species, the parental generations seem to be quite active as fosterers. But the parents probably work mostly by way of positive and negative feedback, and sometimes by way of *demonstration*, not so much by *instruction*, the reason being, of course, that instruction pre-supposes a more developed language than animals seem to have. Thus, the offspring of apes, having been licked by their parents, know how to lick their own offspring, while young apes which have not been licked do not seem to lick their own young. In addition, much animal behaviour and patterns of behaviour are genetically, not culturally, transferred between generations. In a sense, then, animal socialization seems to be literally meaningless. In this way it may be likened to the way computers may be programmed to play chess or to carry on simple conversations.

In contrast, human societal culture is a great reservoir of meaning, which is constantly being drawn upon when human beings communicate and interact – within generations and between generations. This reservoir of meaning defines an important difference between animal and human communication. A defining characteristic of human culture is that it is a product of the human brain. But conceptualized in terms of communication, it is as if it should exist also *between* human brains. Culture lives when meaningfully communicated.

The key word summarizing the difference between human communication on the one hand, and communication between animals and/or plants on the other, is probably *meaning*. Human communication is meaningful – it is full of meaning – but animal communication is not so meaningful, and plant communication has no meaning. Both animal and plant communication can more accurately be characterized as physiological interaction with the environment (see sections 2.1.2 and 2.1.3). What is 'meaning', then?

3.3.2   The meaning of meaning

The concept of 'meaning' could be explained as the whole way in which we understand, explain, feel about and react towards a given phenomenon. Meaning is thus an instrument that is basic to efforts at explaining and understanding alike. It is a concept central to both science and scholarship. For millennia it has been studied by humanistic scholars as well as by social and behavioural scientists. During the last few decades, efforts have been made to unite all studies within this broad field into a discipline of its own: the study of *cognition*. In spite of such efforts, however, meaning is still studied in a number of specific disciplines. Among linguists, for instance, meaning is studied in terms of semiotics, semantics and pragmatics (see section 2.1.). A classic study in the field is Charles R. Osgood et al.'s book *The Measurement of Meaning* (1957), which was followed by a large number of studies by Osgood himself and many others.

When it comes to the defining of the meaning of 'meaning' a distinction needs to be made between *denotation* and *connotation*. The term 'denotation' refers to the specific signification of a given word. The word, 'dog', for example, denotes a fairly well-defined group of four-legged, barking animals, and more specifically, a domestic, canine animal (in strictly zoological terms belonging to the family of *Canidae* which also includes jackals, wolves and foxes). The term 'connotation', on the other hand, refers to the associations or more or less implicit suggestions inherent in a given word. The two words 'dog' and 'doggie' thus have different connotations, although their denotation is one and the same.

Trying to find the dimensions of meaning as actually used by human beings, Osgood applied *factor analysis*, a statistical technique originally devised for finding and/or testing dimensions (see section 1.2) of complex phenomena such as, say, intelligence or attitudes. He did so in order to analyse responses to a special kind of attitude test devised by him, the so-called 'Semantic Differential' or 'Osgood scale'. He found that the meaning of many phenomena could be explained in terms of a 'semantic space' defined by a relatively small number of dimensions, the three most important of which are *evaluation* ('good/bad') *strength* ('strong/weak') and *activity* ('active/passive').

The three dimensions of Osgood's semantic space represent truly basic human phenomena, and at bottom these dimensions are related to the most profound aspects of the meaning of human life. Obviously, any number of dimensions might be found in human meaning. But science and scholarship build on the idea of reducing information as far as possible down to the point where no further reduction can be undertaken. From that point on, additional dimensions may be added to the model, until it becomes unwieldy (see section 1.8).

Osgood and his colleagues did indeed find a number of such additional dimensions of meaning. For many practical purposes, however, the three main dimensions of Osgood's Semantic Space are quite sufficient. Also, the three-dimensional space is more easily grasped, more intuitively understood, by the human brain when reflecting on itself and the meaning that it is continuously producing. For the time being, then, let's stay content with three dimensions of Osgood's Semantic Space – *evaluation* (good/bad), *strength* (strong/weak) and *activity* (active/passive) – three basic aspects of *meaning*.

3.3.3 Agents of socialization

Several specific societal institutions are engaged in the processes of communicating culture from generation to generation, processes which are, in everyday parlance, called upbringing, training and education; in social science, *socialization*. Societal institutions responsible for those processes are called *agents of socialization*.

As mentioned in section 1.5, there are at least eight main types of socialization agents. Three of them may be found in even the the most undifferentiated societies (albeit, of course, in sometimes rather different shapes):

- the *family*;
- the *peer group*; and
- the *working group*.

Three other types of socialization agents are found in somewhat more differentiated societies:

- *priests* (sometimes organized in churches);
- *teachers* (sometimes organized in schools and universities); and
- *law agents* (sometimes organized in courts and police forces).

In modern societies we also have two other main types of socialization agent:

- large *social movements* (sometimes organized in more or less formalized organizations operating at the local, national and/or international levels); and
- general and specialized *media of communication* (ranging from private or semi-private media such as letters and newsletters, to modern mass media reaching virtually all members of a given society).

These eight main types of socialization agents are very dissimilar in their actual *modus operandi*. Socialization in the family is the most basic one, of course. It is often called primary socialization, while socialization by other agents of socialization is called secondary socialization (sometimes including re-socialization). But all agents of socialization are busy storing, developing and sharing culture existing at various levels of society and within different generations (see section 7.3.2). *In so doing, their main instrument is communication.*

This book is primarily about communication. Communication is a very basic process, always taking place in a complex matrix of social relations. To understand communication, we must turn, therefore, from *societal* structure (a structure built on societal institutions such as religion or politics, and on the relations between these institutions) to *social* structure (a structure built on relations between individuals manifested in patterns of action which to a large extent are determined by a small number of characteristics such as age and gender, class and status). We must also relate the concept of *structure* to that of *process*, and we shall do so in terms of the conceptual pair of *agency* and *structure*.

3.4 Agency and structure

Agency is understood as the capacity of acting and willing subjects within existing societal and social structures to exercise choice – 'to be able to act otherwise' – sometimes even to the extent of transgressing the limits established by those structures. More specifically, agency is taken to be characterized by actors' ability to:

- intentionally exercise some kind of power;
- choose between alternatives; and
- reflect on the consequences of acting.

Any study of the interplay between agency and structure over time pre-supposes that both terms are defined independently of each other. Structure and action, then, just as subject and object, must be kept analytically separate. In so doing, we must also observe the distinction between *societal structure* as briefly discussed in the previous sections, and *social structure* as primarily defined by the four basic variables of age and gender, class and status. This distinction is very important.

When societal and social structures have had their say in the social processes, there is some space left for individual choice, within which to form individual actions and patterns of actions (including more or less conscious, and more or less systematically organized attempts at changing societal and social structures). Individual choice, of course, is useless without an individual capacity to realize the choice in action. This capacity is often called *agency*. We thus have three types of patterned action:

- *forms of life*: patterns of action determined primarily by *societal structure*;
- *ways of life*: patterns of action determined primarily by *position in social structure*; and
- *lifestyles*: patterns of action determined primarily by *individual agency*.

The relationships between societal structure, individual position in the social system, individual characteristics and patterns of action are shown in Figure 3.3 (note that in the interest of clarity, arrows symbolizing the no doubt often existing feed-back phenomena, from say, 'patterns of action' to 'individual position' and 'individual characteristics', have been omitted). In section 4.3 below, these relationships will be discussed from a different perspective (see also section 5.1). The so-called beta-coefficients attached to three causal arrows in the model indicate the unique influence of, respectively:

- societal structure;
- individual position in that structure; and
- the influence from personal characteristics and choice, individual 'agency'.

During the last few decades, interest in the notion of lifestyle has been growing. The definition of 'lifestyle' has often been the subject of lively

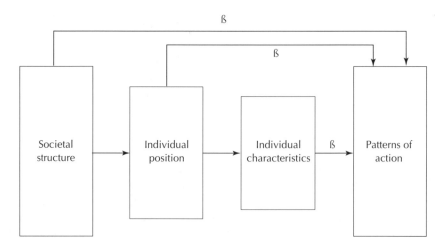

Figure 3.3 Forms of life, ways of life and lifestyles
(*source*: Rosengren, 1994a)

debate, relating naturally to debates that have been raging for years within socialization research. The debates have centred on the characteristics of the two parties involved in all socialization processes: *society* (as represented by its agents of socialization), and the *individual being socialized*. In such debates, society is often characterized primarily by either conflict or consensus. The individual being socialized is often characterized either as a willing and acting subject, or as a more or less passive object of strong forces from outside or within the individual. When combined, the the two distinctions result in a typology of approaches in socialization research which is highly reminiscent of the typology for schools of humanistic and social scholarship and science already presented in Figure 1.1 on p. 8. The similarity between the two typologies offers strong validation to both of them.

Each one of the two dimensions of the typology represents a number of theoretical and practical problems. A partial solution to the *theoretical* subject/object problematics (which is, of course, closely related to the agency/structure debate) is represented by the distinction between structurally, positionally and individually determined patterns of action (see Figure 3.3). The *practical* conflict/consensus problematic is handled in the socialization process by letting objectively existing social differences stand out as morally, politically and/or religiously motivated. In this way, what from a social science perspective may be regarded as a causal relation, from the individual's perspective may appear as subjectively willed, and morally proper action. By thus transforming *causality* into *finality*, *necessity* into *intention*, socialization at the same time may transform *conflict* into *consensus*. It is by this interaction between control and resources that socialization, paradoxically, brings about a process basic to the existence of all of us – *individuation*, the process through which that little brute, the newborn babe, becomes fully human. This individuation process, of course, is not to be mistaken for the process of *individualization*, the immense historical process by which the human individual gradually emerged from the animal group as an integrated and independent being of its own (see section 2.1).

However subtle it may be, the control process of socialization is never perfect. There is always some free space left, small glades in which potential dissidents may find each other and build plans for future change. In most societies, the freedom left to peer groups among young people is perhaps the best example. In addition, there is always more to socialization than *control*. All agents of socialization also provide intellectual, emotional, social and material *resources* which may be used by those being socialized, the 'socializees' – sometimes in ways completely unforeseen by society and its representatives, the agents of socialization.

The control exercised and the resources put at the individual's disposal by the agents of socialization represent two dimensions by which all socialization processes are economically characterized. Indeed, the two dimensions are so basic as to be applicable not only to processes of socialization but to all social groups and their internal and external interactions. In its most general form, the typology is presented in Figure 3.4.

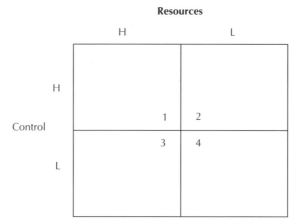

Figure 3.4 Four approaches in socialization research

The types of Figure 3.4 represent so-called *ideal types*, but in their pure form are seldom or never found in reality. This should be kept in mind, but it is no argument against the typology as such. Because of its generality, the typology is relevant to the content, the process, and the agents of that basic process of communication, *socialization* (see section 3.3 above). In empirical research it has to be adapted and modified according to the specific circumstances at hand, and its general dimensions have to be specified. One general problem to be discussed is the crucial one about the relationships between the socializing agents and the individual being socialized. Do the agents of socialization offer a degree of independence to the socializees? How much variation is found in that degree of independence?

A general conclusion to be drawn from the typology is that the dependence of socializees on their agents of socialization will probably tend to be highest in cell 2, lowest in cell 3. Under the conditions of the latter cell, when facing an imminent conflict, there is a high chance of arrival at that sometimes very productive outcome: *to agree to disagree*. Innovations often have their origin in conflicting views on how to solve a given problem facing the group. The typology is thus highly relevant to two characteristics of all groups, all societies: stability and innovation. Processes of innovation are most likely to occur in cell 3, and to some extent in cell 1.

In principle, the same argumentation should be valid when writ large at the societal level. In some societies or parts of societies, for some periods of time, when resources are plentiful, social control is low. Renaissance Florence, and the Vienna of the early twentieth century come to mind, but contemporary examples can also be found, for example some parts of modern California. In all countries and at all times, there seem to be some regions that are more innovation-prone than others. Important agencies of innovative change are the large societal organizations producing and distributing new knowledge, primarily universities and other centres of science and scholarship.

In the final analysis, this line of argument leads us back to the relationship between culture and other societal systems – this time in terms of continuity and change.

3.5 Continuity and change

3.5.1 The rate of societal change

Let us return for a moment to the relations between culture and other societal systems previously discussed in typological terms, and shown in Figure 3.2 above. The figure actually builds on the silent assumption that societies are closed systems. No societies are closed systems, however. Figure 3.5 heeds that trivial and yet basic truth.

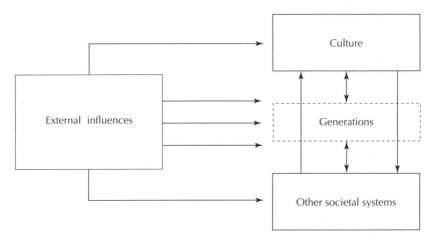

Figure 3.5 A typology of relations between culture and other societal
systems (*source*: Rosengren, 1994a)

It will be seen that the model corresponds to cell 1 of Figure 3.2, characterized by interdependence between culture and other societal systems. Two complications have been introduced, however: external influences from other societies, and a generational filter between culture and other societal systems.

Societies may be conceptualized as systems of ideas, actions and artefacts, but actions are carried out by human beings of flesh and blood, continually producing and/or reproducing ideas and material artefacts. Human beings on average live 'three score years and ten', internalizing societal culture primarily during their first 20 years or so. Our capacity for innovation as a rule being rather low after our first one or two score of years, we then tend to spend large portions of our lives reproducing what was long ago internalized.

A consequence of this is that there is a generational filter between culture and other societal systems, reducing the rate of innovative exchange between society's general culture and other societal systems. New ideas born within and between creative brains, new patterns of actions emerging among innovative groups of people, new kinds of artefacts devised and produced by *homo sapiens et faber*, therefore, are not instantaneously accepted, as innovation research has shown again and again (see section 5.8). Innovations tend to be produced by relatively young generations, and the filter of relatively old generations reduces the rate of change, thus producing a certain amount of societal stability, a precarious balance between continuity and change.

The outcome of this interplay is that overall societal change tends to be relatively slow. In modern societies, all generations seem to feel that they live in a period of rapid change, and perhaps we do. But changes thus perceived are often superficial. The basic characteristics of societal culture tend to change only slowly, often passing by unnoticed until they reach a threshold value at which they are suddenly noticed and vehemently discussed – 'moments of madness', 'periods of clairvoyance'. The years 1968 and 1989, for example, could be said to represent such periods of madness and clairvoyance, each in its own way (see Figure 3.6).

3.5.2   Indicators of societal change and continuity

In order to measure the slow change of society, its trends and cycles, as well as its more or less accidental variations and traumatic climaxes, we need reliable indicators of societal change. In principle, there are four main types of such societal indicators:

* *economic indicators* (measuring phenomena related to *wealth*);
* *objective social indicators* (measuring *welfare*);
* *subjective social indicators* (measuring *well-being*); and
* *cultural indicators* (measuring the development of *basic values* and *other central ideas*).

Although the terms used here to designate them are not very old, economic indicators have been around for centuries or even millenia; social indicators, for at least a century; and cultural indicators for at least half a century. One example of the application of such cultural indicators will be offered below.

As suggested by the American psychologist and sociologist, Milton Rokeach (1918–88), the two values of freedom and equality in combination may be regarded as defining characteristics of four basic societal ideologies, so that, as ideologies,

* *socialism* puts a high value on both freedom and equality;
* *fascism* puts a low value on both freedom and equality; while
* *communism* puts equality above freedom; and
* *liberal capitalism* puts freedom above equality (Rokeach, 1973).

The development of such ideological value systems can be studied in terms of cultural indicators obtained, for instance, from quantitative content analysis of the daily press in a given country. Changes in the value system of Sweden, its 'climate of culture' as it developed during the period 1945–75, were studied in a research program called CISSS (Cultural Indicators: The Swedish Symbol System, 1945–75). The program was based on quantitative content analysis of the Swedish daily press. Examining the extent to which the values of freedom and equality were upheld in editorials in a representative sample of Swedish newspapers during the period 1945–75, Figure 3.6 offers a graphic example of the way such societal change tends to proceed.

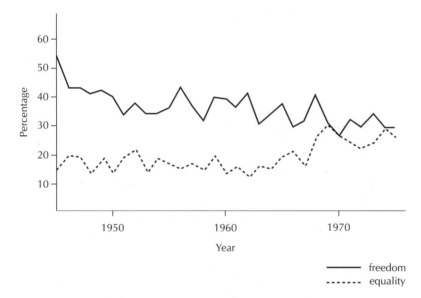

Figure 3.6 The values of freedom and equality as upheld in Swedish editorials, 1945–75 (*source*: Rosengren, 1994b)

What Figure 3.6 tells us is that during the two decades after the Second World War Sweden changed from being a society ideologically characterized by liberal capitalism to being a society ideologically characterized by socialism. Although this period of ideological socialism was 20 years in coming, it lasted only a few years. Contrary to what at the time many people believed, the notoriously famous year of 1968 – a year of social upheavals, not least on university campuses in Europe and the USA – did not mark a beginning, but rather a culmination suggesting an end. The ideological development then took another turn. Two decades later, Sweden experienced an ideologically quite different period, this time of liberal capitalism, the heyday of which (the 'moment of madness' or clairvoyance, see section 3.5.1) probably was not, or will not be, much longer than that of socialism. Although these specific developments have not yet been documented by quantitative and systematic measurements and related to data from other sectors of society, this is by no means an implausible hypothesis, hopefully to be tested in future studies. (Such studies have indeed been prepared by scanning in representative samples of the Swedish daily press during the period 1975–95; see Rosengren et al., 1999.)

Results such as these show that basic changes in societal systems tend to take some time to come about. They also suggest that the results of such slow processes of change, having reached maturity, may be rather short-lived. It is as if the innumerable communicative processes of socialization and re-socialization going on at the individual, 'micro' level are so time-consuming that they do not leave much scope for the overall outcome at the societal, 'macro' level to be very long-lived. Although many of us believe that at the micro level the times are always changing, at the macro level, change is so slow that, paradoxically, periods of stability become rather short. Likewise, this fact contributes to the widespread, but as a rule false, impression that times are changing at a quick pace.

Turning to even more basic types of socio-biological change, we have to expect even slower rates of change. In Box 3.1, the world-famous Italian-American geneticist, Luigi Luca Cavalli-Sforza, together with his son, Francesco Cavalli-Sforza, wonders at the cultural change of Scandinavians. During the Viking period they were the most frightening warriors of their day, while today (according to the Sforzas) they are among the most peaceful people in the world, and this drastic change came within a short period in terms of human population genetics – just a millennium!

To the geneticist, of course, a millennium is a short period of time, but to the scholar of communication and culture in human societies it is a long period. One reason why social and cultural change is so relatively slow is probably because some powerful agents of socialization seem to be conservative almost by definition. What socialization often means is that representatives of old generations (parents and grandparents) hand over the values and opinions of their own generations to representatives of the upcoming generations (their children and grandchildren). In addition, priests, teachers and law agencies, etc. are not exactly known for their high level of general innovativeness (let alone their political convictions).

The most innovative agent of socialization is probably the peer group, especially peer groups composed of young people, who lead for a short period an intermediate, partly secret existence between childhood and adulthood. Two types of socialization agent are variable with respect to their innovativeness: the work group and the mass media. In the work group, a special case is the research group, which exists, in principle, to produce innovations, whether they are new inventions or the discovery of new general knowledge.

The innovative capacity of single groups and types of group is closely related to the culture of the surrounding society: quite naturally, innovative (types of) groups are more innovative in a modern society than in a traditional one, and much the same should go for the individual innovator. We shall return to this discussion in Chapter 6 on mass media and mass communication.

BOX 3.1   THE CAVALLI-SFORZAS ON CULTURAL CHANGE VERSUS GENETIC CHANGE

'If we are looking for examples of cultural change, the present is a rich source; they are now so frequent and fast that it is hard to keep track of them. Ours is an age of strong cultural change, the real benefits, reasons and future of which are hard to identify. . . . Despite sociologists' efforts we are frequently hard put to understand the changes we see around us, or why the changes we would like to see don't come about at all.

'Here is one example: variations in birthrate are far more important for the long-term future of the world than are stock exchange reports, and responsible people would like to see the birthrate drop in regions where there is still out-of-control growth. Unfortunately, there isn't much to be optimistic about. A humane and intelligent form of social engineering able to correct the extremely serious errors committed has yet to be invented. In the meantime, the Chinese system of pressuring women into terminating second or subsequent pregnancies may seem hard to accept, but would it really be better if the population of China, which today numbers more than a billion and represents almost one quarter of humanity, were to double every twenty to twenty-five years? . . .

'Are the changes we see truly cultural? Might they not be genetic?

'Even at its fastest, genetic change is extremely slow. One of the fastest major genetic changes is the increase in the number of people able to use lactose, the sugar present in milk. The highest peak registered is 90 percent, in Scandinavia. This level may have been reached over a period of around ten thousand years, starting from an initial incidence of 1 to 2 percent, or maybe lower. The same time lapse may apply to lightening of skin color and generally to the Scandinavians' virtual loss of skin, eye and hair pigmentation, starting from original colorings that were perhaps similar to the Lebanese of today.

'Fast change is unlikely to have genetic basis. One thousand years ago, southern Scandinavia was inhabited by a race of exceptional navigators and colonizers who were also fierce and fearsome warriors: the Vikings. They occupied Scotland, Ireland, Normandy, and Iceland. They reached Greenland and America and even struck at the heart of the Mediterranean. All of this in marked contrast to their descendants; the Scandinavians of today are calm and mild – Europe's most dedicated pacifists. Some run serious risks and shoulder great responsibility to further the cause of peace in the world. It is difficult to believe this change is genetic, or that all the violent elements have died out in the meantime. Cultural evolution strikes me as a more convincing explanation.'

From: L.L. Cavalli-Sforza and F. Cavalli-Sforza (1995) *The Great Human Diasporas. The History of Diversity and Evolution*. Reading, MA: Addison-Wesley.

PART THREE

LEVELS OF COMMUNICATION

4

Individual Communication: Intrapersonal, Interpersonal and Group Communication

4.1 Individuals in groups and societies

4.1.1 Introduction

The word 'individual' derives from the Latin word *individualis*, meaning *indivisible*. An individual is an indivisible whole: the smallest unit in human societies.

The human body is a *biological* unit, but the human individual is a *social* unit, an actor, a member of society's system of action (see section 3.1). Just like other social units – groups, organizations, communities, societies – the social unit of an individual is constituted by way of *communication* – actually, by way of at least two different kinds of communication:

- intra-individual communication, taking place *within* the individual; and
- inter-individual communication, taking place *between* individuals.

In addition, both intra- and inter-individual communication is affected by communication taking place at higher levels of human life: the group level, the organizational level, the societal level, and the international level. Group communication will be discussed in a later section of this chapter, while the remaining types of communication will be dealt with in the following chapters.

It should be mentioned at once, however, that when discussing group communication, organizational communication, mass communication and international communication, we must not forget the fact that in the last instance, individuals are always involved – one way or the other. When a prime minister or a president speaks to the nation, he often tries to present his message in as personal a way as possible. He pats children on their heads. He bows down to the old woman in her hospital bed, asking how she is. In his famous fire-side chats broadcast on radio, Franklin D. Roosevelt, US president from 1933 to 1945, spoke to a nationwide audience in a personal way.

The importance of individual communication comes to the fore also when the prime ministers or the heads of state of two countries meet and discuss questions of mutual interest. In a sense, France speaks to Germany, Canada to the USA, Japan to India, but the actual conversation takes place between two individuals (although, as a rule, that conversation is backed up by other conversations between the staffs of the two national leaders and is sometimes supported by professional mediators. For example, think of the United Nations' Secretary-General, Dag Hammarskjöld, in the Congo (now Zaire) in 1961, or former Swedish Prime Minister, Carl Bildt, in conflict-ridden Yugoslavia in 1995–96, or UN Secretary-General Kofi Annan in Iraq in 1998.)

Even communication between states by way of conversations between heads of state, then, cannot deviate too much from the basic characteristics of interpersonal communication in general. Indeed, the whole idea of a 'top meeting' is to apply the advantages of interpersonal communication to a strained situation, be it between the prime ministers or presidents of two world powers or between two gang leaders in the dilapidated centre of a large city. In terms of Figure 2.4 on p. 51 above, conversations of this type are actually located in more than one cell at a time. They may be found in both, say, the individual/individual cell and the society/society cell or the organization/organization cell.

International communication is therefore often also interpersonal communication. Conversely, some cases of interpersonal, organizational and mass communication are also international communication – not only at summit meetings. Indeed, all communication between immigrants and natives, between local populations and foreign tourists or business people travelling abroad is, or could be regarded as, international communication. In addition, international transportation of goods and people is steadily increasing, and is always preceded and followed by parallel international flows of information and communication – advertisements, letters, tickets, orders, confirmations, invoices, receipts, acknowledgements, complaints,etc. The levels of communication thus cross each other in occasionally bewildering ways. But that is no reason not to keep them theoretically and analytically apart. On the contrary, only by so doing is it possible to understand not only the basic characteristics of each special type of communication, but also the general characteristics of communicative processes and structures.

4.1.2 Factors influencing individual communication

Individual communication as such is strongly influenced by factors to be found both within and outside the individual: strictly individual characteristics, as well as characteristics influenced

- by both societal and social *structures,*
- by the individual's *position* in the social structure of his society, and
- by the specific *situation* at the moment of communication.

(On the difference between social and societal structure, see sections 3.1 and 3.2.)

A basic characteristic of any individual is his or her *personality* – a structure which is at least partly built by communicational processes (see sections 4.2 and 4.3). In their turn, our personalities affect both our intra-individual communication and our inter-individual communication.

A basic characteristic of the society surrounding a given individual is its *communicative structure,* that is, the organization of the communicative resources available within that society, not forgetting the way these resources are distributed between individuals and classes of individuals. Societal structure offers strong resources for human communication – and also sometimes strict limitations, both quantitatively and qualitatively. In a prehistoric, illiterate society of gatherers and hunters (now almost non-existent on planet Earth; see Box 2.2), patterns of individual communication, in spite of being similar in principle, presumably were different from those to be found in a society primarily based on agriculture, not to speak of communication patterns in today's industrial or post-industrial societies. Under a fascist or communist dictatorship, all communicative structures have to be different from those of a society characterized by parliamentary democracy, free speech, freedom of the press, etc.

The *communicative* structure of a given society, however, is always closely related to the *social* structure of that society, as defined by the four variables of age and gender, class and status (see section 3.4). In its turn, the individual's position in the social structure strongly affects his or her way of communicating, both when it comes to intra-individual and inter-individual communication. Old working-men do not think, feel and communicate in quite the same way as do young daughters of directors-general. Each position calls for a certain 'role' to be played: the roles of men and women, old people and young, workers, clerks and managing directors etc. (see Box 4.3 below).

Roles are ascribed or achieved. Ascribed roles include roles defined in terms of age and gender, race and nationality. Achieved roles include those defined in terms of, for instance, education, job, trade, profession. In all societies, ascribed and achieved roles are related to each other – in some societies more strongly than in other ones. In the public discourse of democratic societies, however, there is widespread agreement that ascribed roles should not form a basis for discrimination. Yet there is no lack of examples of such discrimination – in all sectors of all societies – although the degrees and types of discrimination show some variation between sectors, societies and cultures. In many cases, the discrimination is expressed in communicative terms: mode of address, types of greeting, degree of education, space allotted in the mass media to young and old people, to men and women, to workers and directors-general.

Finally, it should be mentioned that there are hybrid forms of communication at different levels. An interesting hybrid of interpersonal and mass communication is the *mass meeting*, often used by popular movements of protest and reform – and by politicians emerging out of such movements. Cleverly staged mass meetings have again and again demonstrated their capacity for channelling vague individual feelings of unease, dissatisfaction, injustice, giving them direction, a goal, an enemy. Various workers' movements during the early twentieth century used mass rallies to focus and disseminate feelings of injustice and protest. Between the First and Second World Wars fascist and communist politicians alike used rallies as a powerful propaganda tool, for example Nazi Germany's dictator, Adolf Hitler, supported by his Minister of Propaganda, Joseph Goebbels. During the 'Singing Revolution' in Estonia and the other Baltic countries in the late 1980s and early 1990s similar mass meetings were instrumental in bravely manoeuvering these three small countries free from the oppression of the disintegrating Soviet empire. Out of an amorphous mass of individuals may thus emerge or re-emerge, a group, a movement, an organization, a political party, a nation, a country (see Box 4.1).

BOX 4.1 'INTERPERSONAL MASS COMMUNICATION'

'This period [1988–91] is the peak of activities from several competing mass movements. . . . The Baltic liberation movements based their rallies around the traditional cultural form (and the traditional places) of song festivals, known since the first period of national awakening in the 19th century. The traditional form of gathering and the collective rituals of choir singing helped to lift the national spirit and to mobilize people who were alienated from politics during the Soviet era. At mass meetings, thousands of people sang new songs specially written by popular composers for these events, together with the pre-war patriotic songs and the historical, patriotic repertoire of the 19th-century song festivals. The words 'Estonia' (Eesti) and 'freedom' were repeated like a magic formula. The succession of common singing and rhythmic movements with political speeches helped to discipline hundreds of thousands of participants without any external measures. Peaceful rallies of revolutionary people did not need the police to maintain order. . . . After decades of living without 'Voice', without any possibility of expressing their real will, people now enjoyed the feeling of having their own voice, the ability to act as one single body, full of decisiveness and power.'

From: M. Lauristin and P. Vihalemm (1997) 'Recent historical developments in Estonia: three stages of transition (1987–1997)', in M. Lauristin and P. Vihalemm with K.E. Rosengren and L. Weibull (eds), *Return to the Western World. Cultural and Political Perspectives on the Estonian Post-Communist Transition*. Tartu: Tartu University Press. pp. 73–126.

A general conclusion to be drawn from this line of argument, then, is that when, later on, we discuss group, organizational, mass and international communication, we must not forget that at bottom it's all about interpersonal communication – communication between human individuals. At the same time there is no doubt that communication above the individual level is characterized by phenomena not existing at the individual level – so-called 'emergent characteristics'.

In the following sections of this chapter we shall discuss individual communication in terms of intra-personal, interpersonal and group communication, sometimes also examining the social, societal and communicative structure of the surrounding society.

4.2   Intrapersonal and interpersonal communication: some preliminaries

In section 2.2 we discussed a stepwise definition of human communication as follows:

- *interaction* (i.e., mutual influence), which is both
- *intersubjective* (i.e., mutually conscious), and
- *intentional* or *purposive*, and is carried out by means of
- *a system of signs*, mostly building on
- *a system of verbal symbols*, characterized by
- *double articulation*, which in turn builds on fully developed systems of
- *phonology*, *syntax*, *semantics*, and *pragmatics*.

Obviously, in order to define *interpersonal* communication, we have only to add the three words, 'between human individuals', to this stepwise definition – say, after the word interaction'. Similarly, we add the three words, 'within human individuals', to arrive at a definition of *intrapersonal* communication. In this latter case, however, we also have to exchange the word 'intersubjective' (i.e., mutually conscious) against the words 'intrasubjective' or 'conscious', remembering that intrasubjective communication often hovers between conscious, semi-conscious, subconscious and unconscious.

Consciousness, in the sense of being both aware of one's own existence and capable of reflecting on it, is what characterizes the human individual, as opposed to all other animals. The 'stream of consciousness' continuously flowing through our minds is probably unique to all human individuals. It is the basis of the process of *individuation*, the *process* constituting – both forming and being formed by – the *structure* of our individual personalities (see sections 1.3, 2.5, 3.4 and 4.3.1). When we lose our consciousness we lose a defining characteristic of ourselves. In a way, we are no longer fully human.

A phenomenon as important as our stream of consciousness must have been discussed, of course, during millennia. Over the centuries, fictional literature tried to render it in various ways, a high point being reached in James Joyce's famous novel *Ulysses* (1922) (see Box 4.2). The degree of individual consciousness is highly variable, over time and between different situations. Below full consciousness there are also some not immediately accessible, subconscious and/or unconscious processes going on all the time. The techniques for studying such processes, however, have not always reached the levels of intersubjective validity with which more conscious psychological processes may be studied.

BOX 4.2   A STREAM OF CONSCIOUSNESS

'. . . still he had the manners not to wake me what do they find to gabber about all night squandering money and getting drunker and drunker couldnt they drink water then he starts giving us his orders for eggs and tea and Findon haddy and hot buttered toast I suppose well have him sitting up like the king of the country pumping the wrong end of the spoon up and down in his egg wherever he learned that from and I love to hear him falling up the stairs of a morning with the cups rattling on the tray and then play with the cat she rubs up against you for her own sake I wonder has she fleas shes as bad as a woman always licking and lecking but I hate their claws I wonder do they see anything that we cant staring like that when she sits at the top of the stairs so long and listening as I wait always what a robber too that lovely fresh piece I bought I think Ill get a bit of fish tomorrow or today is it Friday yes I will with some blancmange with black currant jam like long ago not those 2lb pots of mixed plum and apple from the London and Newcastle Williams and Woods goes twice as far only for the bones I hate those eels cod yes Ill get a nice piece of cod Im always getting enough for 3 forgetting anyway Im sick of that everlasting butchers meat from Buckleys loin chops and leg beef and rib steak and scrag of mutton and calfs pluck the very name is enough or a picnic suppose we all gave 5/- each and or let him pay it and invite some other woman for him who Mrs Fleming and drove out to the furry glen or the strawberry beds wed have him examining all the horses toenails first like he does with the letters no not with Boylan there yes with some cold veal and ham mixed sandwiches there are little houses down at the bottom of the banks there on purpose but its as hot as blazes he says not a bank holiday anyhow I hate those ruck of Mary Ann coalboxes out for the day Whit Monday is a cursed day too no wonder that bee bit him better the seaside but I'd never again in this life get into a boat with him after him at Bray telling the boatman he knew how to row if anyone asked could he ride the steeplechase for the gold cup hed say yes then it came on to get rough the old thing crookeding about and the weight all down my side telling me pull the right reins now pull the left and the tide all swamping in floods in through the bottom and his oar slipping out of the stirrup its a mercy we werent all drowned he can swim of course me no theres no danger whatsoever keep yourself calm in his flannel trousers . . .'

From: James Joyce (1986) *Ulysses* (the corrected text). London: Penguin Books. pp. 628f.

Dreams are usually regarded as windows for studying otherwise inaccessible, subconscious psychological processes. They tend to occur primarily during sleep and are characterized by 'rapid eye movement' (so-called REM sleep). Various principles for systematic interpretation of dreams have been suggested by psychologists and psychiatrists belonging to different schools and traditions of research and therapy. But the interpretation of dreams still seems to be as much a sophisticated art as a scholarly undertaking, a sometimes pleasant, sometimes unpleasant endeavour. We do know, however, that dreaming is a necessary precondition for a normal human life, and although some brain researchers maintain that dreams are just the way a human computer checks its memory – throwing away, as it were, unnecessary fragments temporarily located there – we will probably continue to regard them as sometimes quite important phenomena. In fictional and religious literature, they were always important, of course – think, for instance, of Joseph's dreams in Egypt as rendered in the Pentateuch of the Bible.

While such partly conscious, rather vaguely perceived and remembered intrapersonal *processes* are thus only with great difficulty accessible to research and scholarship, the intrapersonal *structures* – our personalities – are more easily observed. The study of different types of personality began during Antiquity. Its most famous result was, perhaps, the four classical types of 'temperament': the sanguine and phlegmatic, choleric and melancholic temperaments, supposedly characterized by the domination of one of the four bodily fluids, at the time distinguished between blood and phlegm, yellow and black bile.

Clearly, the four different types of personality are based on strong simplifications. Since all human beings, even one-sexed, genetically identical twins, have had at least slightly different environments and experiences, all of us are indeed virtually unique. At the same time, as human beings we also show some similarities and dissimilarities along a number of important dimensions. Such central individual characteristics may be used to sort us into various types, some of which may be organized in systematic *typologies of personality*.

There are several different typologies for human personalities. Figure 4.1 presents one such typology. It is quite simple, and yet quite striking. Actually, it is very similar to the classical 'temperaments' mentioned above. The two dimensions of the typology should be self-explanatory. The intro/extravert dimension refers to characteristics such as *sociability*, *liveliness*, *activity* and their opposites. The neurotic/non-neurotic dimension refers to variations in characteristics such as *anxiety*, *moodiness*, *emotionality* and their opposites.

The four types of human beings have indeed been found to exist and to be different in other ways as well. What makes the typology interesting in the context of communication is the fact that one of the two dimensions (intro/extraversion) is clearly communicatively-oriented, while the other one (neurotic/non-neurotic) is at least indirectly related to communication. As human beings all of us may thus be meaningfully classified with respect to

	Neurotic	Non-neurotic
Introvert	'Melancholic'	'Phlegmatic'
Extravert	'Choleric'	'Sanguine'

Figure 4.1   Four types of personality (*source*: Leaves et al., 1989)

Note: This typology was originally developed by the German-British psychologist, H.J. Eysenck. A more complex version of the typology includes a third dimension, psychotism. For further information, see, for instance, L.J. Leaves, H.J. Eysenck and N.G. Martin (1989) *Genes, Culture and Personality*. London: Academic Press.

some basic determinants of the way in which we communicate. This truth was intuitively realized thousands of years ago, and it has been verified by present-day communicatively-oriented research.

It should be remembered, however, that such relationships mirror tendencies, not one-to-one relationships. They thus tend to hold true in the aggregate, while they are not very useful when trying to make predictions in the case of a given individual – unless that individual has extreme values on one or both dimensions of the typology. Extremely introvert and neurotic individuals, for instance, may actually be characterized by *communication apprehension* to a degree which may make them need specific help and training.

While the two dimensions defining the typology presented in Figure 4.1 are important, they are by no means the only ones. A number of other dimensions of personality have been suggested, discussed and investigated – for instance, the degree of 'self-monitoring' and 'communication apprehension', 'competitiveness' and 'Machiavellianism' (ruthless goal-seeking). Obviously, such characteristics of personality, such *intrapersonal* structures and processes, must affect the way in which, as individuals, we engage in all sorts of communication, including interpersonal communication.

The experience of one's own personality is important, and so is the experience of that same personality by other persons in our surroundings. The loss of the sense for one's own personality, one's identity, therefore, is a serious blow to the life of an individual, and so is *schizophrenia*, when the mind is disturbed so that one often feels and acts as if there was more than one individual in one's mind. This tragic and complex problem is important, but it is primarily the province of psychiatry, and it will not be discussed here any further.

Finally, it should be remembered that while the personality of a given individual has its roots in biological and psychological phenomena, there is no doubt that it is also affected and modified by material, social and cultural phenomena, and especially by the different roles defined by our various positions in social and societal structure (see section 3.4). The sanguinity of a young stone-age man very probably manifested itself in concrete ways, rather different from that of a sanguine old lady in a modern, post-industrial society, and yet it must have been basically similar.

4.3 Interpersonal communication

4.3.1 Introduction

Interpersonal communication is the primeval form of human communication. It once made us human, for it was a necessary element in the evolutionary process of *individualization* resulting in *homo sapiens* and in the creation of the human group – in its turn a necessity in the individual process of becoming human which all of us have undergone: the process of *individuation* (see sections 1.3, 2.5, 3.4). In the beginning, interpersonal communication was not verbal, although oral sounds were no doubt part of it. Our primeval ancestors communicated by way of grunts and cries and other oral sounds, as well, of course, by gestures and bodily postures – no doubt in ways similar to the way a baby communicates today. As is so often the case, one may thus find a measure of parallelism between *species development* ('phylogeny') and *individual development* ('ontogeny'), although most certainly primeval grown-up members of the species of *homo sapiens* were no babies. The interpretation of such cases of parallelism is a difficult matter indeed. There is no doubt at all, however, that individual development is one of the many variables influencing human communication, and *vice versa*. Also, non-verbal communication – facial expressions, gaze, body language, touch, interpersonal distance, etc. – is still an important part of human face-to-face interpersonal communication. Part of this non-verbal communication is culturally determined; part of it, biologically determined. Not surprisingly, it appears that intercultural agreement is stronger with respect to the *type* of emotion, expressed by a given facial expression, than to the *strength* of the emotion expressed.

When studying interpersonal communication, we must try to find out both its general characteristics and the variations caused by a large number of other variables, the most important of which are age, gender, personality, education, occupation, social class, and nationality. Each variable, in combination with the other variables, defines a number of different social roles to be played (see section 4.1.2).

The influence of *age* as a determinant of interpersonal communication is at its strongest, of course, in the beginning and towards the end of our lives. (For a beautiful and witty presentation of the importance of age as a

BOX 4.3   SHAKESPEARE ON THE SEVEN AGES OF MAN

All the world's a stage,
And all the men and women merely players:
They have their exits and their entrances;
And one man in his time plays many parts,
His acts being seven ages. At first the infant,
Mewling and puking in the nurse's arms.
And then the whining school-boy, with his satchel,
And shining morning face, creeping like snail
Unwillingly to school. And then the lover,
Sighing like furnace, with a woeful ballad
Made to his mistress' eyebrow. Then a soldier,
Full of strange oaths, and bearded like the pard,
Jealous in honour, sudden and quick in quarrel,
Seeking the bubble reputation
Even in the cannon's mouth. And then the justice,
In fair round belly with good capon lin'd,
With eyes severe, and beard of formal cut,
Full of wise saws and modern instances;
And so he plays his part. The sixth age shifts
Into the lean and slipper'd pantaloon,
With spectacles on nose and pouch on side,
His youthful hose well sav'd, a world too wide
For his shrunk shank: and his big manly voice,
Turning again toward childish treble, pipes
And whistles in his sound. Last scene of all
That ends this strange eventful history,
Is second childishness and mere oblivion,
Sans teeth, sans eyes, sans taste, sans everything.

From: W. Shakespeare (1599) *As You Like It*, Act 2, Scene 7, l. 139.
Harmondsworth: Penguin.

determinant of communication, see Box 4.3.) The influence of *gender* is important during all phases of life, of course, not least within the timespan defined by female fertility, during which, in spite of increasing gender equality, the purely biological aspects of motherhood may turn out to be rather taxing. These two biological determinants of interpersonal communication always interact with powerful psychological and social determinants. *Personality*, primarily determined by bio-social circumstances is also important during the whole span of life, and so is *social class* – first, as class of origin, then, as class of destination. The influences emanating from *education* and *occupation* make themselves felt primarily during and after adolescence (see section 7.1). In many or most cases, similarity in terms of *nationality* is taken for granted. But this variable is growing increasingly important, due to the increase in international mobility, facilitated by modern means of communication and transportation and often accelerated by national and international conflict and co-operation. In such cases, the cultural side of nationality is playing a very important role.

Just as in the case of class, there are two basic types of nationality: *nationality of origin* and *nationality of destination*. Most of us have one and only one nationality: our nationality of origin. Increasingly, however, many people have also a nationality of destination, and quite a few have actually lived with more than one nationality of destination. More common, too, is the fact that in many families, wife, husband and/or children have different nationalities of origin and/or destination. A growing number of families are thus actually bi-national, or even multi-national. Some individuals – unfortunate victims of wars and other national and international conflicts – have no nationality at all (see section 7.1).

Each one of the variables just discussed exerts a powerful influence on the kind of interpersonal communication in which a given individual will tend to engage. A graphic model sorting out and grouping some such different types of influence is presented in Figure 3.3 (see also section 5.1). Here we shall add some communicative specifics: one typology for *individual* styles of interpersonal communication; one for *cultural* styles of interpersonal communication.

4.3.2 Individual communication differentiated

At bottom, we are all individuals: human animals whose behaviour and actions to a large extent are biologically determined. In recent years, interest in the biological foundations of human communication has increased. It has been shown, for instance, that individual styles of interpersonal communication are to some extent biologically determined. It has also been shown, however, that such styles are not only *biologically*, but also *culturally* determined. In Box 4.4 you'll find some information about how to conceptualize and measure the way such influences make themselves felt.

In addition to the influence emanating from such individual and cultural characteristics as those just discussed, interpersonal communication is strongly affected also by the communicants' *concordance* or *discordance*, *similarity* or *dissimilarity* in terms of a number of basic variables listed and discussed above and in Box 4.4. As a rule, we tend to prefer communicating with people not too different from ourselves with respect to these variables. A moderate amount of difference may stimulate communication; many large differences tend to reduce it – 'birds of a feather flock together'.

Figure 4.2 offers an instrument for sorting out degrees of similarity and dissimilarity between individual communicators: the social distance between them. It is shaped as a so-called 'Guttman-scale', featuring continuous growth in similarity or dissimilarity. The character and frequence of interpersonal communication will be rather different, of course, if two communicators are identical, or at least similar, on all seven characteristics, or on none at all. Similarity breeds familiarity – a basic condition for truly successful communication. In this sense, true interpersonal communication

BOX 4.4 BIOLOGICAL AND CULTURAL ORIGINS OF COMMUNICATION STYLE

It is only reasonable to assume that our inborn personalities, our 'temperaments', affect the way we communicate, so that there are different *individual styles* of communication. In a similar way, it is quite reasonable to assume that the societal culture within which our communication takes place will affect our way of communication, so that there are different *cultural styles* of communication. Both these assumptions have indeed been tested time and again in communication research. To carry out such tests, we need instruments for measuring communicatively relevant aspects of individual personalities and societal cultures. Several such instruments have been developed.

Studying personality, it is often good strategy to compare 'identical twins' (so-called *monozygotic* or MZ twins stemming from one human egg) with 'fraternal twins' (so-called *dizygotic* or DZ twins, stemming from two different eggs and thus genetically being just ordinary sisters or brothers). In one relatively recent study, a sample of MZ and DZ twins were compared with respect to the temperament of their personality and their style of individual communication. As expected, there were close relationships between temperament and style of communication. Different personalities do indeed communicate differently. In addition, the relationships found between temperament and style of communication were more and stronger for MZ twins than for DZ twins.

The conclusion drawn was that *individual communicator styles are to some extent biologically determined*.

In another study, young adults in Germany, Israel and the United States were compared with respect to their 'listening styles', characterized as more or less oriented towards

- *action* (getting the message quickly);
- *people* (becoming personally involved);
- *time* (being impatient); or
- *content* (concentrate on the facts).

Germans preferred the *Action* style; Israelis, the *Content* style, while Americans favoured both the *People* style and the *Time* style. The conclusion to be drawn is that *individual listening styles are to some extent culturally determined*.

In addition, we know that communication style is also strongly affected by the three basic social variables of age, gender and social class. Similar differences will also be found when in Chapter 6 we turn to mass communication.

From: C.W. Horwath (1995) 'Biological origins of communicator style', *Communication Quarterly*, 43 (4): 394–407.

C. Kiewitz et al. (1997) 'Cultural differences in listening style preferences', *International Journal of Public Opinion Research*, 9 (3): 233–47.

is not a matter of yes or no. It is a matter of degree. The more similar, the more interpersonal in the deepest sense of the word (at least, up to a point).

Then again, we must not forget that social differentiation is less regular than what Figure 4.2 suggests. Actually, the alternatives that are presented offer $2^7 = 128$ different combinations of similarity or dissimilarity between two individuals. In addition, the concept of distance must sometimes be differentially defined. A socially significant distance in age, for instance, must of necessity vary with age, since a difference of five years is, of course, very important in childhood, adolescence and among old people, but much less important between middle-aged people.

Distance in:

	Age	Gender	Personality	Education	Occupation	Social class	Nationality
Age	x						
Gender	x	x					
Personality	x	x	x				
Education	x	x	x	x			
Occupation	x	x	x	x	x		
Social class	x	x	x	x	x	x	
Nationality	x	x	x	x	x	x	x

Figure 4.2   Degrees of social distance affecting interpersonal communication

Studies of interpersonal communication thus often have had to disregard many potential combinations of differences between individual communicators. We have to stay content, with controls for as many variables at a time as possible, and for some effects due to, say, interaction between variables, by means of carefully defining our population of study, as well as by the randomization of experimental and control groups, computerized statistical techniques, etc. Special interest seems to have been given to the unique and combined influences emanating from age and gender, class and nationality, the variables sometimes being discussed and analyzed only one by one.

4.3.3   Variation and stability in individual communication

While the differences just discussed are important, even more important are those characteristics of interpersonal communication which stay more or less constant – in spite of the many differences between individuals communicating and between the situations in which interpersonal communication may take place. The basic characteristics of interpersonal communication are closely related to the fact that interpersonal communication is just that: interpersonal.

One way in which the very interpersonality of interpersonal communication affects its character is by so-called *display rules*. Interpersonal relationships are quite brittle phenomena, and too much truth and sincerity may sometimes be rather harmful to them. We thus all learn sometimes to control the way we display our feelings, especially when convenience, etiquette or just plain humanity so tell us. For better and for worse, we learn how to be dishonest in individual interaction. There are several ways to do so, the three most characteristic being simulation, inhibition and masking: when *simulating*, you show feelings you don't have; when *inhibiting*, although you may have quite strong feelings, you don't show them; when *masking* you show one feeling, although you really experience quite another one. Masking may thus actually be regarded as a combination of simulating and inhibiting.

Small children are not very good at simulating, inhibiting and masking, and not much better at finding out about other people's simulating, inhibiting and masking, but we learn pretty quickly. Nobody is perfect, however, in those noble arts. Besides the *impressions* we want to give, there are always also some *expressions given off*. Our feelings, or lack of feelings, often 'leak out' from behind our simulations, inhibitions and masking. More often than we like to realize, perhaps, our true feelings are thus communicated all the same, an experience which may be quite embarrassing to both parties, indeed, sometimes more embarrassing than plain truth would have been.

An interesting complication to these strategies is that we may both exaggerate and underestimate the extent to which our feelings and actions are perceived as positive or negative – indeed, the extent to which they are perceived at all. Although our way of communicating does reveal a lot about our own inner thoughts and feelings about the content of our messages, it is a fact that we are sometimes capable of hiding such inner thoughts and feelings almost completely – even to ourselves. A very basic, ingenious and yet simple way of sorting out such phenomena is a typology which has been called the *Johari Window* (after its creators, Joseph Luft and Harrington Ingram). It is shown in Figure 4.3.

Attributes

	Known to self	Not known to self
Known to others	1. Open	2. Blind
Not known to others	3. Secret	4. Unknown

Attributes

Figure 4.3 The Johari Window (*source*: Luft, 1984)

Cell 1 of Figure 4.3 represents a theoretically rather unproblematic case: attributes which we ourselves know and which are also known to others. Cell 3 probably represents a rather frequent case. As a rule we know much more about ourselves than anybody else does, one reason being, of course, that people just don't care to know everything about everybody. In addition, rightly or wrongly, we like to think that even if they *should* care to know more about us than they really do, we are capable of simulating, inhibiting and/or masking, that is actively hiding or even misrepresenting things about ourselves. On the other hand, we also tend to be quite clever – indeed, sometimes only too clever – at hiding some truths about ourselves even to ourselves (while at the same time, some of those truths may be visible to other persons in our environment). In that sense, all of us are more or less blind (cell 2).

Cell 4, finally, represents phenomena pertaining to ourselves but unknown to both ourselves and our surroundings. Actually, the size of this cell represents an interesting psychological, sociological, intellectual and epistemological problem, for, paradoxically, cell 4 grows as a result of generally increasing levels of knowledge. *The more we know about the surrounding world and ourselves, the more we also know that there are even more phenomena about which we do not know!* This kind of knowledge is sometimes called 'specified lack of knowledge'.

Specified lack of knowledge is a precious thing indeed, a good starting point for scholarly and scientific activities. Indeed, some specified lack of knowledge is necessary even when in our everyday lives we turn to a reference book or an encyclopedia. And last, but certainly not least, specified lack of knowledge may also be valuable when we communicate about ourselves with individuals in our surroundings. Sometimes, indeed, we may help each other to move some of our characteristics from cell 4 to cell 1. Much therapeutic psychology, of course, consists of attempts to move personal knowledge from cells 4 and/or 2 to cell 1 – or at least, to cell 3. The religious act of confession is a ritualized way of moving individual attributes from cell 3 to cell 1, although, of course, the openness of sins confessed is limited to the confessant and the confessor.

To most people, some cells of Figure 4.3 stand out as 'better' than the other ones. Also, the size of each cell is variable, in at least two senses: the number of phenomena in the cells may vary *between cells*, and also, *within cells*, over time. As a rule, an ongoing positive personal relationship between two people, a dyad, is characterized by a fairly large and growing cell 1. In such a relationship, information tends to flow to cell 1 from both cells 2 and 3. Indeed, the two parties of a positive personal relationship may actually be able to reduce also the size of cell 4, by jointly producing new personal knowledge which previously was unknown to both of them. Such procedures may take quite some time. A simile sometimes used to describe them is 'peeling off an onion'. That seems to be a rather unhappy simile, however, at least to those of us who like to think that we do have an inner core, a few characteristics, tenets and principles which we are not at all willing, or perhaps, are unable to sell out or even show off. Sometimes, we just want them to appear in our actions – naturally, as it were.

An interesting complication of the conceptualization presented in terms of the Johari Window is that the basic categories of the typology are taken to be objectively true. However, many human attributes may be hidden to, or falsely presented by, the owners of the attributes and/or by people surrounding them. Take, for instance, a political viewpoint. An employee may be an ardent anti-feminist, but, since his boss is a successful young woman, he feels he shouldn't show his true opinions on such matters to her. Indeed, he may not only be hiding those feelings, but actually may be exhibiting the exact opposite. This is the strong sense of cell 3 (the weak sense being that he is perceived by his boss as being neutral on those matters, while in fact he is not neutral at all). In principle, the same type of argument may be applied to the other cells of the typology. What has happened is that the *categories* of the typology have been turned into *variables*. We are not talking just open/closed, but 'more or less open or closed', 'more or less' ranging from 'not at all' to 'completely so'. Those new variables may then be related to other variables, say, to a more or less successful career, or to a person's views about truth.

In principle, the Johari Window is applicable also to relationships within groups larger than the dyad – for instance, a circle of friends and aquaintances. As a rule, such processes of gradual, mutual disclosure tend to be quite positive to the life of the group, even if the truths disclosed may sometimes be painful. The positive outcomes of these processes are strengthened by the fact that human communication is also governed by so-called 'reciprocity n orms' ('quid pro quo'). We are thus expected to react to generously open communication in a positive way. A positive 'spiral of interaction' comes about and will gradually find its equilibrium. This is often what family therapy is aiming at.

Such developments are further strengthened by the fact that most of us have been taught to try to avoid escalating a threatening conflict which would otherwise result in a spiral of negative interaction. At some point, an equilibrium must be reached, the negative spiral must be broken. Typical cases of fatal spirals of interaction which are otherwise bound to occur include the vendettas between hostile groups, clans or families – to be found not only in southern Italy, or between families, but also between different groups of, say, managers, scholars and researchers.

4.3.4 Taking turns and other norms of reciprocity

A more peaceful phenomenon is what in communication studies is called *turn-taking*. The term 'turn-taking' refers to the fact that, by definition, all communication processes must be structured so that sooner or later one communicant stops sending messages, letting the co-communicant have a chance – for a while, at least. Actually, turn-taking is a quite subtle phenomenon. In most cases it takes place without much ado. There is an implicit agreement about the length of each speaker's turn in the conversation. As a rule, the speaker signals that the present part of the conversation is approaching an end, by lowering the voice (statement) or raising it (question), thus signalling the expectation of an answer, an objection, an expression of agreement, surprise or protest, etc. In formalized or semi-formalized conversations, there is often an official or semi-official chairperson or other authoritative participant in the discussion who implicitly or explicitly signals that time is out for the current speaker.

Turn-taking may be regarded as a special case of what is sometimes called *reciprocity norms*. Language has specific forms for realizing reciprocal turn-taking – combinations of two speech acts called *adjacency pairs* (on speech acts, see section 2.4 above):

- Greeting   –   Greeting
- Question   –   Answer
- Offer   –   Acceptance/rejection
- Request   –   Compliance/protest/refusal
- Order   –   Obeyance/protest/refusal
- Accusation   –   Admittance/confession/defence/denial.

By playing with such adjacency pairs, a skilful communicator can keep the initiative in a conversation or other iterative processes of communication.

4.3.5   Does the exception prove the rule?

An interesting phenomenon is what happens when somebody ignores, or consciously chooses to break, the habitual, more or less normative pattern of a conversation as usually implicitly agreed upon and schematically described above. In most cases, the other participants in the conversation see to it that the deviance is overcome as easily as possible, half jokingly, for example. In some cases, the offender becomes aware of the fact that he or she has dominated the conversation too much, has initiated it in an untoward way, or has led it astray, etc. He or she then tries to explain, justify or excuse his or her behaviour in various ways. Similar phenomena also occur in mediated interpersonal communication. The implicit norms of interpersonal communication/conversation are thus in the end often honoured even when broken against.

4.4   Group communication

4.4.1   Introduction

The first wave of modern scholarly and scientific interest in group communication started back in the 1950s. A second wave of interest followed a couple of decades later, then as 'network studies' or 'network analysis' (see section 2.5 and 5.1). An increasing impetus to the revival of the field came with the computer which allows quantitative analysis of even large, loosely knitted networks.

In all communicative phenomena, the importance of size is quite remarkable. Obviously, as the number of communicating units (n) in a communicative system grows, the number of potential direct relations (R) between the units of the system also grows. It does so according to the simple but very important formula,

$$R = \frac{n(n-1)}{2}$$

Thus a group with five members has $\frac{(5 \times 4)}{2}$ = 10 different potential two-way links between its five members. But when the group size doubles, it suddenly has more than four times as many different potential two-way links between its ten members (45, to be exact). In parallel with this increasing complexity of group structure (this *quantitative change*), the communicative system of the group undergoes some *qualitative change*. Individual communication rapidly turns into group communication.

The smallest possible group is, of course, a group of two people – a so-called *dyad*. Then comes the *triad*, a group of three people, a *quartet*, a *quintet* and so on. In absolute terms, the difference between a dyad and a triad is quantitatively small. But in relative terms, of course, a triad is 50% larger than a dyad, and that difference is qualitatively quite important. A triad admits the formation of coalitions within the group (actually, three different ones), and if the group has a secret which becomes known outside the group by way of a leak from one of its members, then both members in a dyad know for sure who leaked it, whereas in the triad only one member does. Such differences make communication between two individuals different from communication between three or more individuals. Indeed, some scholars maintain that the dyad is not a group in the proper sense, but a social formation of its own. According to that view, then, a true group has at least three members. Since in this chapter we have made a distinction between individual communication and group communication, we are at least indirectly backing up this view.

As the size of the group grows, as its goal is made more explicit and formalized, and as its structure is becoming increasingly formalized (a growing hierarchy of increasingly differentiated leadership covering different functions, etc.), the group is gradually turning into an *organization* (see Chapter 5).

Now, where is the upper limit for a group? Strictly theoretically, there is no such limit. A clever orator may turn even a large amorphous mass of individuals momentarily at least into a group with a leader and a joint goal (see section 4.1). Some sociologists even regard a whole society as a group, since, in principle, it has characteristics in common with a small group. But most scholars agree that as a rule it is practical to restrict the definition of a human group to a fairly small number of people having certain characteristics in common. A human group may be defined, then, as

- a *small number of individuals* (at most a dozen or, perhaps, 20),
- having a *joint identity* based on
- a common, implicit or explicit *goal*, as well as
- a more or less informal *structure*, including
- some sort of informal or semi-formalized *leadership*.

Group communication may thus be described as (a) communication within social entities having at most a score or so of members; and (b) communication between such entities and their societal surroundings (including, of course, other groups and individuals, as well as organizations and society itself). Just like all other group activities (the *processes* of this little system), group communication is both forming and formed by the *structure* of the group, defined by a number of various group characteristics.

4.4.2   Group structure

Just like all other groups, even a completely informal group of friends has a certain *structure*, although that structure is by definition unformalized.

Time is an important element of group structure. The age of the group as such (the period of time during which the group has existed) is a basic characteristic of its structure, affecting the character of its activities, even disregarding the age of the individual members of the group. In addition, all group activities, including group communication, vary over time, sometimes following the seasons of the year and/or the economic and political situation of society, always and inevitably following the biological process of ageing common to all human group members.

Not all members are exactly alike, however. Some members, for instance, are more active than other ones. They are often found in the centre of the group, sometimes forming what is technically called a *clique*, a tightly knit sub-group within the group. On the periphery we find more passive members, more or less openly accepting or rejecting the suggestions from the leading members of the group. Such peripheral members sometimes club together to form an oppositional clique.

Group structures may be described, measured and analyzed by various so-called sociometric techniques, techniques which were originally introduced into social science in the 1930s by the Italian-American psychotherapist, J.L. Moreno. The results of these analyses can be visualized in *sociograms*, graphic figures based on the preferences of all group members, for all group members as measured in interviews or questionnaires (those preferences often mirroring actual interactions). In the 1950s, sociometry was revived as computer technology permitted the detailed quantitative analysis of large amounts of sociometric data, that is 'network analysis' (see sections 2.5 and 5.1). Figure 4.4 presents a simple sociogram, offering an abstract picture of

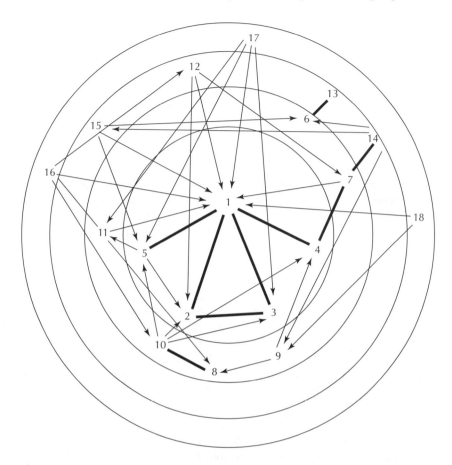

Figure 4.4 A target sociogram (*source*: Rosengren and Arvidson, 1997)

the structure of preferences and interactions in a small group of college students.

The sociogram is a so-called 'target sociogram'. In the centre of the target we find the *group leader* as a member of a central *clique*, who is surrounded by satellites and peripheral group members. In principle, this type of structure is characteristic for all groups of this size. Such a sociogram can be translated into a matrix which can then be formally analyzed in terms of *matrix algebra*. This kind of analysis is often used in a research tradition called 'communication network analysis' (see section 5.1).

4.4.3 Societally institutionalized groups

Some groups are societal institutions in the sense that society provides a more or less institutionalized set of norms and rules for each of these types of group (see section 1.3). The most basic groups are the family, the peer group, and the working group (these groups being more or less differentially defined in different cultures).

There are two main types of family: the *core family* of man, woman, children; the *extended family*, including more than one generation and/or more than one core family belonging to the same generation. The difference between family and kinship is thus relative. It is further complicated by the possibility of *polygamy* (one husband, more than one wife) and *polyandry* (one wife, more than one husband), both of which are rare today, although the former is more common than the latter, which is so rare that each case calls for a special explanation.

The human core family might be said to offer a primeval prototype for all human groups, as well as for all human organizations. Its basis is both highly biological and highly social, not to say economic: in principle, an exclusive right to sexual intercourse between spouses, and a binding responsibility for jointly bringing up and socializing new members of society. It is thus a unit for both production and reproduction.

One important consequence of the combined biological and social character of the family is that (in principle, and as a rule) its members are not exchangeable, in contrast to those of most other groups or organizations. You cannot really leave that strange organization called a family, for you have one and only one biological mother, one and only one biological father. Also, your daughters and sons will always be your daughters and sons. There is thus no true substitution and no succession in a core family, although, of course, there is not only biological, but also social heritage, and also divorces and re-marrying, phenomena which have sometimes been called 'consecutive polygamy/polyandry', and which in general parlance are expressed in terms of the prefix 'step-', as in 'stepmother', 'stepfather', etc.

In the strictly juridical sense, a marriage may be dissolved in practically all modern societies, and both parties may marry somebody else, a procedure sometimes repeated more than once, thus introducing what might be called 'temporal polygamy'. But according to some religious beliefs, marriages can never be dissolved. Indeed, many people still adhere to such beliefs. In addition, biological inheritance cannot be done away with. Your mother may indeed have divorced your biological father and re-married, so that socially you may have a new father, but he is not your biological father, and in most cases the three of you know that. This knowledge, in its turn, affects your relationships, one way or other. Similarly, adopted children often, or perhaps even as a rule, come to know that they have other, biological parents in addition to those in the family in which they live. Their feelings towards those biological parents may sometimes be rather mixed, sometimes strongly romanticized. They may sometimes prefer to regard their adoptive parents as the 'real parents', but they also know whose children they 'really' are. In some societies you may disinherit a wayward son, but he will always be your biological son, and when he returns to his parents, the joy in the family is great. You may tell your mother you don't ever want to see her again, and you (and she) may even live up to that decision, but she will always be your mother. In this sense, the family is a prison in which all of us serve for life. Most of us would be quite unhappy, however, if we ever had to leave that prison and its inmates. We would be even more unhappy if our children denounced us.

4.4.4 Group leadership

All groups are more or less hierarchically arranged, within groups and between groups. The strength of the hierarchical pattern varies between types of group, with the type of main activity of the group, and over time. Significantly, the smallest unit in an army (a 'squad') is often called just a 'group', three or four groups forming a platoon, three or four platoons, a company, three or four companies, a battalion, and so on. Similar levels are found in other types of organization, for example, in business enterprises, and at local, regional, national and international levels, etc. And, at the bottom of such large organizations, we always find the human group.

A group hierarchy is characterized by two types of leadership: *instrumental* and *expressive* leadership. Instrumental leadership focuses on the instrumental functions of the group: production, survival, formal relations within the group and between the group and its surroundings. The instrumental leader thus sets the goals of the group and sees to it that these goals are realized.

Expressive leadership is primarily concerned with the social relations within the group, as well as with the basic values held by the group. Expressive leadership is thus important not least in creating and providing acceptance of, and consensus about, the goals set or at least formulated by the instrumental leader. Goals thus tend to be set from above, while they have to find acceptance from below. Neither instrumental nor expressive leadership, therefore, can ignore the views and opinions of the rest of the group.

Both types of leadership are fundamental for the survival and success of the group. They are functionally defined. Thus (especially in some small, tightly knit groups) both can be exerted by one and the same individual. Leadership manifests itself primarily by communication, sometimes realized in concrete action: 'leadership by example'. Good leadership presupposes both firmness and flexibility, and not least *empathy*, the capacity to recognize, respect and adequately respond to other people's thoughts and feelings, without necessarily sharing them.

4.4.5 Socialization and the family communication climate

All groups have to train and teach their members: teaching them what is good, true, productive, beautiful, healthy, normal, etc.; training them in the art of acting so as to realize these precious values (see the Great Wheel of Culture in Society (Figure 3.1) in section 3.2). As mentioned above, such processes of teaching and learning form what is called *socialization*. They are immensely important.

There are two main types of socialization. Socialization carried out during childhood, especially within the family, is called *primary socialization*. Later on, socialization carried out in groups other than the family is so-called *secondary socialization* (see sections 1.3, 3.3, and 6.4). Primary socialization is primary in at least two senses: (a) it is the first one: and (b) it concerns very basic skills and manners – how to behave in a small group, how to eat, when to sleep, etc. Obviously, all socialization builds on various processes of communication.

The basic agent of socialization, then, is the family. As primary socialization is carried out within the family, it is naturally influenced by the *family communication climate*. This climate structures the interaction and communication going on in the family, not least the processes of socialization. There are two main types of family communication climate. These have been called 'socio-orientation' and 'concept-orientation'. The former stresses social harmony, trying to avoid controversy. The latter stresses intellectual values, encouraging flexibility and tendencies to challenge other people's views, in spite of potential differences in status, knowledge, capacity, etc. Crossing the two dimensions, we get a typology for socialization processes (see Figure 4.5).

The socialization processes going on in the four different types of family communication climate tend to be rather different. In *laissez-faire families* the amount of active and conscious socialization is reduced to the minimum necessary to make family life bearable and to keep the family together. In *protective families* children are protected as much as possible from meeting opinions different from those of the family (and sometimes even shielded from knowledge about some of life's harsh realites). In *consensual families*, although children are allowed to express and defend their own ideas, children's and parents' opinions about the best way of leading one's life tend to coincide. Family consensus prevails. In *pluralistic families* children are themselves encouraged to seek, accept or reject knowledge, and to have and defend their own opinions, even if these do not coincide with those of the parents. A plurality of views and opinions is found.

		Socio-orientation	
		Low	High
	Low	*Laissez-faire*	Protective
Concept-orientation			
	High	Pluralistic	Consensual

Figure 4.5 Family communication climates (*source*: Chaffee et al., 1971)

Obviously, the results of these different processes of family socialization must in themselves be different. Empirical communication research measures these differences. It has been shown, for instance, that boys and girls growing up in *laissez-faire* families have a somewhat more negative self-image than other youngsters.

Finally, it should be mentioned that these four main types of communication climate may be found, of course, in other small groups and not just in family groups. In such cases, they are sometimes expressed in the more general terms of 'control' and '*resources*' (see Figure 3.4 on p. 64).

The amount of common control and resources varies immensely between groups. This is so not least for geographically defined groups, the most basic of which is the neighbourhood group. Obviously, the informal control to be found in a village neighbourhood is rather different from that of a neighbourhood in a dilapidated city centre. The informal control in a neighbourhood of a successfully renovated city centre offers yet another picture. The interplay between the two dimensions of control and resources may thus appear in many different shapes.

4.5   Functions of group communication

We have already mentioned that, in addition to such *qualitative* differences as discussed above, *quantitative* phenomena are also important to group communication. We have also seen that the arithmetic of the simple formula $\frac{n(n-1)}{2}$ has important consequences for communication in groups, networks and organizations (see section 4.4.1). One weapon against the iron law formula is increasing differentiation within the group, based on increasing specialization by different group members. Within a large group, various sub-groups emerge, sometimes with more or less formally agreed upon tasks. The group is on its way to becoming an organization. Such processes of differentiation and specialization have a common root in the basic distinction between instrumental and expressive functions of the groups mentioned above (see Figure 4.5, also the Great Wheel of Culture in Society in Figure 3.1). It should be noted, however, that groups communicating asyncronically, by way of a more advanced technology, such as groups of people chatting on the Internet, may have many more members than a traditional 'natural group'. The number of theoretically possible links between group members grows much more rapidly than the number of members. Very properly, such groups are often not called groups, but 'networks' (see section 4.4.1).

As far back as in the 1950s, the various functions of group communication were most ingeniously studied in a series of theoretically well-founded experiments by Robert F. Bales of Harvard University. He distinguished between a dozen different types of speech act (see section 2.4), ordering them in the meaningful pattern shown in Figure 4.6. It will be seen that the 12 interaction categories are neatly organized in various types of instrumental and expressive communication, so that the instrumental functions are found

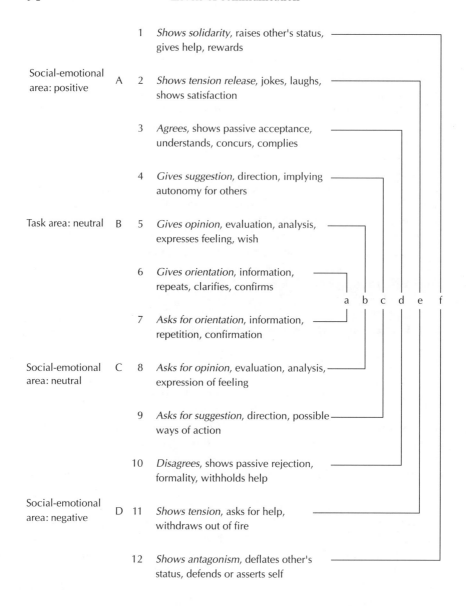

1 *Shows solidarity*, raises other's status, gives help, rewards

Social-emotional area: positive   A

2 *Shows tension release*, jokes, laughs, shows satisfaction

3 *Agrees*, shows passive acceptance, understands, concurs, complies

4 *Gives suggestion*, direction, implying autonomy for others

Task area: neutral   B

5 *Gives opinion*, evaluation, analysis, expresses feeling, wish

6 *Gives orientation*, information, repeats, clarifies, confirms

7 *Asks for orientation*, information, repetition, confirmation

Social-emotional area: neutral   C

8 *Asks for opinion*, evaluation, analysis, expression of feeling

9 *Asks for suggestion*, direction, possible ways of action

10 *Disagrees*, shows passive rejection, formality, withholds help

Social-emotional area: negative   D

11 *Shows tension*, asks for help, withdraws out of fire

12 *Shows antagonism*, deflates other's status, defends or asserts self

a   b   c   d   e   f

Key:

a   Problems of communication
b   Problems of evaluation
c   Problems of control
d   Problems of decision
e   Problems of tension reduction
f   Problems of reintegration

A   Positive reactions
B   Attempted answers
C   Questions
D   Negative reactions

Figure 4.6   Robert Bales's Categories for Interaction Process Analysis
(*source*: Bales, 1976)

in categories 4–9; the expressive functions, in categories 1–3 and 10–12. The main dimensions of the Bales typology are very basic indeed. They operate at all levels of human social life, and we have already discussed them in terms of the Great Wheel of Culture in Society (see Figure 3.1 on p. 55).

Depending upon the more or less explicit goals of the group, different groups vary considerably in the time they spend on the various kinds of inter-group communication. Quite naturally, working groups have to spend more time on instrumental functions. Groups of friends and acquaintances who have concrete tasks to solve may also spend considerable portions of their communication on instrumental functions, while as a rule they tend to spend most of their communication on the expressive functions. (In addition, the expressive function may, paradoxically, become so important to the existence of groups of friends that it actually might be regarded as highly instrumental to the life of the group.)

4.6 The strength of the weak tie

4.6.1   The concept of the weak tie

Bales's typology for acts of communication refers to within-group com-munication ('intra-group communication') but it could also be applied to communication *between* groups ('inter-group communication'). By definition, most group communication is intra-group communication, but all groups also have to communicate with their surroundings, and some groups spend considerable time on inter-group communication.

In communication between groups, the group leaders are often very important, but other members may be quite important in such cases, too. Indeed, even rather peripheral group members may be valuable due to the fact that they sometimes have relatively strong relationships with other groups. A special case of this phenomenon has been called the 'strength of the weak tie' (the term and concept introduced in the early 1970s by the US sociologist, Mark Granovetter).

For one reason or another, some group members have especially good relations with other groups, displayed in frequent contacts with members of those other groups. If a given group member is the only one who has such an external link to another group, his or her position may become a very important one, even if he or she happens to be a marginal figure in each of the two groups. The reason why this group member is so important is that he or she is the only person to join the two groups into one system. The strength of his or her position lies in this one tie. It is an example of the 'strength of the weak tie'. Such ties are especially important if there is a need for collaboration between the two groups; more generally, they represent a liaison, a bridge, a gateway to the surroundings of both groups. They may thus be regarded as a special variant of what in other connections is called a 'gate-keeper' (see section 6.4.2).

Now, if an individual represents the only link between two networks, he or she may sometimes be the only link to other networks as well. Such a person occupies an important position within the group. Where individuals occupy a central position within their own group and have a number of unique links to other groups they tend to be even more valuable to the group, and are often so valuable that they hold a leading position in the group. Why does this happen? Do people who have many 'weak ties' to other groups become group leaders, or is it the other way round? As so often, the answer may well be both ways.

4.6.2 Some functions of the weak tie

Disregarding the problem of how people with many weak ties achieve their position, it is obvious that occupants of this position serve in numerous capacities. They act as valuable links in a number of social and societal processes, for instance, negotiation processes, or processes of diffusion and adoption of innovations, or, say, the spread of more or less well-founded rumours (see Box 4.5; for rumours in organizations called the 'grapevine', see section 5.4).

Group linking also has another communicatively interesting consequence. Although most groups are, almost by definition, local, some groups may be very international indeed – for example, research groups. Also, the fact that virtually all groups must have at least some direct or indirect links to their surroundings suggests that the gigantic 'group of groups', making up the whole world population, might actually form a surprisingly efficient communicative system. US psychologist Stanley Milgram devised an ingenious experiment to test whether this is so. Wanting to measure the capacity of interpersonal networks, he asked people to send a given message to an unknown, geographically distant person by way of personal contacts. As it turned out, the number of personal links necessary to connect two individuals living on the East and West coasts of the USA, respectively, was quite small (on average, about half a dozen). Also the number of links that are needed to connect two individuals of different nationality, living in different parts of the world, and unknown to each other is surprisingly low.

This problematic and its surprising outcome has been dubbed *The Small World Problem*. In its way, it is rather comforting, although it may be difficult intuitively to understand it. An important role in such cases is again played by the strength of the weak tie. Most of us know somebody living in another part of our country, and even if not all of us have personal friends abroad, many people do have, and many people know somebody who has friends overseas. Thus the chain tends to start with an often weak but certainly important link. Much the same argument holds true for contacts with the inhabitants of a large city some distance from where we ourselves may live. Once more, we see 'the strength of the weak tie'.

Weak ties sometimes bridge both time and space. You may no longer associate with that old school-friend, but she did become a doctor in the end, didn't she? And now your child has stomach pains, and your family doctor

BOX 4.5   ON THE TRUTHS OF RUMOURS

Rumours represent an important type of communication in modern societies whether in individual, group or mass communication. They tend to feature in situations when something important has happened (or is believed to have happened) and when information about what has happened is scarce and/or contradictory. Probably the most famous rumour was the so-called 'invasion from Mars' panic, which resulted from a science-fiction radio broadcast by a young Orson Welles (1915–85), later to become known as a creative if somewhat wilful *auteur* of a series of motion pictures. In 1938, Welles's radio broadcast, 'The War of the Worlds', based on a story originally written in 1898 by the English novelist H.G. Wells, featured an invasion from Mars. Many people thought the program was real, quite naturally becoming very scared. Some actually tried to flee, jumping into their cars with their families and belongings. Not surprisingly, these phenomena were vividly reported on the radio and in newspapers. Subsequent studies, undertaken soon after the radio broadcast, revealed that the panic was indeed genuine in some instances, although, again not surprisingly, it had been greatly exaggerated by the media.

In 1973, a similar phenomenon occurred in Sweden. As part of an ongoing debate about nuclear power plants, Swedish Radio broadcast a fictitious news report about an accident in a nuclear power station then under construction at Barsebäck in southern Sweden. Leakage was said to have occurred, with the result that radio-active material was being carried in the wind across southern Sweden and towards Copenhagen, the capital city of Denmark some 15 miles distant. The fictitious radio program was mistaken for a real news bulletin by a tiny portion of its large audience (in absolute terms, a sizeable number of people, however). Within an hour, several Swedish and Danish radio stations reported widespread panic in southern Sweden. Television broadcasts later followed up the story. Next day, the newspaper carried page-wide headlines on the panic, in some cases using the exaggerated versions of the Orson Welles panic as a model.

At the request of the Swedish Board of Psychological Defence, an investigation based on personal interviews with a representative sample of the population in the area, as well as qualitative and quantitative content analyses of mass media reports etc., was undertaken at the University of Lund in southern Sweden. It showed that less than 1% of the population had in fact been scared. No-one in the sample had panicked and no-one had seen anything remotely similar to the panic reports of the media. However, an extremely tiny portion of the population admitted being scared for a short while.

These results are in agreement with studies carried out in connection with real disasters. Mass reactions may appear, of course, but rarely do panics of the kind and scope presented by the mass media in the two cases of the 'War of the Worlds' panic and the Barsebäck panic actually occur. From time to time, however, such panics are reported by the media, often the result of the pressure of deadlines, hear-say information and poor source control by the journalists.

From: K.E. Rosengren, P. Arvidson and D. Sturesson (1978) 'The Bärseback Panic', in C. Winick (ed.), *Deviance and Mass Media*. Beverly Hills, CA: Sage.

doesn't answer the telephone. What about contacting her? She still lives in her home town, doesn't she? Why not call her, talk about the good old days, just as if the tie between you and your former school-friend should still be multifunctional, and when time is ripe throw in a casual question about appendicitis?

Useful as they may be, it should also be mentioned that weak ties are often weak in more than one sense. By definition they are weak in the sense that they are not thoroughly embedded in the communicative networks of your primary groups (family, work group, etc.). It may thus take quite some time to activate the weak tie. In addition, these ties are weak in the sense that they are often limited to one specific function. They are seldom multifunctional in the way in which ties between members of a closely knit group of friends and relatives are multifunctional.

There is a special term for positions likely to generate weak ties, *familiar strangers* – people you meet regularly but sometimes without even knowing their names. They are often so-called 'urban agents' working in more or less public positions: local officials, teachers, service attendants, shop assistants, bartenders, hairdressers, bus drivers, etc. The strength of such 'uni-functional' weak ties may sometimes be such as to admit not only exchange, of small-talk but, if need be, even serious advice in a critical situation.

Weak ties within and between groups may thus represent powerful instruments even for communication at a distance (see also the following section). Then, again, the sad truth is that in the end, no matter how closely knitted their networks may be, all groups die, especially small, informal groups of friends, colleagues and neighbours. Some groups have longer lives than other groups, however. Formally organized groups, for example – often called organizations (see section 5.1) – tend to survive longer than do informal groups, and some organizations have survived for centuries. A large Swedish company, STORA, having recently merged with other companies, traces its origins from *c.* 1000 AD. Two very old, very large, and highly formalized groups are the Roman Catholic Church and the Greek Orthodox Church, the former being some 1,500 years old, the latter some 800 or 900 years younger.

Before turning to organizational communication, which is the subject of the next chapter, let us shortly discuss yet another type of communication: mediated individual and group communication, mediated in a different sense, that is, from the one implied in arguments about 'the strength of the weak tie'.

4.7 Mediated individual and group communication

4.7.1 Introduction

During the last 150 years or so, the means of both communication and transportation have been freed from their previously earthbound, locally restricted existence. Whole military expeditionary forces – tanks, hospitals, etc. – can now be transported between continents in a matter of weeks. You can have a telephone conference with three friends and/or colleagues on three different continents at the same time, the only restriction being time differences between continents. Such developments in the means of transportation and communication have tended to run in parallel, partly because the transportation of goods, as a rule, must be followed by information – information not only about the goods themselves, but also about the type of transportation used in the specific case, the time in transit and the actual status of the transportation process at a given moment. Originally, the transportation of information equalled the transportation of people and/or goods. For thousands of years wanderers, slow ox-waggons and rapidly riding couriers used the rough roads and narrow paths provided by the large empires and small countries on the African, American and Euro-Asian continents. Pilgrims walked to far away temples in Eleusis and Delphi, Jerusalem and Rome, Mecca and Medina, Kyoto in Japan, Sergiev Posad outside Moscow, Lourdes in France, Santiago de Compostela in Spain, Nidaros in Norway, and to very many other places. And then they walked home again, if they didn't die *en route*. Even important news took weeks or months to arrive at the central administration from the outskirts of an empire. For centuries people have sought faster means of transportation. The fast clipper ships represented perhaps the acme of this development, as did the short-lived Pony Express, launched in mid-nineteenth-century USA, only to be quickly outmoded by the steam-engine on its railway. Later on, means of transportation and communication became mutually interdependent and complementary. A good example is the telegraph/telephone lines which originally ran parallel to the railway lines.

At the individual level, if we have no time or are not able to make a personal visit, we can, of course, make a telephone call.

4.7.2 Telephone communication

The telephone technology was invented in late nineteenth century, and it has been developing ever since. While the telephone was originally a completely synchronic medium – tied to the simultaneous attendance of two people – the answering machine has made us incessantly available for incoming messages – a means for synchronic/asynchronic communication. In addition, the filtering capacity of the answering machine makes us both available and unavailable at the same time, as if we have private secretaries. Similarly, a display on some telephones (or an additional gadget) allows us directly to check who is calling, without even answering. The mobile telephone has also made us always synchronically available for both incoming and outgoing messages, wherever we are.

The telephone was always a handy means of keeping contact, if not eye-to-eye, at least ear-to-ear. It was thus always a good family medium, a supplement and a complement to, and also a substitute for, eye-to-eye contact. Important family events – births, deaths, illnesses, new jobs, loss of jobs, unexpected travels etc. – are still often announced over the traditional, stationary telephone, allowing intimacy at a distance. It is the natural medium of contact for families in which, for long or short periods of time, one family member has to be far away from home. For circles of both close and distant relatives and friends, it was always a means of maintaining social contact. A 'telephone visit' follows more or less the same stages of communication as a real visit.

In modern times, where many families have been broken up by divorce, the telephone has become a necessary means of keeping in contact. In such cases, the telephone and the car complement each other in that both facilitate keeping in contact over sometimes considerable distances. Recent French studies have shown that a large portion of domestic telephone calls are actually related to daily geographical mobility: replacing it, generating it, or organizing it.

By way of the telephone-based modem, we also have access from home to the World Wide Web and messages can be sent from computer to computer anywhere in the world by email (see section 7.7). Such developments increase the possibility of working at home, even in jobs previously necessitating a personal presence in the office. The fax machine offers additional help in such cases. All these developments reduce the significance of distance in time and space, just as the trains and the telegraph services did in the nineteenth century, and still do, of course.

Quite naturally, age and social position affect our telephone use, and indeed our use of all those gadgets of communication. Single people use the telephone more than other people do, and it is even more important to people isolated by illness or other restrictions. Other individuals and groups of individuals also use the telephone much more than other people do. For example, recent French research reported the almost compulsory use of the mobile telephone among some tightly-knit groups of young people who feel they always need to know what everybody else in their group is doing at any one time. More formalized, professional networks regularly use the tele-conference facility for semi-formalized meetings, sometimes also including video-conferencing. Indeed, this technique is now being developed into what has been called long-distance surgery: an expert in one location may actively take part in an operation carried out in another hospital. In general, however, group meetings by telephone are now gradually supplemented by, and indeed, sometimes taken over by, electronic communication over the Internet (see the next section).

Finally, the telephone is also a very important *mercantile* medium: lots of professional business deals are made over the telephone, and it is also used for retail trading of certain standardized products, including other means of communication, such as books, journals and newspapers. In France, a combination of a telephone and a small computer – the so-called *Minitel* – was distributed for free to all telephone households, offering many standardized services to large parts of the population: ordering and buying tickets, providing informational services, etc. Similar services are now found in many countries, including standardized, pre-recorded advice in cases of mild illness.

4.7.3 Individual communication by computer

In parallel with such telephone–computer based developments, individual and group communication by way of direct and mediated communication between computers is developing at an even faster rate. Communication between computers has always been possible. Gradually, more or less formalized networks for computer communication were also developed. Later on, networks of networks were developed. What is today called the 'Internet' grew out of a number of US computer networks, in a long and complicated process of development, starting from the late 1960s. The system was given its present name in 1990. It can be described as an open international network of large computers, each of which is the hub of other networks. All that is needed to join the club is to follow a common communication standard, a so-called 'protocol' (see Box 4.6).

The basic element of the Internet is thus the computer. What was originally conceived as a calculating machine has become a means of communication, and the Internet, originally conceived as a military and/or academic

---

BOX 4.6 INTERNET PROTOCOLS

'A communications protocol is a set of rules governing how computers exchange information with each other. . . . The Internet protocols became widely accepted standards in an unconventional way. Unlike the . . . protocols developed by the International Standards Organization (ISO), [they] did not have the official imprimatur of an internationally recognized standards authority. Unlike commercial networking protocols . . . they did not have the marketing resources of a large company behind them, nor was their design oriented toward any particular vendor's hardware. Instead, they were developed by researchers funded by the U.S. government, and consequently were made freely available to anyone who wanted to use them – in other words, they became *open standards*. They were developed in an iterative fashion and approved over time in a process that was not controlled by financial interest, leading to a free quality product that people wanted to adopt. The seemingly ironic outcome of this process is that the free choices of millions of individuals led to much more universal adoption of the common Internet protocols than any of the other more centrally mandated alternatives. . . . Open standards are key to the Internet's juxtapostion of interoperability with distributed power and control.'

From: S.E. Gillet and M. Kapor (1997) 'The self-governing Internet: coordination by design', in B. Kahin and J.H. Keller (eds), *Coordinating the Internet*. Cambridge, MA: The MIT Press. pp. 8–9.

enterprise, has become a medium of public services (see section 7.7). Its rate of growth has been, and still is, incredible – 100% a year. Every year its size has been doubled. It is thus the latest in a series of media which started with the letter, the book, the journal, the newspaper and included the cinema, radio, television and video. The Internet is also a gateway to other media, offering access to all conceivable forms of computerized texts, pictures, programs, museums, libraries. On top of all this, it is a highly efficient medium for interpersonal communication. It may thus be called an 'interpersonal mass medium', a medium creating 'virtual communities'. In 1998, the number of Internet users was estimated by the *Computer Industry Almanac* to be some 150 million people, from all around the globe although mostly in industrial and post-industrial societies. That is quite a lot of people, but just a small percentage of the global population, of course.

In 1993, the World Wide Web (WWW) was created: a network of host computers 'talking the same language' – the Hypertext Transfer Protocol (HTTP), a 'hypertext program' able to distribute text, sound and moving pictures over the Internet. In 1995 it had become the dominating program of its kind with some 300 sites, 'home pages', etc. on the Web, presenting companies, authorities, organizations and individuals. By the next year there were four million sites, and the acceleration goes on.

Small wonder that the Web was immediately complemented with various programs for reading Web pages: NETSCAPE or MOSAIC, for instance. The huge amounts of information available soon called for a number of 'search engines', for example *Lycos* (available at www.lycos.com).

The Web also offers opportunities for 'chatting' in real time about virtually everything with individuals known and unknown, and within groups of fairly well-known individuals. Chatting may be the most common way for individuals to use the Web, the chatters being distributed over a great number of different 'sites' and often appearing under more or less witty and/or affronting pseudonyms. A special type of site is so-called MUDs, 'Multi-User Dungeons' – sites for networked interpersonal and group interaction in 'virtual reality'. MUDs have many attributes that are characteristic of real places, but basically, they are different, of course, and this may lead to new social phenomena not found in traditional reality (see Box 4.7).

The World Wide Web is also being used for advertising and in this way can be likened to a listing in the *Yellow Pages* telephone directory. Using a search engine, we are able to find virtually anything for sale, and to buy it. Naturally, the products themselves have still to be sent by mail, unless they are electronic products, of course. We may also contact various authorities over the Internet, say, in order to get all those forms that are necessary to apply for this or that permit to be sent directly to our home computer.

The effects of such developments have already been noticed by various national mail services, which have now started to restructure their activities towards packages and parcels rather than towards letters. Many national mail services have also created their own Internet sites, offering various types of electronic services. In the long run, such tendencies will inevitably have some

---

BOX 4.7   ON MUDS

'MUDs are networked, multiparticipant, user-extensible systems most commonly found on the Internet, the international network that connects many thousands of educational, research, and commercial institutions. Using a MUD does not require any of the paraphernalia commonly associated with virtual reality. There are no visors or gloves, let alone body suits. The MUD interface is entirely textual, and a simple PC can act as a gateway into this kind of virtual world. Instead of using sophisticated tools to see, touch, and hear a virtual reality, users of MUD systems are presented with textual descriptions of virtual locations. . . . There are many hundreds of individual programs running on the Internet, each depicting a different virtual environment. The name, MUD, is now used to refer to the entire class of such text-based virtual world systems, and the original expansion to Multi-User Dungeon has been commonly replaced by the more generic Multi-User Domain or Multi-User Dimension.'

From: E. Reid (1995) 'Virtual worlds: culture and imagination', in S.G. Jones (ed.), *Cybersociety. Computer-Mediated Communication and Community*. Thousand Oaks, CA: Sage.

'A MUD (multi-user dungeon or multi-user dimension) is a networked virtual reality whose user interface is entirely textual. Participants log into a MUD through their computer workstations. Since it is text-based, a MUD is rather like old-time radio: you are given a verbal description and visualize the scene with your imagination. The text describes an artificial place. Each participant has a separate character, and the subject matter stems entirely from interactions, which occur in almost real time, being limited only by typing speed. Thus MUDs are *social* worlds, not *solitary* ones.

As virtual gathering places, MUDs have many of the social attributes of real gathering places. However, certain of their attributes are different and lead to new social phenomena not usually seen in real life.'

From: P. Curtis (1996) 'Mudding: social phenomena in text-based virtual realities', in M. Stefik (ed.), *Internet Dreams. Archetypes, Myths and Metaphors*. Cambridge, MA, and London: The MIT Press.

---

consequences for the retail trade, just as email has already affected the location of some office work, with more people now working at home – a trend that is likely to continue for the next few decades. Historically, this may be compared to working at home as an independent craftsman or craftswoman, delivering one's more or less finished product to an agent for some emerging industry or other. This so-called 'putting-out system' was a widespread phenomenon during the transition between the period of mercantilism and that of industrialism (periods which, of course, have occurred at different times in different parts of the world).

Finally, it must be remembered that, in spite of all these new media, no medium of communication has completely disappeared. For every new medium of communication, the old ones have been able to adapt themselves. We write in stone and wood more than ever, for example on gravestones. Diplomatic couriers are still rushing between continents with this or that important document in the sealed portfolio. We still scribble our graffiti on the walls, much as people did in ancient Rome. And lovers will always like to hear the voice of their beloved close by.

5

Organizational Communication

5.1 Organizations, groups and networks: an introduction

One way or the other, most of us are active in some organizations and belong to others. As individuals, all of us are also of interest to a number of quite different organizations (authorities, corporations, companies, unions, clubs, etc.). But we do not philosophize very much about these organizations. As a rule, we take them more or less for granted. And yet, an organization is a quite complicated structure (see Box 5.1). In order to understand the concept and phenomenon of an organization, it is useful to return to our definition of the concept of a group.

In section 4.4.1 we defined the human group as

- a *small number of individuals* (at most a dozen or, perhaps, 20),
- having a *joint identity* based on
- a common, implicit or explicit *goal*, as well as
- a more or less informal *structure*, including
- some sort of informal or semi-formalized *leadership*.

We added that group communication may thus be described as (a) communication within groups, as well as (b) communication between groups and their societal surroundings (including, of course, individuals and other groups, as well as organizations and society itself). These definitions may be used as starting points when defining the concepts of organization and organizational communication.

We have just seen that a group is a social structure defined in terms of a relatively small number of *individuals* whose characteristics and interrelations constitute the structure of the group. An organization, on the other hand, may be regarded as

> a social structure defined in terms of the relations between a number of more or less interrelated *positions*, the individual incumbents of which have to play *social roles* more or less distinctly defined by the position in question.

Organizations may thus be regarded as a special type of group, namely, a group which has

---

BOX 5.1   ON THAT STRANGE MACHINE, AN ORGANIZATION

Imagine a machine where some of the parts walk away every evening or whenever it stops operating, only to come back when it will start again. And while they are away they may change. An organization is a jig-saw puzzle that has to be put together again and again. Its human parts cannot be glued or screwed together once and for all. Nor can they be inscribed into a microchip as integrated circuits.

Since the parts of an organization are not fixed together once and for all, there is some fragility in all organizational constructions. The reiterated assembling of parts can be understood in relations between the dependence of affiliates on an organization and their dependence on other organizations or people in the surrounding social landscape where they spend some of their time. How an organization is fitted together can thus be seen in the tension between centripetal forces within the organization and centrifugal forces in the environment. However, there may also be centripetal forces at work outside an organization that contribute to its stability.

From: Göran Ahrne (1994) *Social Organizations*. London: Sage. p. 88.

- a formalized, more or less hierarchical structure of communication, and
- an explicitly defined goal (often laid down in a founding charter, see section 2.5), as well as
- a system of standardized procedures for recruitment and exclusion, for decision-making, for communication with the surroundings of the organization, etc.

Organizations often cross boundaries between other social units, be they small or large (groups, societies, nations, etc.), thus forming multinational, multicultural social units. Simplified, it could be said, then, that in a group the *individuals* and their characteristics define the positions and the roles tied to the positions, while in an organization the *positions* define the characteristics necessarily (or, at least, preferably) to be possessed by the individual enacting the role defined by a given position. In this sense, although we do not usually regard it that way, a traditional family is really an organization:

- its *goal* is defined in terms of the formal wedding ceremony (be it religious or civil), common law and generally accepted mores;
- its *structure*, in terms of positions and social roles calling for very specific characteristics of their incumbents: wife and husband, mother, father, daughter and son (and, in extended families, grandparents, grandchildren, cousins, in-laws, etc.);
- its *procedures of recruitment*, in terms of the mores and family laws of the land;

- its *structure of communication*, to a large extent by the formal structure as understood in terms of traditional mores.

In most common-sense theorizing, however, a family is not regarded as an organization, and in this special case we have preferred to follow common-sense rather than formally defined theory (see sections 2.5 and 4.4.1) – a decision also affected by the fact that co-habitation without any formal ceremonies at all is becoming increasingly frequent, thus making some of the criteria listed above obsolete.

Our general definition of the concept of organization covers a number of different kinds of organization. Besides that primeval group/organization, the traditional family and established, old organizations such as the Roman Catholic Church, the nineteenth and twentieth centuries have seen an immense growth in the number and types of organization. In addition, there is a growing number of a special kind of large and important organizations. These organizations have been around only for a few decades, or sometimes for about a century. They may be found in all societal sectors. Some are national, some are truly international, or have close international relations, and all of them are *organizations of organizations*. In an organization of organizations, of course, the role in a traditional organization played by the individual is played by an organization. Many organizations of organizations are international (see section 7.4.3). In its way, this type of organization signals both the increasing complexity of all human societies and the increasing internationalization which characterizes all human existence today. Best known among the international organizations of organizations is perhaps the United Nations: an organization of national states, founded in 1945, now having some 170 members. In fact there are several such international organizations of organizations, and they may be as different from each other as, for instance,

- the International Telegraphic Union (ITU), founded in 1868;
- the Fédération Internationale de Football Associations (FIFA), founded in 1904;
- the International Labor Organization (ILO), founded in 1946; and
- the International Bank for Reconstruction and Development (World Bank), founded in 1946.

The World Bank, in its turn, is a member of the World Bank Group, including also the International Finance Corporation and the International Development Association.

Before ending this introductory section of our chapter on organizational communication, it should also be mentioned that there are indeed some intermediate forms of groupings situated between informal groups and formal organizations: so-called *networks* (see sections 2.5, 4.7.3 and 7.7). The conceptualization and its corresponding terminology is not quite clear in this area, but networks are often regarded as being closer to groups than to formal organizations. Sometimes the term is reserved for groups composed of geographically differently located individuals held together by way of mediated communication (letter, telephone, email, etc.). Networks tend to operate without any formal rules of decision, so, strictly speaking, they cannot take any formal decisions at all. All the same, networks may sometimes be large and influential. Members of the 'Old Boys' club' may be found in the most unexpected positions.

The sociograms discussed in section 4.4 can be taken to represent abstract models of relatively small individual networks. Recent developments in transportation and computerized communication have stimulated the growth of very large networks. Almost by definition, communication within and between such large networks has to be mediated, today often by way of computers. At the same time, the analysis of communication in especially very large, geographically dispersed networks within and between organizations have been immensely facilitated by computerized techniques – actually to the extent that the computers themselves deliver the data about the cases of network communication under study. As a result of such developments, classical sociometry (see section 4.1.1) may now be regarded as a sub-specialty within a large field of research often called 'communication network analysis'. As the name tells us, in this tradition of research the interest is focused directly on the communicative aspects of networks.

So much for the definitions of the basic concepts of *group, organization, network,* and for empirical examples hopefully illuminating the theoretical definitions. In reality, however – always much more fuzzy than our relatively neat theories – there is no sharp limit between groups and organizations. Many organizations began their existence as groups, and within all formal organizations there are informal groups of individuals who have formed friendships or other personal relations based on similarity, vicinity, personal preferences, love, common interests, common enemies, and so on.

Similarly, there are no sharp limits between the roles and their incumbents. The role shapes the incumbent, and *vice versa*. In his book, *Social Organizations* (1994; already quoted in Box 5.1 above), a Swedish sociologist of organization, Göran Ahrne, has very aptly expressed this phenomenon of dual influence in terms of a striking simile: as members of an organization, all of us are *centaurs* – both 'individual individuals' and 'organizational men and women'.

A centaur is a mythical being: half man, half horse. It may not be quite clear, however, which part of the centaur would represent the so-called 'organization man' (originally, by the way, the title of a well-known book published in 1956 by the American sociologist, William H. Whyte, Jr). But these and similar ideas may be best expressed in the somewhat more precise terms of the causal model presented in Figure 3.3 on p. 62. The arrow from the box 'individual characteristics' visualizes the 'individual individual', while the arrow from 'individual position' might be taken to symbolize, among many other phenomena, 'organization man'.

5.2   Some historical examples of organization and organizational communication

The biblical book of Leviticus (*c.* 1,200 BC) tells us how during the travails of the people of Israel, while wandering away from Egypt, through the wilderness and towards the Promised Land of Canaan, Moses had to organize the administration of law in a bureaucratic pattern in order to be able to handle all the quarrels and complaints arising from the hardships. Moses was not the first one to realize the problem and its solution, however. Already a millennium or so previously, among the forefathers of his Egyptian masters, somebody (or some people) wrote a manual about how, as an individual, to deal with different bureaucratic problems, the *Precepts* of one Ptah–hotep.

Formal organization thus has a history which dates back at least to the times when the first large river states developed out of a number of local farming communities (see section 2.3 above). The co-ordination of large watering systems called for advanced formal organization. So did the collection and distribution of surplus value in the form of grain and other agricultural products which emanated from small and large farming units and were delivered to the authorities as taxes in kind. Similarly, the huge Egyptian pyramids, for instance, built some 4,500 years ago and still being some of the most impressive buildings ever created by human beings, could not possibly have come into existence without an elaborate system of a large number of co-operating – and, sometimes, competing – organizations, each one of which specialized on specific functions ranging from

- keeping the populace alive and submissive, to
- regulating and distributing the enormous water masses of the Nile, to
- distributing the large masses of grain to large and small buyers and consumers, to
- collecting taxes in kind and money, to
- book-keeping in general, to
- defending the river state against enemies from within and without, to
- creating ideologies and mythologies to justify the large differences in wealth and power which were necessary to maintain all these activities, and to
- innumerable other, more specific tasks and activities emanating from these overarching organizational patterns and demands, tasks including the construction of the pyramids.

Organization thus *was*, *is* and *will always be* needed in all sectors of the Great Wheel of Culture in Society (see section 3.2 above):

- for reasons of production and transportation;
- for technical and administrative reasons;
- for political and military reasons;
- for ideological and religious reasons; and also
- for artistic and other more or less purely symbolic reasons.

Such needs have been following humanity right from the beginning, not only during the times of the Egyptian Pharaos or Emperor Shi Huangdi (some 200 years BC), known as the creator of the Chinese Wall, the 'Chang Ching' (actually having been built, partly destroyed and rebuilt both long before and after Shi Huangdi's time). Over centuries and millennia, different but basically similar ways of satisfying those needs have been found in innumerable small and large organizations around the globe.

The *normatively*-oriented sectors in the Great Wheel of Culture in Society – religion and politics – very early got their own, more or less rationally organized bureaucracies – priesthoods and governmental agencies – often working under conditions of mutual co-operation and/or competition. Also the *instrumentally*-oriented sectors – economy and technology – were quick to develop corresponding bureaucracies: guilds, crafts, more or less highly-organized fraternities, etc. During the late Middle Ages, for instance, a number of large trading houses in some prosperous towns and cities in what is now northern Germany founded a powerful, co-operative organization, a guild called the 'Hanse'. At the top of its career in the late fifteenth and early sixteenth centuries, the Hanse actually dominated all trade around the Baltic Sea, thus also affecting the organization of semi-industrial craft production going on in the area at about the same time. Presumably, there was no explicit theory of organization and organizational communication around at the time, but those sturdy craftsmen, business people and town politicians surely knew what they were doing. Indeed, the Hanse organization was powerful enough to form alliances with, and actually even to wage war against, the national states then emerging around the Baltic. The Hanse is thus an early example of a type of organization which has recently been called a 'BINGO' (see section 7.4.3).

The *cognitively*-oriented sectors – science and scholarship – followed in the footsteps of the other bureaucracies, offering their services wherever needed and/or asked for. The first universities of the European model were established in the twelfth century, while the clearly *expressive* sectors of society – art and literature – as a rule developed their bureaucracies in later periods of time. Various schools and academies of the fine arts had their roots in Renaissance Italy and perhaps their best-known organization was *L'Académie Française*, in the seventeenth century, later on to be followed by similar institutions around the world. The Swedish Royal Academies of science and literature, for instance, which since 1901 have granted the Nobel prizes in sciences and literature (see section 7.6), were founded in the eighteenth century. (Both universities and academies have a venerable pedigree, with roots going back to a grove in the vicinity of classical Athens, to the *Akademeia*, where Plato (427–357 BC) is said to have taught.)

The positive functions of a smoothly working organization have often been used also for criminal purposes, in order to draw on the same instrumental advantages of organizations as lawful organizations do – and also to minimize the risk of being found out and, if having been found out, to minimize the risk of total disaster. In some cases, secrecy has been carried to its extreme:

the *very existence* of some organizations or parts of organizations has been kept secret, since outside knowledge about their existence would have made them less fit for their purpose. The same purpose of secrecy is approached not only *vis-à-vis* the surrounding society, but also within the organization itself, so that one part of the organization may not even be aware of the very existence of another part of that same organization. Secrecy may also be used to increase the status of sometimes rather trivial organizations.

The best-known example of organized crime is probably the Sicilian mafia ('cosa nostra'), which over centuries has represented a serious threat to the monopoly on violence and taxation traditionally associated with that very large organization called a state. The mafia probably owes its existence partly to the fact that during its long history Sicily has belonged to so many continental states that the otherwise legitimate power of the state has come to be regarded with great mistrust. The word 'mafia' has also become a general term for various kinds of organized crime. The US mafia flourished especially during the prohibition period in the late 1920s and early 1930s, and was partly influenced by the Sicilian mafia. More civilized but less important than the mafias are some secret societies, for example, the *Masonic Order* whose origins date back to the 1790s. The rumours of grisly ceremonies, which circulated for centuries, were probably never true.

Secrecy is sometimes regarded as something immoral, a breach of normal rules of communication, but a minimum of secrecy both within an organization and between organizations and large parts of the society surrounding them is a *sine qua non* for both large and small organizations – not least when negotiating with other organizations. Actually, many or most organizations, just as all societies, have some more or less secret, more or less informal parts whose function is to produce information on real or imagined enemies among other organizations and/or societies – or, indeed, within their own organization. Such information agencies sometimes work both inside and outside the limits drawn by the law (witness Watergate, and other scandals in many other countries, some truly terrible examples being provided by the Soviet secret police in the 1920s, the *Cheka*, and by Nazi Germany's *Gestapo* in the 1930s and 1940s). As is well known, even more secret *counter espionage* is to be found, not only at the national level, but also within and between organizations.

Finally, it should be mentioned that in the end the rationality of bureaucracies has been turned against the bureaucracies themselves. Not only have physical production systems been rationalized, so have all types of bureaucracies, and not least their administrative systems, even to the extent that a special philosophy of *administrative rationalization* (AR) has been developed. Attempts to reduce the number of bureaucratic levels have been undertaken in various kinds of organization, sometimes successfully. Recently, rather different tendencies have been observed, however. The organizational pyramids may have become somewhat flatter, but the power of the executives of large business organizations does not seem to have diminished.

5.3   Theories and models of organization and organizational communication

Organizations have been around for millenia, but modern, systematic theories of organizational communication appeared only in the late nineteenth and early twentieth centuries. At that time, the industrialization processes which had developed from the eighteenth century had come to dominate modern society to the extent that it became urgent to study them systematically in terms of economic, social and political theory. These studies of organization had their background in classical disciplines such as economics, political science and sociology.

In 1776, the Scottish economist and philosopher Adam Smith published his treatise, *The Wealth of Nations*, in a famous passage of which he stressed the importance of industrial organization to progress (see Box 5.2). In 1848, the English philosopher John Stuart Mill (1806–73) published his path-breaking study, *Principles of Political Economy*. Another pioneer was the German philosopher, Karl Marx (1818–83), who in 1867 published the first

---

BOX 5.2   ORGANIZATION AS THE DIVISION OF LABOUR, AD 1776

The effects of the division of labour, in the general business of society, will be more easily understood by considering in what manner it operates in some particular manufactures. . . . To take an example, therefore, from a very trifling manufacture; but one in which the division of labour has been very often taken notice of, the trade of the pin-maker; a workman not educated to this business . . . could scarce, perhaps, with his utmost industry, make one pin in a day. . . . But in the way in which this business is now carried on, not only the whole work is a peculiar trade, but it is divided into a number of branches, of which the greater part are likewise peculiar trades. One man draws out the wire, another straights it, a third cuts it . . . it is even a trade by itself to put them into paper; and the important business of making a pin is, in this manner, divided into about eighteen distinct operations, which in some manufactories are all performed by distinct hands. . . . I have seen a small manufacture of this kind where ten men only were employed. . . . Those ten persons . . . could make among them upwards of forty-eight thousand pins in a day. Each person, therefore . . . might be considered as making four thousand eight hundred pins in a day. But if they had all wrought separately and independently . . . they could certainly not each of them have made twenty, perhaps not one pin in a day. . . .

   In every other art and manufacturer, the effects of the division of labour are similar to what they are in this very trifling one.

From: Adam Smith (1776/1976) *The Wealth of Nations*. London: Penguin.

version of his classic work, *Das Kapital*, which discussed the role played by the general societal conflicts between the owners of industrial capital and those without any capital at all, the proletarians: 'the haves' and 'the have-nots'. Between them, Mill and Marx introduced those two great political philosophies, Liberalism and Marxism. (The last heyday of scholarly Marxism occurred in the late 1960s and early 1970s, and the revolutions in Eastern Europe starting in 1989 put an end to Marxism as a viable political philosophy. Liberalism remains, in many countries now competing with an originally Marx-inspired social democracy, which has turned almost as liberal as the liberals themselves – witness, for instance, the British Labour Party under Tony Blair.)

Later practitioners and theoreticians in the area focused on more specific aspects of the overarching industrial problematic. When the large industrial companies in Europe and America emerged in the late decades of the nineteenth century and the early decades of the twentieth century, the only other models of large organizations were the state bureaucracies, the military organizations and religious organizations such as the Roman Catholic Church, all of which in principle were (and still are) very hierarchal. The industrialists primarily used the military model, gradually adapting it to industrial conditions. (Interestingly, one of the most successful of the many religious revival movements of the late nineteenth century, the *Salvation Army* (founded in England in 1865), also used the same military model.) In so doing, they were supported by the pioneers in organization theory of the early twentieth century, men such as the American, Frederick W. Taylor (1856–1915), who in 1911 published his book, *The Principles of Scientific Management* (based on sometimes extremely detailed time-and-motion studies), the Frenchman, Henri Fayol (1841–1925), who in 1921 published his book, *Administration industrielle et générale (Industrial and General Administration)*, and the German, Max Weber (1864–1920), whose book, *Wirtschaft und Gesellschaft (Economy and Society)* appeared posthumously in 1922, having first been published in a series of journal articles.

For a long time Max Weber's theory of organization was the dominant one, having being translated into English in the late 1940s. Weber liked to think and argue in terms of so-called 'ideal models': theoretical constructs verbally expressing the general principles governing the phenomena under study. The ideal models, it should perhaps be noted, are not formalized in the sense that, say, a statistical model is formalized (see section 1.8 above). Nor do they represent a morally, economically or aesthetically preferable ideal. They are *verbal models*, and they are ideal in the sense that they clarify the 'pure case' of a phenomenon: what the phenomenon would have looked like if existing in a world of precise ideas, not complicated by empirical reality's many specific, more or less haphazard circumstances. By comparing empirically existing phenomena to such 'ideal models' it becomes possible to better understand, clarify and explain, for instance, a specific case of an organization, be it an economic, political or religious organization, or some other type.

This is what Max Weber's ideal model of an organization amounted to:

1 Hierarchical authority, no diffuse authority.
2 Regulated division of labour.
3 Rules (preferably written ones) for how work should be done.
4 No direct individual ownership of organizational assets and rights.
5 Recruitment based on specified qualifications, not on personal relations.
6 Tenure: employees on the permanent staff cannot be fired without formal procedures.
7 Fixed wages and salaries for the employees of the organization; no other rewards.
8 A right of appeal, by means of which the individual member is protected against potential misuse of power.

Each one of the eight defining characteristics is more or less self-explanatory, yet all of them are never completely to be found together in the real world. Indeed, we would be hard put to find an organization always – completely and strictly – following even a single one of these defining characteristics. Also, assuming that each one of the eight characteristics would have two values, 'high' and 'low', there would be $2^8 = 256$ different types of organization. Allowing more than two values for each characteristic, the number of variations would become very high indeed: thousands of types. Nevertheless – or rather, precisely because this is so – the ideal model may be used for better understanding all those concrete cases of organizations and organizational communication which we may find in real life, for instance, if we want to understand the development of organizations during the last century or so, or to compare the precise character of two different organizations found in one society at a given point of time.

The ideal model of an organization is often expressed in a diagram offering a schematic overview of the organizational framework. All of us have seen such charts. They may be compared to the sociograms discussed in section 4.4. In small, spontaneously created groups, *the group structure is a function of the individuals in the group, their characteristics and preferences* (cf. the definition of group quoted in section 5.1). If there is a 'born leader' in the group, he or she tends to be located at the centre of the group, and his or her preferences for, and types of relations with, other group members tend to exert a sometimes strong influence on the structure of the group as it may be visualized in a sociogram. *An organizational structure, however, is a function of the task of the organization.* The positions in that structure exist before their incumbents, so to speak (see section 5.1). In the ideal case, theoretically and practically highly qualified people are supposed to be located at the top and less qualified people among the lower echelons of the organization.

Basically sound as it may be, this line of argumentation is complicated by the distinction between *formal* and *informal* organization. The fit between (a) the demands put on the incumbent of a given position in a bureaucracy and (b) his or her actual capacity may be less than perfect, and the misfit may work both ways. The too low capacity of an incumbent of a relatively high position may thus be contrasted with the really high capacity of an incumbent of a relatively low position. In addition, the contrast will stand out as even more stark, if the inefficient incumbent of the relatively high position should happen to have tenure, in contrast to the efficient incumbent of the relatively low position. In such and similar cases, an informal structure tends to appear. In that informal structure, a formally lowly positioned individual with high capacity may rank high, often using informal communication to his or her advantage – for instance, in his or her efforts to get promotion and/or to attain tenure.

In the long run, over-large discrepancies between formal and informal structure may be threatening to the organization, sometimes so threatening that changes may stand out as the only possible solution. Actually, as advances in the rationalization of industrial production continued to develop, as productivity increased, and as the workforce became increasingly better educated, better off, and consequently more demanding, the traditional organizational models had to be revised. In general, it may be said that the original, more or less militarily-oriented solution was gradually abandoned for less mechanical, more human and humane, civilian alternatives. These developments were due to rational economic calculations, in their turn to no small extent due to protests from industrial workers, clerks and other employees, from their labour organizations, as well as from their political parties. To an unknown extent they were also due to protests from artists and authors, presented in such classic works as Aldous Huxley's *Brave New World* (1932), George Orwell's *1984* (1949) and, not least perhaps to Charlie Chaplin's successful movie, *City Lights* (1936).

A pioneer in the theoretical and practical developments which resulted from such emerging insights and protests was the Australian-American, Elton Mayo, who already in the mid-1920s, together with Fritz J. Roethlisberger and William J. Dickson, had started a series of path-breaking studies of industrial work and workers in the Hawthorne Works of the Western Electric Company in Chicago. More than a decade later, in 1939, Roethlisberger and Dickson published the main results of these now classic studies, *Management and the Worker*, thus providing the so-called Human Relations School with an impressive platform.

In principle, the message was simple. Industrial and clerical workers are not machines. After all, they are human beings, and they have to be dealt with as such: in 'human relations'. A striking proof of this almost ridiculously simple thesis turned up at a very early stage: the very fact that social scientists started to take an interest in factory workers' concrete work tended to raise the productivity of those workers, whatever changes the scientists proposed. Not many people had really communicated with the workers as workers before, unless in terms of rules, orders and prohibitions. The mechanical processes were still in focus, of course, but interest gradually moved to the psychologically and sociologically founded *processes of communication* necessary to carry out the productive processes as smoothly as possible. Communication in organizations thus became a subject of increasing interest.

The Human Relations tradition was at least partly continued within a broader specialty, the psychology of organizations. The main themes in these lines of research have concerned the notions of individuality, alienation and so-called 'limited rationality'. Since by definition the positions in the organizational structure define the activities pursued by the individuals located in those positions, there is less room for individual initiatives, individual creativity, and indeed for individuality at all. A rather limited rationality may gradually turn into its own goal. As a result, a feeling of alienation, a sense of *Verfremdung* (individuality lost) may become widespread. You go by the book, not as a means of protest (see section 5.4 below), but as a matter of your everyday work, indeed, your everyday life. It is as if you are no longer an individual, but just a cog in the wheel.

So far, we have been discussing primarily the basic *structural* characteristics of an organization. Now we shall turn to the *processual* side of those important systems called organizations. We shall discuss organizational communication.

5.4 Formal and informal organizational communication

From the fact that there are two basic types of organization, formal and informal organization, it follows that organizational communication always has at least two forms of existence:

- formally defined communication between individual incumbents of different positions; and
- informally defined communication between individuals *qua* individuals (although, by definition, of course, always being located at a specific position in the organization).

The latter form of communication – a special case of individual communication – is often called 'grapevine'. The meticulously planned organizational structures may be large and impressive, but the grapevine will find its way to the most unexpected places, creeping from window to window according to rules more often than not unknown to the powerful bosses of the large organizations. Actually, there are at least two forms of grapevine, one in which *individual relationships* have the upper hand (as when, for their own benefit, two old friends share secret knowledge which actually should be tied to a given position), and one in which the *organizational relationships* have the upper hand (as when, for the benefit of the organization, a director is told by a rank-and-file member of the organization that there is foul play going on somewhere among other ranks and files in the organization). The grapevine is the organizational equivalent to the spread of rumours at the group and societal levels (see section 4.4 above). Just as with rumours, it may be beneficial or negative to both individuals and societies and just as with rumours, the grapevine may build on true or false information.

Regarded in this light, the informal type of organizational communication may be looked upon as both functional and non-functional or even a-functional. But the fact is that, however skilfully it may have been planned and created, no organization can handle all contingencies by means of formal communication only. Informal communication is thus necessary to the very existence of even the most cleverly formalized organization. This becomes clear in the seemingly simple but powerful method of protest used by lower echelons of large organizations called 'working to rule', 'working according to the book', etc. If mechanically followed in great detail, even the best organizational plans and rules may turn out to be fatally dangerous to the very existence of that carefully planned organization.

In addition, we have already mentioned that the roles played by the incumbents of given positions, within even a very large, highly formalized organization, are necessarily affected by the personal characteristics of the incumbents (witness, for instance, the United Nations under different Secretary-Generals). On the other hand, individual incumbents of given organizational positions are affected not only by the *opportunities* which that position may offer to its incumbent, but also by the *demands and restrictions* put by a given position on every incumbent of that position. Such combined effects may sometimes be disastrous, their worst forms being known by terms such as 'megalomania' or 'imperial lunacy' (see Box 5.3).

While the communicative relations between individuals within organizations are very important *per se* – and as objects of scholarship and research – the relationships between organizations and the society surrounding them are no less important. No organization can deviate too much from the basic social, economic and cultural conditions prevailing in the surrounding society. Similarly, no society, and especially, perhaps, no modern society, can neglect the developments within and between the many organizations to be found in all societies. Sometimes society has to adapt to organizational developments; sometimes organizations to societal development.

A special case of such adaptations is represented by organizational change and developments caused by the basic, long-term changes in the climate of culture and opinion as discussed in section 3.5 above. Obviously, in a society ideologically characterized by a strong emphasis on equality, organizations and their way of operating must be somewhat different from that of organizations operating in a society with other priorities. Thus, towards the end of the 1960s, organizations in many countries had to heed the fact that in many quarters there were at that time strong feelings against the very idea of hierarchy dominating traditional organizational theory. Not surprisingly, about the same time there was also a tendency to make the organizational pyramids flatter by way of reducing the number of organizational levels.

BOX 5.3 A CASE OF MEGALOMANIA – IMPERIAL LUNACY

. . . and there, chained by the waist to a ring bolt, with irons on his wrists and ankles, was el Supremo.

He was in rags – half naked in fact, and his beard and hair were matted and tangled, and his own filth lay on the deck about him. . . .

'You see I wear these chains', he said. 'It is a strange whim on the part of myself and my servants that I should do so. I hope you agree with me that they set off my figure quite admirably?'

'Y-yes, sir', stammered Hornblower.

'We are on our way to Panama, where I shall mount the throne of the world. They talk of hanging; these fellows here say that there is a gallows awaiting us on the bastion of the Citadel. That will be the framework of my golden throne. Golden, it will be, with diamond stars and a great turqouise moon. It will be from there that I shall issue my next decrees to the world.'

. . .

'The sun grows in his splendour every day' said el Supremo. 'He is magnificent and terrible, as I am. He can kill – kill, as he killed the men I exposed to him – when was it? And Montezuma is dead, and all his line save me, in the hundreds of years ago. I alone remain. And Hernandez is dead, but it was not the sun that killed him. They hanged Hernandez even while the blood dripped from his wounds. They hanged him in my city of San Salvador, and as they hanged him he still called upon the name of el Supremo. They hanged the men and they hanged the women, in long rows at San Salvador. Only el Supremo is left, to govern from his golden throne. His throne! His throne!'

El Supremo was staring about him now. There was a hint of bewildered realization in his face as he jangled his chains. He peered at them stupidly.

'Chains! These are chains!'

He was bawling and shouting. He laughed madly, and then he wept and he cursed, flinging himself about on the deck, biting at his chains. His words were no longer articulate as he slobbered and writhed.

'It is interesting, is it not?', said the Spanish captain.

From: C.S. Forester (1937/1975) *The Happy Return*. London: Penguin.

5.5 Models of organization

5.5.1 Introduction

There are millions of organizations around the globe. The different empirical types of organization (as well as their corresponding, more or less well-developed theories, some of which have been presented above) have been expressed in terms of various, more or less formalized *models of organization*. During the last few decades a number of different organizational models have been discussed in theory and tried in practice. They go under different, sometimes rather fancy names. Although the dimensionality of organizations is a complex problematic, for our purposes the various types of organization and parts of organization may be described in terms of a few, basic dimensions:

- *hierarchy*, which is an expression of power;
- *function*, the primary tasks of the organization and its different units: production, sales, research and development, etc.;
- *product*, the kinds of goods emanating from the organization and its different units; and
- *space*, the location in geographical space of the various organizational units.

Obviously, the four dimensions are interrelated. All of them are also affected by two basic variables: the size of the organization and its *variation over time*. As organizations grow in size, they also grow in complexity. The hierarchy gains more levels. The functions increase in number. The spatial location expands so that the various units of administration, production, selling, etc. become located in different places, different regions, different countries – sometimes, indeed, in different parts of the world.

Not surprisingly, space and time are basic dimensions of any organization. The middle-sized grocery shop round the corner may have been started by one individual, a small-scale *entrepreneur*, but as time went by, it grew, and the shop-owner asked the widow round the corner to take care of the cleaning, a task he previously did himself. It continued to grow, and he asked his teenage son to step in as an errand-boy. A few years later, that boy was a young man who enjoyed dealing with the customers. A new errand-boy was on his way in. Also, the book-keeping had grown more complicated, so the owner asked his accountant friend from the pub to take care of it. Some years later, his son was ready to go into business on his own, and since there was a similar shop for sale in the same town, his father borrowed some money, bought the shop and put his son in as the boss of that second shop. This has happened thousands of times, and sometimes it was the way an international chain of stores – a very large organization indeed – was created. Such a chain has a specific structure, the general characteristics of which tend to be similar to those of thousands of organizations which perform very different tasks in very different sectors of the Great Wheel of Culture in Society (see section 3.2).

5.5.2   Three models of organization

In this section, we will discuss some models of organization which represent different variants of the general organizational pattern previously examined. Three such variants are shown in Figure 5.1. Model A corresponds most closely to the traditional, strictly hierarchical type of organization, during millennia used and gradually refined in armies, governmental agencies, various units of production, etc. Our example refers to a traditional company producing goods for a market. At the uppermost levels of the model, all units are functionally differentiated (production, marketing, administration, etc.). At the lower levels, some units are differentiated with respect to the goods produced, be it physical products or social and human products (recruitment and training of office and factory workers). Although not shown in the model, each unit features some internal hierarchical patterns.

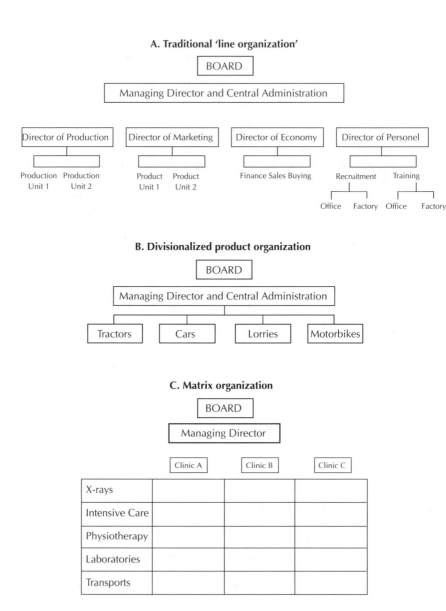

Figure 5.1 Three simplified models of organization

Model B features an organization primarily built around the goods produced and sold. The four main units – often called divisions – represent four main types of product. As modelled here, the organization has only three levels, but looking into the four divisions, within each one of them we would find functionally-oriented units dealing with broad functions such as buying, producing, selling, etc. And within these units, the usual hierarchical patterns will be found as a rule. In addition, just as the managing director needs a staff taking care of a number of different functions of support, etc., so must the divisional heads, and probably also management at lower levels in the organization. Some such support functions may be common to the various product areas. This means that the organization is not really unidimensional (indeed, how could it be?) but at least two-dimensional, and very probably actually features more than two dimensions. Organizational structures, then, should not be understood as being as unidimensional as they may appear in Models A and B.

An attempt to pay attention to the more than unidimensional character of almost all organizations is shown in Model C, featuring a so-called 'matrix organization', which has two explicit dimensions: a hierarchical dimension, and a functional one. There are three 'production units' (Clinics A, B and C rather traditionally organized around bodily parts and functions, say, heart, lungs, brain) and five units providing the specialized services needed by all three production units. In addition to a relatively small overarching hierarchy (Board, general manager with a staff, etc.), the hierarchies necessary to all largescale production are to be found within each unit of production, each functional unit – not between them.

Obviously, the models of Figure 5.1 are very schematic. Figure 5.2 offers a somewhat more realistic example (although still schematic, of course, since it is a model). It will be seen that this organization is fairly large and complex. The principles of structuring are based on geography, product, business function and work functions, the latter being fabricating and assembly. The fabricating functions are exemplified by three special functions, turning, milling and drilling. Note that only one of three geographical areas has been rendered in some detail, and only one of the two work functions. However, all such charts are only crude pictures of what is really going on in the organization.

5.5.3 'Adhocracy'

There is no organizational type that best fits all purposes. In addition, the type of societal climate prevailing in society is very important. In a climate characterized by high equality and high freedom, organizations tend to be somewhat different than in a climate of culture characterized by low equality and low freedom. Furthermore, changes in the basic modes of production also affect the type of organization which tends to be preferred. Thus, while all production was originally production of one unit at a time, during the

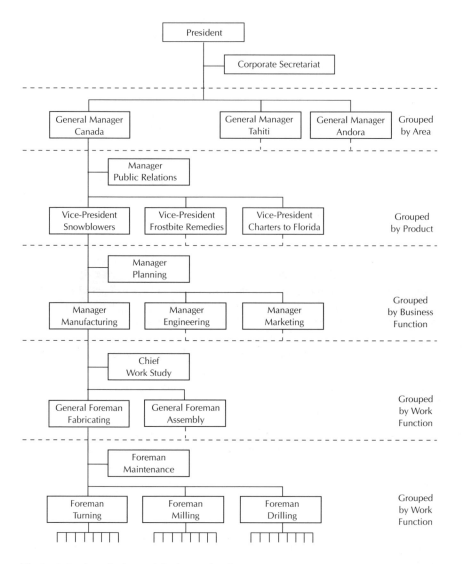

Figure 5.2   A realistic model of organization
(*source*: Mintzberg, 1993: 57)

nineteenth and twentieth centuries *mass* production entered the scene, dominated it, and is now experiencing increasingly heavy competition from *process* production, and also from returning integrated production of one complex unit at a time. Obviously, these basic processes of change must affect basic organizational patterns. Also, the types of communication going on in the different types of organization must be different from each other.

A general consequence of all these processes has been that all organizations now have to be flexible, not rigidly clinging to organizational charts established, perhaps, long ago (see Box 5.4). Thus, the three types of organization discussed here are often combined so that small-scale hierarchies may be found, and indeed have often been consciously created, within the separate units and sub-units of a divisionalized organization. As the organization suddenly meets new demands, it must be prepared to change, to adapt, to re-organize. In short, it must work in an *ad-hoc* fashion.

BOX 5.4   ON THE ROAD TO ADHOCRACY

There was a time when a company's Tables of Organization (formal and informal) stayed put for long periods, even during periods of depression, war and economic growth. By the time a company had successfully transitioned from the one-man-rule of its founder to a many-layered hierarchy, it had also, most likely, bolted into place a permanent departmental structure. There were departments for manufacturing, marketing, sales, research and what-have-you. Line and staff were clearly delineated. Sub-organizations reporting to the top of the hierarchy provided fixed corporate services, such as legal, financial, and personnel. Serried ranks of vice presidents held it all together.

Once this iron framework was installed, the company might shrink or grow, according to its fortunes, but the basic elements of its structure usually held firm. Reorganizations – usually implemented when a new chief executive took over – were few and far between.

By 1970 . . . the frequency of corporate reorganization had increased. . . . I quoted a business consultant to the effect that 'one major restructuring every two years is probably a conservative estimate of the current rate of organizational change among the largest industrial corporations.' Today the pace has grown hotter and the stakes bigger. Successive reorganizations not only occur more frequently. They cut deeper. In fact, we are witnessing the most rapid, complex and thoroughgoing corporate restructuring in modern history.

From: A. Toffler (1985) *The Adaptive Corporation*. Aldershot: Gower. p. 4.

– And a Note of Scepticism
Let's quickly review recent history to understand the current love affair with task forces. Although they undoubtedly existed previously in many unlabeled forms, NASA and the Polaris program gave them a good name. NASA invented the *ad hoc* team structure and in early programs delivered the goods. The Polaris submarine program worked even better. The task force notion then diffused to industry and was used for everything. By 1970, it had become incorporated so pervasively in many large companies that it had become just one additional part of the rigid system it was meant to fix.

From: T.J. Peters and R.H. Waterman, Jr (1984) *In Search of Excellence*. New York: Harper & Row. p. 128.

The expression 'ad hoc' may be translated from the original Latin as 'for this specific purpose'. As societal change increases in amount and tempo, specific, ad hoc solutions to organizational problems must often be quickly found. These tendencies have been well expressed in the term *adhocracy*, denoting a flexible organization, that can change its structure as changes in its environment dictate.

In traditional organizations the general pattern of the organization was not, and is not, changed very often. When specific problems unexpectedly turn up they are frequently solved by what is called informal organization (see section 5.3). Adhocracies, however, are systematically created with a view to being able to respond to the dynamic societal environment today surrounding most organizations. Few organizations are pure adhocracies, but relatively small organizations built for creative tasks – say, a new advertising agency – are often typical adhocracies. They solve their tasks as they come along, and the basic organizational structure is not rigidly followed but adapted to the task in hand.

In larger, more differentiated organizations, the need for adhocracy is often solved by creating specific, so-called ad-hoc groups for specific purposes: special 'task forces'. In some lines of business and trade, there has always been a strong need for similar types of organization. As a consequence of its very nature, for instance, the building sector was always working to its own ad-hoc pattern: a new sub-organization is created at the start of each specific building project – a 'one-at-a-time' pattern. Paradoxically, military organizations, although often accused of being very rigid organizations, may actually be regarded as classic examples of applied adhocracies, detaching this or that 'task force' to solve this or that military problem. As the Duke of Wellington, who defeated Napoleon at Waterloo in 1815 said: 'I'll cross that river when I come to it.'

5.5.4   Academic adhocracies

While the terminology used here may have been created during the twentieth century, some of the organizational types or sub-types discussed above have been around for centuries, not to say millennia (see section 5.2). An early example of a divisionalized product organization, for example, is the European university which has its roots in the Middle Ages. Its four classic faculties (theology, philosophy, law and medicine) correspond to the four divisions (tractors, cars, lorries, motorbikes) presented in Figure 5.1 (Model B); its hierarchical dimension appears in terms of assistants, junior and senior lecturers, assistant, associate and full professors, deans and (vice-)chancellors; its product differentiation appears in terms of Bachelors and Masters degrees and Doctorates of various academic subjects and faculties. Obviously, universities have developed immensely since the Middle Ages. The present university system is just a few centuries old, by and large stemming from traditions established in nineteenth-century Germany and further developed in other countries, not least in the USA.

During the last few decades a strong element of vitalizing adhocracy has been introduced to the traditional European university system: any number of institutes and centres have been created for the solution of this or that special task, calling for a number of different specialists working more or less closely together. Then again, while it may be difficult to start a new university centre, it would seem that it may be no less difficult to close it down. Having solved its task or perhaps having been made obsolete by other societal developments, as a rule the leading circles of that once successful university centre are not slow in coming up with new problems to be solved by the centre – a general process which has aptly been called 'displacement of goals'.

5.5.5   Organizations in time and space

Finally, let's return for a short while to those basic dimensions, time and space. When the owner of that small private organization, the shop at the corner, opens another shop in a different part of the town, the basic pattern of the organization has to be drastically changed. There is a joint leader of the organization (the original owner), two subordinated positions (the bosses of the two shops; the original owner sometimes being one of those bosses, thus enacting two different roles in the single organization), and possibly a third level of shop assistants at the two shops. The fact that the two main parts of the organization are differently located requires the transportation of people and goods between them, in a way which is quite different from the case when the original organization is located at one point in space. Consequently, also the overall pattern of communication has to be changed.

In this connection, it may be useful to consider the fact that patterns of communication are always heavily dependent upon patterns of transportation, and *vice versa* (see sections 1.1 and 4.5 above). Before the moveable steam engine, the 'locomotive', information could not move more rapidly than a galloping horse or a fast-sailing ship. International organizations such as the Hanse (mentioned in section 5.2 above) thus had formidable difficulties to overcome in their internal communication, difficulties which were multiplied many times, of course, in the communication systems of, say, a large empire. News about battles, upon which the very existence of the empire might depend, could take weeks to reach its capital. The telegraph changed all this in a way which is difficult to grasp today (see section 4.7). More recent developments in communication technology have changed society's structure of communication in ways which already are often taken for granted but in the future might, perhaps, be difficult to understand (see Chapters 2 and 8).

5.6   The climate of organizational communication

In section 3.5.2 above we discussed various climates of culture prevailing in a given society during different periods of time. We distinguished between two basic dimensions, freedom and equality. When dichotomized and combined, the two dimensions resulted in four ideologies, four types of climate of culture:

- *socialism* puts a high value on both freedom and equality;
- *fascism* puts a low value on both freedom and equality; while
- *communism* puts equality above freedom; and
- *liberal capitalism* puts freedom above equality.

When, in section 4.4.5, we discussed family communication, we mentioned the existence of different family communication climates. Two basic dimensions of family communication climate were identified: socio-orientation and concept orientation. When combined, the two dimensions resulted in four different types of family communication climate:

- A *consensual* family communication climate is high on both socio- and concept orientation.
- A *protective* family communication climate is high on socio-orientation, low on concept orientation.
- A *pluralistic* family communication climate is high on concept orientation, low on socio-orientation.
- A *laissez-faire* family communication climate is low on both socio- and concept orientation.

In a similar vein, attempts have been undertaken to identify the basic dimensions of various organizational communication climates, and to combine those dimensions into typologies. The most widely known and applied typology of this kind is probably the one presented by the Dutch scholar and businessman, Geert Hofstede, who for decades was theoretically and practically engaged in the field of organizational communication, developing a series of organizational typologies. A late version of these typologies has five dimensions:

- Power Distance
- Collectivism/Individualism
- Femininity/Masculinity
- Uncertainty Avoidance
- Long-term/Short-term Orientation.

The main characteristics of the five dimensions are presented in Box 5.5.

Paradoxically, although Hofstede originally was interested in phenomena at the organizational level, he describes the five dimensions as phenomena existing primarily at the societal level, and he actually measured them at the individual level, within national branches of a large international company (IBM). The intuitive appeal of his results offers increased support, however, to those professionally designed studies which have been carried out in more than 50 countries over the last 25 years. Figure 5.3 shows the location of a number of IBM personnel nationalities in a fourfold table based on the two dimensions, *uncertainty avoidance* and *power distance*. Once we see the results, we tend to find them rather convincing, by and large in line with our

BOX 5.5   DIMENSIONS OF ORGANIZATIONAL CULTURE

In his book, *Cultures and Organizations: Software of the Mind* (London: McGraw-Hill, 1991), Geert Hofstede shortly describes five main dimensions of organizational culture, and the measurement thereof:

Power Distance Index (PDI)

'PDI scores inform us about *dependence* relationships in a country. In small power distance countries there is limited dependence of subordinates on bosses, and a preference for consultation, that is, *interdependence* between boss and subordinates. The emotional distance between them is relatively small: subordinates will quite readily approach and contradict their bosses. In large power distance countries there is considerable dependence of subordinates on bosses.' (p. 27)

Individualism Index (IDV)

'*Individualism* pertains to societies in which the ties between individuals are loose: everyone is expected to look after himself or herself and his or her immediate family. *Collectivism* as its opposite pertains to societies in which people from birth onwards are integrated into strong, cohesive ingroups, which throughout people's lifetime continue to protect them in exchange for unquestioning loyalty.' (p. 51)

Masculinity Index (MAS)

'*Masculinity* pertains to societies in which social gender roles are clearly distinct (i.e. men are supposed to be assertive, tough, and focused on material success, whereas women are supposed to be more modest, tender and concerned with the quality of life); *femininity* pertains to societies in which social gender roles overlap (i.e. both men and women are supposed to be modest, tender and concerned with the quality of life).' (p. 82f.)

Uncertainty Avoidance Index (UA)

'Uncertainty avoidance can . . . be defined as the extent to which the members of a culture feel threatened by uncertain or unknown situations. This feeling is, among other things, expressed through nervous stress and in a need for predictability: a need for written and unwritten rules.' (p. 113)

Long-term/Short-term Orientation (LTO/STO)

'Long-term orientation stands for the fostering of virtues oriented towards future rewards, in particular perseverance and thrift. . . . Short-term orientation stands for the fostering of virtues related to the past and present, in particular respect for tradition, preservation of face, and fulfilling social obligations.' (pp. 261, 263)

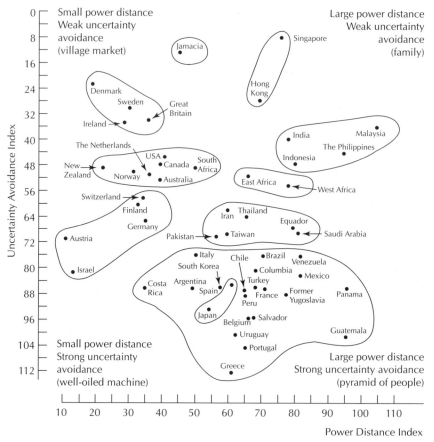

Figure 5.3 Organizational communication climates in 50 countries
(*source*: Hofstede, 1991)

expectations or, if you will, our prejudices. According to Hofstede, then, in organizational communication: Scandinavians and Anglo-Saxons tend to have *small power distance* and *weak uncertainty avoidance*; Germans, Austrians and Israelis tend to have *small power distance* and *strong uncertainty avoidance*; people in some African and Asian countries tend to have *large power distance* and *weak uncertainty avoidance*; and people in many Latin countries tend to have *large power distance* and *strong uncertainty avoidance*.

Obviously, the kind of organizational communication going on in cultures with *small power distance* and *weak uncertainty avoidance* must be rather different from the kind of organizational communication going on in cultures with *large power distance* and *strong uncertainty avoidance*. Presumably, organizational communication in cultures characterized by small power distance and weak uncertainty avoidance should be more open than in cultures characterized by large power distance and strong uncertainty avoidance. It goes without saying that in a world characterized by increasing social, economic and political contacts between different cultures, Hofstede's typologies are becoming more relevant to more people engaged in more kinds of differentiated activities.

An interesting problem is the relationship between the three typologies summarized above: climate of culture, family communication patterns and climates of organizational communication. How might the climate of societal culture, the family communication climate and the organizational climate be related to each other – if at all? This has never been systematically studied, but it would make a demanding task of research, and an extremely fascinating one.

On the face of it, it does not seem unrealistic to assume that a given societal climate of culture would tend to favour a given type of organizational communication and a given pattern of family communication, so that in a given society, a given type of family communication pattern would also tend to go together with a given type of organizational communication. Tentatively, it might be suggested, for instance, that

- a societal climate of culture characterized by high equality and high freedom would tend to go together with organizational communication characterized by small power distance and low uncertainty avoidance;
- a societal climate of culture characterized by high equality and high freedom would tend to go together with a family communication climate characterized by pluralism;
- a societally predominating family communication climate characterized by pluralism would tend to go together with organizational communication characterized by small power distance and low uncertainty avoidance.

Such society, such models of organizations, such family communication patterns. There are no data around to test these grand hypotheses, but future research will hopefully be able to throw some light on the fascinating relationships between societal climate of culture, type of organizational communication, and type of family communication patterns. For the time being we must stay content just speculating about them.

Finally, it should not be forgotten that Hofstedes's typology of organizational communication is highly relevant also to the formal models of organization discussed in previous sections of this chapter. Obviously, a strictly one-dimensional organizational hierarchy as depicted in Figure 5.1 (Model A), calls for different types of organizational communication than does, say, a matrix-type organization as depicted in Figure 5.1 (Model C).

5.7 Organizations especially designed for communication

All units of all organizations – all individual members as well as all sub-groups, sections, etc. – must of necessity spend large parts of their time communicating with other individuals, groups and organizations, not only inside their own sub-group or organization, but often even more so outside that sub-group or organization. For some individuals, groups, organizational sections, etc. the special task of communicating becomes so important that it stands out as their main task, or even the only one. Even in a small human group, for instance, communication – inside the group and outside it – is one of the main tasks of the group leader (see sections 2.5 and 4.4.1).

Similarly, in a small, weakly differentiated organization, the chairperson may stand out as the natural spokesperson. As the organization grows in size, however, its functional differentiation also tends to grow. Increasingly often, specific tasks are allocated to specific positions within the organization, occupied by specific members of the organization. The chairperson of the organization may find it convenient, for instance, to delegate specific communicative functions to a special person or role-incumbent, say, to the secretary of the organization. The organization may thus get a more or less formally recognized spokesperson, acting more or less on his or her own initiative, and that spokesperson is not necessarily the leader of the organization. (Similar tendencies may sometimes be found in otherwise rather informally organized groups.)

The role of the spokesperson may be formulated in terms of the general model of communication presented in section 2.6 above (Figure 2.3). It also shows some similarities to that of the gate-keeper (see section 6.4.2 below). But while the gate-keeper is focusing on incoming messages, the spokesperson is focusing on outgoing messages, of course.

As the organization continues to grow in size and complexity, the spokesperson will need some assistance, and soon the organization may acquire a unit of information and communication. If the organization continues to grow, so will that unit, and after some time we may have a large organizational unit of information and communication, headed by a 'director of information and communication'. At some stage in such developments the individual or unit responsible for the organization's internal and external communication may find it convenient to use part of the resources available for communicative tasks for buying communicative products and services from outside the organization.

Organizations and roles specially designed for acting as providers of communicative services of different kinds have been around for millennia, serving different sectors of the Great Wheel of Culture in Society (see section 3.2). Think, for instance, of the ambassadors of the large river empires during Antiquity, or the bards of northern Europe's early history, or the missionaries sent out from Rome to convert the heathens north of the Alps, or the newsletter services offered by large merchant houses during various epochs of history. But during the nineteenth and twentieth centuries such organizations and roles multiplied at a very rapid rate (see Chapter 6 on mass communication).

Now, we shall briefly discuss organizations created especially for serving other organizations with their communicative problems. Such organizations include, for instance, those specializing in providing services in public relations, marketing, and advertising. Often they are special units within large organizations which often have quite different functions. Increasingly often, however, they are more or less independent companies offering their services and goods on the open market. Their professional expertise is becoming increasingly indispensable to producers wanting to reach a market willing to buy what they have to sell.

The terminology is by no way completely agreed upon in this area, but one way of understanding these communication activities is to look at the time perspective applied. In *consumer research*, what one is after is knowledge about the existence of markets for the goods that will ultimately be offered for sale. Obviously, such studies must be undertaken at a fairly early planning stage, preceding the actual production, sometimes by years. When the existence of a potential market has been certified, there is a need to find out more about that market. *Motivation research* tries to identify the population categories that will be most inclined to buy the potential product, in what quantities, and for what reasons or motives.

But motivation is not enough. Potential buyers must know about the existence of the product, and about its comparative advantages in terms of quality, costs, etc. When time is ripe to launch the product on the market, it is also time for heavy *advertising campaigns*, to be carried on in media found by the experts to be suitable for the product at hand: mass media for mass products, specialized media for specialized products, etc.

At each and every point in these long processes, there are communicative specialists available, experts at the research needed in their specific part of the marketing and selling process. To get a general understanding of such processes, however, it may be useful to compare these types of research to research of a more general kind: innovation and diffusion research.

5.8 Research on innovation and diffusion

However special and even esoteric it may be, every new product to be brought to the market may be regarded as just another special case of a very general phenomenon: the diffusion of innovations. Every new product may thus be regarded as an *innovation* which in order to be successful has to pass through both a large number of individual processes of *adoption* (you adopt the new phenomenon in the sense that you start to buy it and use it) and a societal process of *diffusion* (the innovation spreads in society until it has found its maximum level of diffusion). For more than a century, large amounts of research on adoption and diffusion processes have been carried out in a number of disciplines such as geography, history, anthropology and sociology etc. During the last few decades these problematics have also generated much interest in various branches of media and communication studies – not least in research on organizational communication. An important, special type of diffusion and adoption research is *epidemiology*, a medical speciality with a

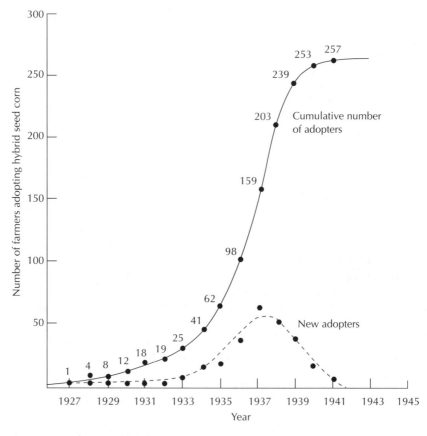

Figure 5.4 Processes of diffusion and adoption
(*source*: Rogers, 1995: 258)

tradition stretching back at least to the seventeenth century. In that tradition of research a basic distinction is made between the two notions of *incidence* and *prevalence*: incidence denoting the frequency of new cases during a given period of time; prevalence, the absolute or relative number of people suffering from a given illness at a given moment in time. Prevalence is the product of incidence, the longevity of the illness, and its death rate. Chronic diseases may have a low incidence and a high prevalence. Obviously, this basic distinction is applicable to all kinds of innovation research as well.

Figure 5.4 offers a visual presentation of the character of the processes of diffusion and adoption in the example of farmers adapting hybrid seed corn. The diffusion process should be understood in terms of the large figure, the adoption process, in terms of the small figure. The so-called S-curve depicted in the figure is characterized by a general pattern of slow–rapid–slow diffusion as various population categories adopt the innovation during different phases of the diffusion process. The adopters are distributed over time according to a normal, roughly bell-shaped curve of probability, showing that there is a small number of early adopters who are willing to take some risks for the chance of making wind-fall profits, while the laggards prefer to stay content with a less risky, later adoption.

Both the individual process of *adoption* and the societal process of *diffusion* may be understood in terms of communication. Neither process can take place without a lot of communication, engaging the individual or organization launching the innovation to this or that segment of society, the adopter of the innovation as well as other individuals and groupings in society, for one reason or another wishing to further or prevent the diffusion of the adoption. Obviously, the type of communication to be used by those wishing to further the innovation varies with the phase of diffusion in which the new product is located at a given moment. In addition, it goes without saying that the specific character of the innovation must be heeded.

Important characteristics of an innovation are who will use the innovation, and who decides what and who is to be rewarded for the innovation, as well as the kind of reward provided to the innovator – material or symbolic rewards, for instance. The character of an innovation is thus to a large extent defined by the reward system applicable to the innovator and his or her innovation.

The central characteristics of different reward systems may be used to create a typology for innovations. Such a typology is shown in Figure 5.5. It will be seen that the innovators' power over their innovations varies considerably within the five different sub-systems. Only in basic and applied science do the groups of innovators themselves have a decisive influence over the rewards given for innovations within their area of expertise. This influence is expressed not least in the sub-system of symbolic rewards. (For some information about the most prestigious scientific symbolic rewards, see Box 7.9 on p. 195.)

Yet another problem in this connection is that the character of the innovation and its consequences for the potential adopters may stand out as different to different people. Two key variables in this connection is the potential adopter's degree of involvement in the innovation (high/low), and his or her attitude towards it (positive/negative). Some other important variables include whether the innovation may be adopted gradually or in one step, and whether the adoption of the innovation entails abandoning previous patterns of action or may be regarded as an additional pattern of action.

All these circumstances, and some other ones as well, affect the type of communication to be directed towards potential adopters by those wishing to further the diffusion of the innovation at hand – as well as by those who, for one reason or another, wish to prevent or at least delay the diffusion process. Finally, as the process of diffusion proceeds, the various promotional activities must, of course, change character, as must those activities aimed at preventing or delaying the diffusion of the innovation. (The latter type of activities are especially important in connection with the special type of diffusion called epidemics.)

Innovative product consumed mainly by fellow innovators	Material rewards allocated among innovators mainly by fellow innovators	Symbolic rewards allocated among innovators mainly by fellow innovators	Norms for innovations set mainly by fellow innovators	Ideal type of reward system	Tentative examples
Yes	Yes	Yes	Yes	Esoteric	Basic science
No	Yes	Yes	Yes	Independent	Applied science
No	No	Yes	Yes	Semi-independent	Technology, elite art and literature
No	No	No	Yes	Sub-cultural	Jazz, radical science
No	No	No	No	Hetero-cultural	Mass media culture (literature, music, etc.)

Figure 5.5 A typology for innovators' reward systems (*source*: Rosengren, 1994c)

5.9 Organizations for furthering adoption and diffusion

5.9.1 The general pattern

A large number of organizations are busy with the tasks of furthering adoption and diffusion processes. Think, for instance, of all the advertising agencies, communication consultants, etc. A useful way of gaining a quick overview of this type of communicative organization and its activities is to try to express it in terms of Figure 2.3 in section 2.6 on p. 50, offering an abstract model of communication between three levels. Obviously, the organizations of communication just discussed are represented by the box in the middle of the figure, while the upper box can represent the organization wishing to communicate with the public and the lower box represents the public. The simple reason why the box in the middle is useful is that for a number of reasons the four direct arrows, 1–4, in many situations do not work very well.

Quite naturally, in the beginning of the relationship between the organization at hand and the service organization specializing in communicative activities, communication of types 5–8 are predominating. But what is discussed in those types of communication is often communication of types 1–4. And when the service organization has accepted the job, communication of types 9–12 starts appearing. This stage often begins with informal, so-called qualitative interviews undertaken with selected, more or less typical potential customers or clients of the originally initiating organization.

When the service organization and its client have discussed the results of the preparatory interviews, these are sometimes followed up by a full-blown survey study (type 12). More formalized interviews and/or questionnaires are distributed to a representative sample of the segment of population regarded as including the potential customers or clients of the initiating organization. The results of the survey study are analyzed in quantitative and qualitative terms, interpreted and presented to the client (type 5). After one or more rounds of discussion (types 5–8), the results of the survey serve as one of several bases for launching a campaign presenting the client company and/or its products to the public in as positive and enticing a way as possible (type 2). Real business may begin for the client. The service organization turns to other clients, hoping that its activities will have been so successful as to make the client return for more business later on.

5.9.2 Lobbying

These types of relationship between a producing and selling organization and a consulting organization take different concrete shapes, but by and large they tend to follow the pattern just described. The pattern may become rather different, however, when an organization wants to affect the opinions of really powerful groups of decision-makers, trying to get an innovation or new idea

---

BOX 5.6 ON PRESSURE GROUPS

'Until the 1960s the prevailing model of pressure-group activity in developed democracies focused on relations between organizations representing the diverse interests of a pluralistic society and the agencies of government, in which news media publicity played little part. Direct and regular access to decision processes was the favored goal. . . . Since the 1960s, however, because of the combined impact of several political, social, and communicative transformations, a more "media-centric" model of pressure-group activities has come to the fore. Without displacing the more traditional patterns, this new model has often supplemented, bypassed, and penetrated them. According to this model, media attention is a vital source of potential influence and power, creating perceptions of public support that policy-makers must heed. Groups must therefore give much higher priority to the publicity field, recognizing that it is a competitive arena in which many rivals are also seeking footholds and that it is dominated by the standards of journalism to which their own media materials must conform. This in turn

- generates pressure to develop self-conscious news-management strategies,
- influences the kinds of appeals and demands that will be ventilated,
- can provoke conflict inside groups over what is thought necessary to break into the news as distinct from what would be more true to an organization's purposes, and
- may redistribute overall power and status differentials among groups in society.'

From: J.G. Blumler (1989) 'Pressure group', *International Encyclopedia of Communications*, vol. 3. 350–1.

---

accepted by them. The problem has to be handled much more delicately, often by various kinds of so-called *lobbying*.

The term 'lobbying' originally stems from activities connected with the British parliament. In the lobby of that parliament it was, and still is, possible for selected representatives of other authorities, companies, organizations, media, etc. informally to meet the parliamentarians, collect valuable information and, if possible, try to influence the parliamentarians in one way or the other. These types of activities have grown ever more widespread and important. They are now carried out not only in parliamentary lobbies or similar localities around the globe, but in a number of different ways as well.

The basic idea, of course, is that by means of more or less informal, personal contacts it is possible to speak for this or that opinion, this or that potential solution to an economic or political problem, in ways, as a rule, not used in more formal connections. Today, special *pressure groups* formed for such purposes are sometimes also called 'lobbies' (see Box 5.6). Such groups often combine the informal methods just described with other methods such as producing promotional material and also making presentations to various groups and to the mass media. Their activities thus include all or most of types

1–12 in Figure 2.3 on p. 50. Of course, not all groups and organizations can afford to carry out such campaigns. Obviously, the increasing use of the mass media as a complement to more direct lobbying activities may imply a risk to the overall societal functions of the mass media. These and a host of related problems will be discussed in the next chapter.

6
Societal Communication, Mass Communication

6.1 Types of societies, types of communication

In previous chapters we have noted in passing the close, almost tautological relationship existing between *type of society* and *type of communication* prevailing in society (see, for instance, section 2.3). A given technology of communication admits a given type of society. A given type of society calls for a special type of communication.

So-called primitive societies may have quite efficient technologies for mediated communication *over space*, sometimes even over fairly large distances (beacons, smoke signals or drumming, for instance). They may also have some means of communication *over time*: tombs, memorial stones, etc. (see section 2.3). But they have no means of mass communication beyond meetings at the village square, the market-place, before a holy shrine, or a similar place, and communication at such meetings may often be better understood as group or organizational communication than as mass communication (see sections 4.4 and 5.1). In such societies, audiences are bound with respect to both time and space.

Inherent in the arts of reading and writing, however, is not only the capacity to communicate over large distances in space and time, but also *to multiply a given message*. Once a message has been written down – in however primitive a medium – it may be multiplied. Already in classical European Antiquity (and for centuries afterwards) written texts – sometimes quite long texts, 'books' – were multiplied by groups of scribes (often, slaves) working in so-called *scriptoria*. The scribes wrote on rolls of parchment ('scrolls') or, much later, on paper what was read to them from an original manuscript. (Parchment was made of hides from goats, sheep or calves.) Similar arrangements were to be found in other parts of the world as well. They were good enough as far as they went, but they could never produce and reproduce verbal messages in really large quantities. Only an efficient printing technique could do that. To really move on, the writing revolution thus needed another epoch-making revolution: the printing revolution.

Printing as a technique for duplicating pictorial and verbal messages has actually been around for more than a millennium. Early ways of doing this was to carve pictures or letters on wooden blocks which were then covered with ink (sometimes, of different colours) and pressed against cloth, parchment or paper. Paper was invented in China about 2,000 years ago and came to Europe in the twelfth century. The art of printing on paper by means of moveable and re-usable types arrived much later, however. The first versions of this technique were being used in East Asia already in the eleventh century, but it was Johannes Gutenberg, a goldsmith in Mainz, Germany, who in the mid-fifteenth century created a highly efficient technique for casting re-usable types of lead (also developing a better printing press and better printing ink), thus starting a new era in the history of communication. Gutenberg himself used his new technique to print the most important book there was: the Bible. Several versions of the famous 'Gutenberg Bible' appeared in the mid-1450s.

Johannes Gutenberg had produced an innovation that was to change the world forever. At long last, the writing revolution, which during Antiquity began in the Eastern Mediterranean area, had received a viable follow up, which was to change virtually all human societies. For more than four centuries, the printed word was the only true mass medium. Gradually developing, it was differentiated into two main types of mass media:

- the *book media*, in principle built on unique, one-of-its-kind publications; and
- the *periodic media*, in principle built on publications repeatedly published with new contents on similar themes over a regular time frame: every day, every week, every month or every year.

In the nineteenth century, the 'century of inventions', the door opened for new, decisive developments in the drawing, writing, calculating and printing technology. For example:

- the cylinder press (*c.* 1810);
- photography (*c.* 1840);
- the rotation press (*c.* 1860);
- the typewriter and the calculator (both *c.* 1870); the calculator for some time having a rival in the now obsolete *slide-rule*, and very old predecessors in various types of the *abacus*, advanced forms of which are still in use in some countries;
- the punched-card tabulator, the 'Hollerith' (*c.* 1890);
- the offset technique (*c.* 1900).

All these inventions made the production, reproduction and distribution of messages in words, figures and pictures faster and cheaper. In addition, schooling was gradually becoming compulsory and children stayed at school for longer periods, with the result that literacy levels rose creating a large reading public (see section 6.5).

In the 1940s, this stepwise and accelerating development took a giant leap forward with the development of the electronic computer, the 'electronic brain' as it was often called at the beginning. When mechanical machines for handling large amounts of information were superseded by electronic ones – by computers – not only the *physical* production, reproduction and distribution, but also the *intellectual* and *artistic* production of all sorts of information was drastically changed – a breakthrough indeed in the history of information and communication. During the last 50 years and in innumerable ways, the computer has changed all parts of all modern societies, not least their communicative systems. The computer is therefore on a par with such epoch-making inventions as the steam-engine (*c.* 1770), the railway (*c.* 1830), the internal combustion engine (*c.* 1860) and the aeroplane (*c.* 1900). These inventions affected the *production* and *transportation* systems of practically all human societies. The computer affected the *information* and *communication* systems of practically all human societies. In combination with the reproduction technologies mentioned above – plus the xerox type photocopier (*c.* 1950) – it ushered in what has been called the *information society*.

During the last 50 years, this breakthrough has been continuously followed up by a stream of communicatively-oriented innovations as different as, for instance, the computerized telephone switchboard, the personal word processor, and the 'World Wide Web' (see sections 2.3 and 4.7.3). It goes without saying that, directly and indirectly, all these inventions and developments changed all media of communication, not least, the media of mass communication (see also section 7.7 below).

6.2 A necessary precondition

Since the first true mass media were the book and the newspaper, a necessary precondition for the great leap of true mass communication was widespread literacy: the art of reading and writing. The notion of literacy is not as simple as it may seem. At the individual level, there are degrees of literacy. Also, different texts vary immensely in terms of 'readability', a characteristic measured by a number of specific indices. Some people may only be able to read even a rather simple text with great difficulty, while others can read extremely complicated texts with great speed.

Societies characterized by more or less general literacy have existed for only about 150 years. Previously, all societies were characterized by very different degrees of literacy. As a rule, only small portions of the population showed complete mastery of the arts of reading and writing, with various types of specialist serving religious, political or economic elites. Outside these narrow circles, oral communication dominated almost completely (see sections 2.3 and 4.3). The huge processes of industrialization in the nineteenth century, starting in north-western Europe and the USA, called for increased literacy among the population at large; consequently, compulsory schooling was introduced in those countries.

Even with a relatively modest definition of literacy, the degree of population literacy still varies immensely around the globe, and sometimes between different parts of the same country. It is true that the religious reforms of sixteenth-century Europe called for increased literacy in north-western Europe in particular: the individual was supposed to meet her God in this Holy Scripture. But only with the introduction of general, compulsory schooling in the mid-nineteenth century was something like general literacy within reach. Naturally, however, it took decades for European and North American literacy to reach the present rate of close to 100%. Several South American, Asian and African countries have reached similar figures, although in some countries, of course, literacy is still not the norm in spite of impressive national and international efforts. These are gaps of information and knowledge writ large (see section 2.3.4 above).

Nobody knows whether – and if so, when – 100% global literacy will ever be achieved, but the growth of literacy goes on. Paradoxically, as literacy is continually growing, the media which do not call for any literacy in the traditional sense of the word – radio and television – are also experiencing world-wide diffusion and penetration. In that specific sense, then, literacy seems to be becoming less important, while what might be called 'pictorial literacy' is becoming more important. At the same time, however, the increasing complexity of modern society makes literacy more important than ever.

6.3 Media of sounds and pictures

In the late nineteenth century and the first half of the twentieth century, all types of print media got three powerful competitors, the three new mass media: radio, cinema film, and television.

The medium of *radio* was a result of the discovery of electromagnetic waves, first theorized by the Scot, James Maxwell, and observed by the German, Heinrich Hertz, in the 1860s and 1880s, respectively. Radio was thus originally a scientific discovery. But around the turn of the century, in the creative hands of inventors such as the Italian Guglielmo Marconi, these waves were turned into the medium of wireless telegraphy, a point-to-point medium far superior to the original, electric, wire-borne telegraphy which had been launched a couple of decades earlier by the US inventor, Samuel Morse, whose code, the 'Morse alphabet', built on points and dashes, remained, however. After the First World War, the new electronic medium was further developed from a point-to-point medium to a mass medium – broadcast radio, as we know it today.

In North and South America, the new mass medium was quickly commercialized, advertising being its main source of income. But in many European countries, and in some other parts of the world as well, radio originally became a 'public service medium', financed by licence fees and state support. From the late 1920s onwards, under the dynamic leadership of Sir John Reith, the British Broadcasting Corporation (BBC) offered a much-copied prototype for this form of mass communication. Today, all parts of the world have both commercial and public service radio.

Cinema film, offering moving pictures, had several more or less ingenious predeccessors, but it was the Lumière brothers in Paris in 1895 who demonstrated the first viable version of this medium. Their invention was an immediate success, quickly spreading world-wide, not least in the USA. In the beginning the films were very short, and without sound. After the First World War there was increasing competition from a number of countries in all parts of the world, especially Germany, France, the Soviet Union, the Scandinavian countries, Japan and India. Cinema film that offered both sound and pictures became general around 1930. It quickly adopted a then relatively new theatrical genre which was to prove very viable indeed: the musical. The musical was able to assimilate modern forms of popular music, and in the end this genre became a serious threat to other types of stage music theatre, especially the light opera, the *operetta*. But media developments continued.

The ever-increasing costs of film production soon led to a process of concentration among production companies and a tendency increasingly to rely on a partly international star system (British-American Charlie Chaplin (b. 1889), German-American Marlene Dietrich (b. 1901), Swedish-American Greta Garbo (b. 1905), etc.), a few, expensive productions (*Gone with the Wind* (1939)) and, wherever possible, a world-wide distribution aiming at global success. These general tendencies were soon to be epitomized in the film studios mushrooming in a Los Angeles suburb called Hollywood. After the Second World War the Hollywood system became even more internationally dominant, although national film industries, especially in England, France and Italy, were still able to come up with world-wide successes. Also, several individual talents were able to compete successfully with their American counterparts for an international public (for instance, some Italian, French, Scandinavian and Japanese film directors and their favourite star actors). With the advent of *television*, however, the international media scene was again drastically changed.

As a technical possibility, television had been around since the 1920s, but it was only just before the Second World War that television as a mass medium was launched in the USA and a few other countries. The war imposed a moratorium on the medium, but around 1950 it was ready for its world-wide, rapid diffusion process. In less than a decade, TV became *the* mass medium. Right from its beginning, the new medium of television was closely related to, and dependent on, the film medium, often re-distributing cinema film. Time and again it was invigorated by additional developments such, as colour television, the portable video camera, and the home video cassette, admitting 'time shifting' and encouraging private video filming.

Just like radio, TV appeared in a commercial and a public service format. Not surprisingly, countries with public service radio tended to prefer public service television; countries with commercial radio preferred commercial television. (In some countries, however, there were two viable systems right from the beginning: both public service and commercial TV.) In addition, large parts of the programming were commercially produced, also in public service television countries. Later on, commercial television was also introduced into countries which originally started with monopoly public service systems, one reason being the fact that satellites allowed individual downloading of commercial TV from the skies. In many countries, however, public service television is still a highly competitive medium, and in some countries the policy is to try to ensure that public service television keeps 50% of the audience, an ambition which has to pay a price in terms of increasing investments and gradual adaptations to a commercially viable level of taste.

With the arrival in the mid-1970s of the portable video camera and the home video cassette, two older mass media, cinema film and broadcast television, got yet another formidable competitor. But just as in previous introductions of new media of communication, the old media did not disappear. They adapted to the new situation. Facilitating the recording, transferring and editing processes, the portable video camera was quickly accepted as a handy method of TV news journalism, capable of offering live visual coverage of even rather unexpected, rapidly evolving critical situations in various parts of the world. In addition, large numbers of old cinema films were transferred to the new medium, thus being given a second life – a development very welcome to the film industry at a time when public cinema viewing had been heavily reduced by television viewing, and today still welcome by TV viewers and cinema film producers alike. Also, the video cassette recorder (VCR), allowing individual 'time shifting' in television viewing, has actually increased numbers of TV viewers in that viewers can record programmes they would otherwise have missed, to watch later. Finally, video is not just another mass medium. Much like the previous still and film cameras, video cameras developed into a family medium, offering the possibility of recording private experiences, including important so-called 'rites of passage': christenings, graduations, weddings, even burials. Thus video may be said to bridge the technical differences previously existing between the mass media of film and television, as well as those between family filming and television.

The traditional mass media scene as we now know it seems to be set at least for a decade or so – unless, of course, some new, unexpected innovation should appear: digital television has already arrived offering better visual quality and new programming. At the same time, of course, all traditional mass media are experiencing increasing competition from the World Wide Web (see sections 4.7 and 7.7).

6.4 From society to individual and back again

6.4.1   Different perspectives of time

In sections 1.3 and 3.3 above we discussed the process of *socialization*. We noted that there are two main types of socialization: primary and secondary socialization. Primary socialization is the process by which culture is transferred from generation to generation – the process by which the newborn baby is gradually transformed into a fully competent member of human society. Secondary socialization is the ongoing process by which all members of society are taught new knowledge and specific skills necessary to adapt to general societal culture and overall societal change. Mass media are important agents of socialization, transferring culture from the level of society to that of the individual. Since the definitive breakthrough of mass media in the late nineteenth century, their importance as agents of socialization has been continuously growing, not least in the process of secondary socialization to which all of us are always subject.

As agents of socialization, present-day mass media are unique in many ways:

- acting for several hours each day of the year in virtually all homes of the society;
- offering virtually endless flows of entertainment and information;
- establishing the agenda of political, economic and cultural discussions;
- providing formal, educationally-oriented socialization (see section 3.3);
- helping to conserve existing structures of power at the same time as preparing the ground for those ongoing processes of change so vital to any modern, industrial and post-industrial society and presumably, to all postmodern ones as well.

These fundamental facts of modern and postmodern society have not been left unnoticed by communicatively-oriented research and scholarship. Actually, a number of different traditions of research have been studying these phenomena for quite some time. Two broad and large traditions of mass communication research have been around for at least half a century. So-called *uses and gratifications research* focuses on the individual use made of the mass media, while *effects research* focuses on the short- and long-term effects on the individual of his or her mass media use. These traditions of research will be discussed at some length in section 6.6 below.

In addition to the two main traditions, five different, explicit and rather specialized traditions of research have been busy describing and explaining the various processes by which mass media content reaches and affects individuals and groups of individuals. The main difference between these five traditions is the time perspective applied within them. These are the five traditions, and their time perspective:

- diffusion of news (hours and days);
- agenda-setting (weeks and months);
- spiral of silence (months and years);
- cultivation research (years and decades); and
- *Öffentlichkeit à la* Habermas (decades and centuries).

Diffusion of news is the process by which news that is collected and presented by the mass media spreads ('diffuses') to individual members of the population. This is a very rapid process, its time scale being measured in *hours and days*. The first news diffusion studies were carried out in the USA, after the death of President Franklin D. Roosevelt in 1945. Since then, a number of such studies have been undertaken. (For a somewhat more recent example of world-wide diffusion of news, see Chapter 7, Figure 7.2 on p. 185).

Agenda-setting is the process by which the mass media 'tell' members of society what to think about, what to discuss with family members, friends, colleagues, etc. Its time scale is *weeks and months*. Its originators are two US scholars of communication, M.E. McCombs and D. Shaw, who published the first scholarly article on the subject in 1972.

The spiral of silence is a process related to agenda-setting. While agenda-setting tells us what to think *about*, the spiral of silence tells us which views and opinions are the 'correct' or 'proper' ones when discussing issues with family members, friends, colleagues, strangers, etc., and which opinions are less correct. Quite naturally, it is easier to voice 'correct' views and opinions than more questionable ones – especially among strangers. Incorrect views may thus become the object of a spiral of silence, being gradually 'hushed up'. Very probably, the spiral of silence varies in strength between individuals and groups of individuals. For instance, in more or less avant-garde circles of, say, students, artists and intellectuals, the 'correct' views to be voiced may be exactly those which in more traditional circles tend to be regarded as 'incorrect'. Obviously – and happily – the spiral of silence thus does not work in any absolute sense. Its time scale is *months and years*. This tradition was exhibited by the German scholar of communication, Elisabeth Noelle-Neumann, her first publications on this subject appearing in the 1970s.

Cultivation is the process by which the common culture of society (its mainstream views about the world at large, society, human beings, etc.) is 'cultivated' by the mass media, that is, implanted and strengthened within all or most members of society. The concept was defined by the Hungarian-American scholar of communication, George Gerbner, in the late 1960s. This process is less concrete than the previous ones. It has also been discussed and criticized more than the previous ones, but all the same it is a quite striking idea. In a way, it can be characterized as the opposite of the spiral of silence. Its time perspective is *years and decades*.

The German concept of *Öffentlichkeit* is less dynamic than the previous ones and, perhaps, also less clear-cut. It was first defined in the 1980s, in particular by the German philosopher-sociologist, Jürgen Habermas. *Öffentlichkeit* best translates as the *public sphere* in English. The public sphere, of course, is the ever-dynamic result of the different processes briefly described above. The public sphere thus builds on general societal knowledge. Inevitably, it is shaped by the overall institutional structures of society. It changes only slowly, over decades and centuries, although in revolutionary times, of course, the *Öffentlichkeit* undergoes rapid and drastic change.

The shape and content of the *Öffentlichkeit* at a given moment in time are closely related to what has been called 'the climate of culture' (see section 3.2 Figure 3.6). Obviously, in a society putting the value of freedom clearly above that of equality, the debates going on in the public sphere will be rather different from those going on in the public sphere of a society putting equality above freedom (to the extent that such societies do have any public sphere at all unless, of course, we recognize that in such countries there tends to exist an 'underground public sphere', manifesting itself not least in subtle and sometimes quite sophisticated humour).

In a modern, strongly sectorized democratic society there is more than one *Öffentlichkeit*. Simplified, it could be said that there is at least one *Öffentlichkeit* for every sector of the Great Wheel of Culture in Society (see Figure 3.1 on p. 55): religion and politics, economy and technology, science and scholarship, art and literature. The different societal sectors develop differently over time, and yet they follow the overarching framework pre-scribed by general societal culture, today having its most important propagator system in the mass media.

A case of development within one sector of one society is presented in Box 6.1, which features developments within the Swedish literary system, its 'literary *Öffentlichkeit*'. Such large and slow societal processes are the cumulated results of innumerable individual acts and decisions taken in various sectors of society, often in a rather unreflected way. One important type of such decision is represented by the many decisions every day very quickly taken by 'Mr Gates'.

6.4.2   Gate-keeping and access

In the previous section we discussed a number of processes by means of which mass media content reaches and affects individuals and groups of individuals. Two phenomena common to these processes are the notions of *gate-keeping* and *access*.

The concept of gate-keeping was introduced into communication research in the 1950s. It is a very general one, however. Originally a sociological term, referring to the role of a traditional housewife *vis-à-vis* the rest of her family, she kept the gate open for each family member to enjoy his or her favourite dish, not being tempted by the offerings presented by the supermarket or delicatessen. In media and communication studies, the term 'gate-keeping' refers to a special journalistic function: the task of dealing with the large number of messages from news agencies, etc. that arrive at the various editorial offices ('desks') of the newspapers, often by way of cables forwarded by a teleprinter, a telex or a fax machine or, more often than not, by the computer sitting at the desk of a rather powerful person in communication research called '*Mr Gates*'.

The first decision to be taken by 'Mr Gates' for each one of all those incoming messages is a seemingly simple one: to stop the message or to pass it on (possibly in reduced and/or re-written shape). You open the gate, or you close it. In reality, the task is a rather difficult one. As a rule it is also carried out under considerable pressure of time. To be a really good gate-keeper in

**BOX 6.1 ON THE GROWTH AND DECLINE OF
LITERARY TRADITIONS**

In sections 5.8 and 5.9 above we discussed research on innovation and
diffusion within the framework of organizational communication. General as
they are, the phenomena of innovation and diffusion also deserve some
reflections in terms of mass communication and the concept of *Öffentlichkeit*,
the 'public sphere'. We have already mentioned that there is one
Öffentlichkeit for each sector of the 'Great Wheel of Culture in Society'. All
these specific public spheres change over time. The study of those processes
of change is an important task of communication science and scholarship.

One way to study a specific *Öffentlichkeit* is to take a look at what is being
publicly discussed in a given sector of society. In the sectors of art and
literature, these discussions are to a large extent carried out in newspapers
and journal reviews of new works such as, for instance, new novels, dramas
and collections of poems. In such reviews, the reviewer often mentions
different authors from the one under review: 'Obviously, Mr X has learnt a
lot from Mr Y, who likes to write about similar themes, in a similar way.';
'Unlike Ms Z, Mr U does not seem to know this type of social problem very
well.' Such mentions carry valuable information to the reader of literary
reviews – and also to the student of literary communication.

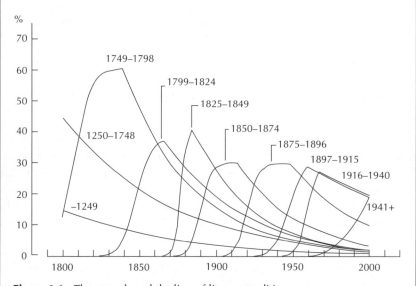

Figure 6.1 The growth and decline of literary traditions

A mention is an expression of an association made by a reviewer of
literature in newspapers or journals. A collection of such mentions may thus
provide some information about the field of associations, the 'literary frame
of reference' of one or more reviewers. A representative sample of all such

continued

mentions in leading journals and newspapers may thus be used to characterize the 'literary climate' of a given country in a number of ways, say, the way the reviewers' literary frame of reference changes over time, stressing this or that literary tradition, from this or that literary period.

The growth and decline of literary traditions as captured by the mentions technique follow curves of growth and decline well known from other cultural phenomena, especially the so-called 'S-curve' of growth (see Figure 5.4). An example of such processes of literary growth and decline is offered in Figure 6.1. The point at which a rising curve crosses a formerly dominant curve, in its turn becoming the dominant curve, is important, of course. It marks the definitive break-through of a new literary tradition. The locations of such break-throughs in Figure 6.1 coincide fairly well with the traditional history of literature, thus offering valuable validation to the mentions technique, to the sociology of literature and to traditional history of literature. (It will be seen that according to the figure, the Swedish generation of writers born after 1940 can expect such a break-through about the year 2000. In their fifties or sixties, they have finally achieved a position of domination.)

The mentions technique is a special case of an important tradition of research called 'citation analysis', mostly applied within a specialty called 'bibliometrics': the study of scholarly communication.

From: K.E. Rosengren (1998) 'The climate of literature: a sea change?', *Poetics*, 25: 311–26. On bibliometrics, see, for instance, C.L. Borgman (ed.) (1990) *Scholarly Communication and Bibliometrics*. London: Sage.

this sense, therefore, you must have sound journalistic judgement, backed up by long experience. Preferably, you should also possess that hard-to-define characteristic called journalistic flair.

'Mr Gates' is still to be found in his original role, throwing most of the cables, faxes and other messages arriving at his desk into his waste-paper basket, or deleting them at his computer screen. At bottom, however, the function of gatekeeping is a very general one. Roles similar to that of Mr Gates's are being played within a number of societal institutions – including, for instance, all university departments: is a particular student worthy of being accepted into a department?

A phenomenon opposite to that of gate-keeping is *access*. To have access to the mass media is a *sine qua non* for many professions and in all sorts of social roles. Access to key people or important information not only to politicians but to each and everybody gives power and influence – a chance to affect this or that societal condition to further the interests of this or that grouping and, more generally, to have a voice in societal debates to let one's voice be heard. The need for access is thus the basis for the importance of the function of gate-keeping.

In advanced societies, access to important social functions such as decision-making, general debates preceding societal decision making, etc. is

strongly dependent on technical communicative resources. Without a telephone, a modem and a computer, you cannot reach all that knowledge, all
those debates taking place on the World Wide Web.

Both access to and gate-keeping within the media are also related to more
general societal and social phenomena. By and large, the better your social
situation, the easier your access to the media, the more lenient the gate-
keepers. Poor, old and uneducated women from an ethnic minority have
more problems with media access than have rich, young and well-educated
men from the dominant ethnic grouping. By definition, the gate-keepers
attempt to keep out people from all social groupings, but much more so
the former than to the latter. In more general terms, of course, the two
phenomena of access and gate-keeping tend to turn up wherever scarce
resources are to be found.

6.5 Homogeneity and heterogeneity

Box 6.1 refers to developments within a specific sector of society: the fine arts
as represented by literature, more specifically by literary criticism in Swedish
quality newspapers. Obviously, literary criticism in leading quality newspapers is a rather special case of societal culture. By definition, this type of
communication is of interest to a relatively narrow section of the population
(although people primarily active in other sections of society may scan the
literary reviews just in an attempt to keep up to date). Mass media and mass
media content thus tend to be structured and stratified in a way which directly
and indirectly mirrors overall societal stratification. Literacy, of course, is the
prime dimension of such stratification.

Societies characterized by general literacy have been around only for about,
say, 150 years (see section 6.1). In parallel with the increase in literacy, the
existing media system was drastically changed. There had always been some
publications for the masses, of course. Especially in Protestant countries,
three books – the Bible, a book of hymns, and a collection of sermons – were
invariably to be found in many lower-class households. But with increasing
literacy a new, vast market for various popular publications was opening up.
Enterprising businessmen were not slow to take the opportunity, drawing on
the possibilities for creating a mass media society, offered by the new printing
technologies. Implicit in these tendencies was a duality: the rift between, on
the one hand, the educated middle and upper classes, and on the other, the
newly literate but otherwise not very well educated lower classes. The media
quickly adapted to this rift. In the latter half of the nineteenth century, large
numbers of popular newspapers were created, tailored to the tastes and
capacities of the newly literate masses. Books, as well as weekly, monthly and
yearly periodicals, were published to suit the various tastes and purses of the
huge reading market that was gradually opening up. The *mass* media were
thus differentiated into *class* media. By and large, these tendencies were
to be found in most capitalist societies during the late nineteenth century,

and the greater part of the twentieth century. (In fascist and communist dictatorships, of course, these basic tendencies are, and always were, modified to suit the political system. But in principle, much the same tendencies prevail also in such countries.)

In parallel with these tendencies towards *differentiation* among the mass media and their publics, there has been a strong tendency to both *concentration in ownership* (fewer owners of many separate dailies and weeklies, etc.) and *integration of ownership*, resulting in very large publishing houses (*'conglomerates'*) directly or indirectly controlling the production and distribution of a large number of publications in different media operating at different levels of taste (books, journals, newspapers, magazines, cinema pictures, videos, etc.). Such conglomerates are thus both vertically and horizontally integrated: vertically, from production to distribution; horizontally, from popular television series to esoteric modern poetry.

In the last decades of the twentieth century, a similar tendency is making itself increasingly strongly felt at the receiving end of the mass communication processes: the tendency among broad groupings not to specialize on either high-brow or low-brow mediated culture. The 'omnivore' is becoming an increasingly common type of media user, reading both literary or even scholarly journals and popular magazines, looking at both popular television series and Shakespearian drama. (Note that such general tendencies, of course, are always modified by national, regional and local conditions.)

In terms of programming, the conceptual correspondence to the omnivore is the demand for diversity that is traditionally directed towards public service channels – both radio and television channels. *Diversity in programming* may be measured in quantitative terms, and such measurements have been carried out from time to time. On the whole, diversity in programming is larger in public service channels than in commercial channels, both for overall output and during prime time. Public service channels also have been shown to *increase* the overall diversity of national television systems in countries as different as Canada, Japan, Sweden, the UK and USA, while the commercial channels rather tend to *reduce* the overall diversity of a national TV system (see Box 6.2).

The detailed study of individual mass media use, its causes and consequences, has become a specialty of its own within the broad field of communication studies. In the next section some results produced within this scholarly specialty will be presented.

BOX 6.2 ON DIVERSITY IN TELEVISION PROGRAMMING

The quality of mass media output is a subject of interest to most of us, and especially so to media politicians, scholars and researchers. A problem in this connection, of course, is that what is high-quality output to one group of people may be low-quality output to another group, and *vice versa*. A solution to this problem is offered by the concept of *diversity*. Diversity

continued

presupposes variation. A program schedule characterized by a reasonable level of diversity has a chance to offer something of value (some quality) to everybody, even within a public characterized by different types and levels of tastes and preferences.

How can we measure diversity in programming, then? That was the question put to a group of scholars of communication from Asia, Europe and the USA, brought together by Japan's television network, the NHK, and its resourceful 'Broadcasting Research Institute'. The group met a number of times in the early 1990s. Several different measures were suggested, discussed and tested in formalized simulations. In the end, what has been called 'relative entropy' was chosen: an index used to calculate the average quantity of variation in a given programming output during a given period of time (after controls for the number of program categories in the schedule applied). The index varies between 0 and 1, zero denoting no diversity at all; 1 denoting, maximal diversity. High relative entropy in a mass media channel – say, a television channel – implies that in that channel there is indeed some diversity, something for everybody – for adults, children and adolescents, for so-called high-brows and low-brows.

The diversity of the program output was measured during one week in March 1992, in 26 TV channels in five countries: Japan, the USA, the UK, Canada and Sweden. Relative entropy for a whole day of programming varied between 0.84 (Sweden's Channel 1) and 0.44 (Japan's Educational TV channel, which in spite of its obvious focus on informative programs did not have much lower entropy than some channels in other countries focusing more entertaining types of content). In general, public service-oriented channels had high entropy; commercial channels, low entropy. During prime time – often dominated by various types of entertainment – relative entropy tended to diminish.

The contribution given by a specific channel to a country's overall diversity in programming was also measured. By and large, public service broadcasting channels contributed to overall diversity, while commercial channels did not. At the national level, the UK had the highest entropy; the USA, the lowest.

Obviously, these results are valid for the period of time and the countries studied. But the general tendency has probably remained and supposedly will continue to do so, despite the fact that some public channels have found it convenient to adapt their programming schedules to those of the commercial channels, at the same time as (because of the satellites) the number of channels available to large portions of a given population has drastically increased.

From: Ishikawa (1996) *Quality Assessment of Television*. Luton: Luton University Press, see also Hellman (1999) *From Companies to Competitors*. Tampere: University of Tampere Press.

Hillve, P., Majanen, P. and Rosengren, K.E. (1998) 'Quality in Programming: commercial and public service diversity', *European Journal of Communication*, 12(3) 291–318.

6.6 Individual use made of mass media:
quantity and quality, causes and consequences

6.6.1 The study of individual media use

In today's societies most individuals spend considerable amounts of their time reading, listening to and viewing various types of mass media content. Far from being as simple as at first glance it may seem to be, the measurement of these considerable amounts of time represents a difficult problem. Even more difficult, of course, are the attempts to study the causes and effects which may precede and follow from the individual's use of this or that mass medium. A number of different techniques for the measurement of individual mass media use have been employed. The techniques may be classified along several dimensions.

One important dimension concerns *what is being measured*: actual media use at a given moment or period of time (yesterday, for instance), or habits of media use during, say, the last few weeks or months. Another dimension concerns the *general type of data collection*: personal interview, telephone interview, or mail survey. A third dimension concerns *the specific technique used for the data collection*: the character and pattern of the questions put to the interviewees or the respondents in a survey. The more precise and detailed the questions, the better the answers (within reasonable limits, of course).

Most figures circulating about the amount of individual media use stem from commercial agencies which specialize in opinion studies based on telephone or mail surveys of (more or less) representative population samples. These agencies work for the media companies commissioning the studies. In some cases, studies are undertaken by government agencies, such as the National Bureau of Statistics, often at regular intervals, but sometimes on an *ad hoc* basis depending on the research being undertaken by a particular government organization. Political parties often have opinion research companies carry out studies specially designed for their specific purposes, and so do many other large organizations and companies. Also, many university departments in the social sciences and humanities undertake such studies for their own specific scholarly purposes.

Results vary between countries, the time of the year and the technique of data collection etc. Some data about mass media use in different countries are presented in Table 6.1. Due to a number of causes (e.g. different media systems, different national cultures, etc.) they show considerable variation between countries. In some countries, newspaper reading and public service TV viewing are relatively strong, in others, relatively low. But they also show considerable similarity and consistency. In all modern societies, at all times of the year, most people spend large portions of their time in the presence of mass media. Within this overall similarity between populations, there is considerable individual variation in the amount and type of media use. Not surprisingly, the three variables in all societies most strongly affecting that

Table 6.1 *Aspects of media use and media structure in seven European countries*

	Newspaper copies per 1,000 inhabitants	Minutes of TV viewing a day	Minutes public service TV viewing a day	Percentage of public service TV viewed a day
Norway	611	148	64	43
Sweden	518	139	71	51
Germany	426	186	76	41
UK	362	216	93	43
France	157	181	78	43
Italy	115	214	103	48
Greece	83	194	17	9

Source: S. Hadenius and L. Weibull (1997) .

variation is social class, age and gender. Variations in individual mass media use among young people will be discussed in the following section.

6.6.2 Media use among young people – how much?

In this section, some concrete and detailed examples of variation in individual mass media use and its causes and consequences for young people will be presented. This is a field of research which, during the last few decades, has drawn an immense interest in many countries in all parts of the world. It is also a field of research which deals with the habits of many readers of this book. Since effects and consequences of individual mass media use may cover many years, it is also a field of research which has some relevance for their future lives. Therefore, this section has been made somewhat more detailed and precise than other parts of the book.

The data that is presented stem from a longitudinal research program, the Media Panel Program (MPP), which since 1975 has been carried on at the University of Lund in Sweden. The MPP was started by the author and professor Sven Windahl. Its present director is professor Ulla Johnsson-Smaragdi, of the Media and Communication Studies Department at the University of Lund, who has been active within the program since it started.

Within the MPP empirical measurements of media use among samples of children and adolescents (as well as among their parents) have been taken in the city of Malmoe and the town of Vaexjoe, both of which are situated in southern Sweden. The various waves of measurements have been organized so as to admit both cross-sectional comparisons (between various age groups during the same period of time) and longitudinal comparisons (within the same panel of children and adolescents at different periods of time). Over the years, a number of reports, journal articles, dissertations, and other books have been published within the program. For a list of publications in English emanating from the Media Panel Program, see Box 6.3.

BOX 6.3 CHRONOLOGICAL LIST OF SOME PUBLICATIONS FROM THE MEDIA PANEL PROGRAM*

Johnsson-Smaragdi, U. (1983) *TV Use and Social Interaction in Adolescence. A Longitudinal Study*. Stockholm: Almqvist & Wiksell International.

Roe, K. (1983) *Mass Media Use and Adolescent Schooling: Conflict or Co-existence?* Stockholm: Almqvist & Wiksell International.

Jönsson, A. (1986) 'TV – a threat or a complement to school?', *Journal of Educational Television*, 12 (1): 29–38.

Johnsson-Smaragdi, U. (1989) 'Opening the doors – cautiously', in L. Becker and K. Schönbach (eds), *Audience Responses to Media Diversification. Coping with Plenty*. Hillsdale, NJ: Lawrence Erlbaum Associates.

Rosengren, K.E. and Windahl, S. (1989) *Media Matter: TV Use in Childhood and Adolescence*. Norwood, NJ: Ablex.

Johansson, T. and Miegel, F. (1992) *Do the Right Thing. Lifestyle and Identity in Contemporary Youth Culture*. Stockholm: Almqvist & Wiksell International.

Roe, K. (1992) 'Different destinies – different melodies: school achievement, anticipated status, and adolescents' tastes in music', *European Journal of Communication*, 7: 335–57.

Rosengren, K.E. (ed.) (1994) *Media Effects and Beyond. Culture, Socialization and Lifestyles*. London and New York: Routledge.

Johnsson-Smaragdi, U. (1994) 'Models of change and stability in adolescents' media use', in K.E. Rosengren (ed.), *Media Effects and Beyond. Culture, Socialization and Lifestyles*. London and New York: Routledge.

Rosengren, K.E. (1995) 'Substantive theories and formal models: Bourdieu confronted', *European Journal of Communication*, 10: 7–40.

*Only publications in English have been listed.

The MPP is dedicated to the study of individual media use during the most dynamic periods of human life – childhood and adolescence. Small wonder, then, that the variation in amount and character of media use during those periods is quite striking. This variation is related, of course, to the various needs, tastes and wishes characterizing the individual during different periods of childhood and adolescence (and, as usual, to traditional background variables such as gender, social class, etc.). As we shall see, however, it is also related to the media structure surrounding the youngsters (and, indeed, all of us), as well as to changes in that structure.

Obviously, the results gained within the MPP are influenced by the specific temporal, geographical and cultural conditions of the study. The phenomena of individual mass media use, its causes and consequences are so general all around the globe, however, that the general tendencies should be much the same in many or most other industrial or post-industrial societies.

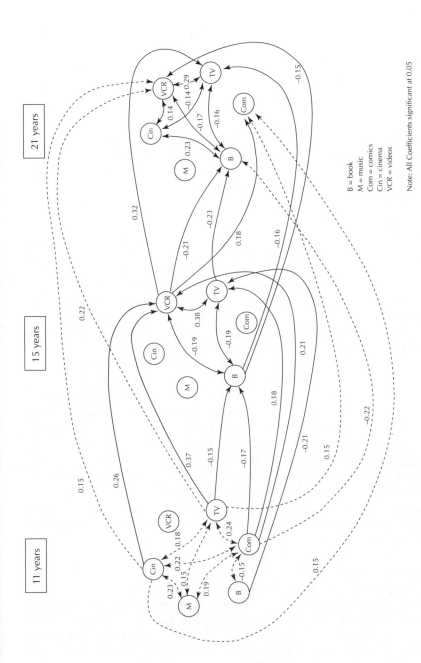

Figure 6.2 Relationships between the use of various media – simultaneously and over time
(*source*: Johnsson-Smaragdi, 1994)

B = book
M = music
Com = comics
Cin = cinema
VCR = videos

Note: All Coefficients significant at 0.05

Figure 6.2 offers an overview of the relationships between the use of a number of mass media by children and young people in southern Sweden during the period 1980–90. The coefficients of correlation attached to the arrows between the media within a given period of life and during different periods of life show the extent to which the use of different media go together, so that the use of one medium tends to correlate with that of another, within or between periods of time. (Note that, since they would have cluttered the figure beyond legibility, correlations between the uses of one and the same medium at different ages have not been included. Obviously, these correlations tend to be relatively high.)

The figure clearly shows that the individual use of different media forms a rather complex pattern, partly stable over long periods of time, partly changing as society's media structure changes, and as the users of mass media pass through different periods of life. Although the figure deserves a more detailed analysis, suffice it to note: first, that the individual patterns of media use are more complex during the relatively stable ages of 11 and 21, while during the more turbulent age of 15, there are not many significant relationships between the use of various media (few correlation arrows); and secondly, that the use of specific media during different periods of life hangs together, both within and between media, so that there are a number of correlation arrows not only *within*, but also *between* the three periods of time represented in the figure. No less than five statistically significant arrows run directly from the age of 11 to that of 21. We thus see that, just as in so many other facets of life, the child is the parent of the adult also when it comes to the use of mass media. For an example, take a look at the arrow running between the circles marked 'TV' in the first wave, 'B' in the second wave, and 'TV' and 'VCR' in the third wave. They show that the more the youngsters were looking at TV at the age of 11, the fewer books they read at the age of 13. And the fewer books they read at the age of 13, the more they looked at TV at the age of 21, both directly and by way of the video cassette recorder (VCR). This was in the late 1980s and early 1990s. Today, the same tendencies would no doubt be found – very probably, however, even stronger.

Figure 6.2 visualizes the *relationships* between the use of different mass media during childhood, adolescence and young adulthood. It does not tell us anything about the *amount of use* of a given mass medium during a given period of life. Quite naturally, however, there are sometimes rather drastic changes in the amount of use of some mass media during the often rather dramatic periods of childhood and adolescence. For a long period of time, for instance, perhaps the most striking result regarding the media use of children and adolescents was the fact that there was a dramatic *decrease* of television viewing during the early teenage years, accompanied by an equally dramatic *increase* in listening to music. A typical result from this period is presented in Figure 6.3, featuring the amount of TV viewing and listening to music among young Swedish people (from age 11 to age 15). (Note that in order to admit comparison, the amounts of TV viewing and listening to music have been standardized so as to make the means of the two variables equal:

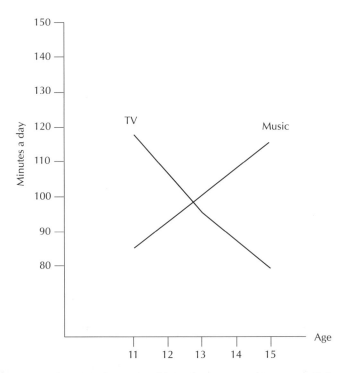

Figure 6.3 Television viewing and listening to music among Swedish children and adolescents, 1976–81 (*source*: Rosengren, 1994c)

100.) Figure 6.3 offers a good picture of the state of affairs in this area in Sweden from the mid-1970s to the early 1980s, and presumably also in many other countries around the globe about the same time. We see the typical increase in listening to music and the equally typical reduction in TV viewing during the early teenage period.

Figure 6.4, however, offers a radically different picture. What is the difference between the two figures? One difference, of course, is the fact that Figure 6.4 covers a longer period of childhood – adolescence and early adulthood. More important, however, is that it also covers a different period of societal time: from the early 1980s to the early 1990s. What happened during this period of time?

What happened was, *first*, that during these years, cable television (CTV) and the video cassette recorder (the VCR) became widely available in Sweden. The technology was enthusiastically received, especially by the young generations, not least because it gave them greater access to favourite outlets such as popular music. Secondly, youngsters increasingly had their own television sets in their own room. Thirdly, in the face of the vigorous competition from CTV and VCR, the staid Swedish public service television channels slowly adapted its output so that it became more suited to the taste of a previously neglected segment of the public: those aged between 15 and 25.

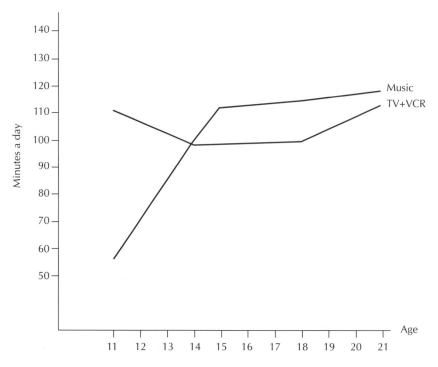

Figure 6.4 Amount of TV plus VCR viewing and listening to music,
1976–90 (*source*: Rosengren, 1994c)

In more general terms, there was a change *from* a system characterized mainly by supply/output control, *to* one increasingly characterized by demand/receiver control. As a result of these structural changes, the young generations watched more television during adolescence. While large portions of their parental generation gradually complemented their interest in popular culture with at least some sprinkling of high culture, the television generations do not seem to be very inclined to follow that pattern. (On the relationship between high culture and popular culture see also sections 3.2 and 7.6.)

This is a finding interesting *per se*, but above all it teaches us that many results from the social and behavioural sciences are somewhat less general than sometimes assumed. *To a considerable extent, they are dependent on the time and space in which they have been collected.* The tendencies shown in Figure 6.4 may well have been further strengthened during the last few years.

So much for the quantity of TV viewing among children and adolescents. What about its qualities?

6.6.3 Relations between viewers and the content viewed

We have just seen that the *quantity* of individual TV viewing varies considerably over time and between individuals but shows some stability within individuals over time. In this section we shall look at variations in the *qualities* of TV viewing, and the variation over time in these qualities. An important quality of TV viewing is the relationship which tends to be established between the viewer and content viewed.

There are a number of different types of media relations which have been discussed in scholarship and research. The two relations which have been the most preferred by media scholars are probably *identification* and *para-social relations* (PSI). The latter type of media relations could be characterized as a quasi interaction between viewer and a person on the screen, be that person is real or fictitious. Identification may be short-term or long-term. Short-term identification prevails during the moment of viewing. In long-term identification the viewer tends to identify, more or less superficially, with an individual on the screen – say, the hero or heroine of a series or serial – often for relatively long periods of time after the viewing. A combined index of PSI, short-term and long-term identification called 'TV relations' has been used in most MPP waves of data collection.

Figure 6.5 presents a model of the causal relations between the amount of TV consumption and TV relations during childhood, adolescence and early adulthood. It offers a simplified picture of an analysis undertaken by means of an early version of the advanced statistical program package called LISREL. The program shows the strength of the unique influence exerted by one variable on other variables of interest in the analysis, after controls for the influence of other relevant variables in the model. It thus admits the study of complex causal relationships. We recognize, for instance, the well-known fact that gender and social background are relatively powerful determinants of media use (beta coefficients of –0.28 and +0.23 indicating that girls tend to watch less TV than boys; on the other hand, girls are somewhat more prone than boys to establish TV relations).

Also in Figure 6.5, we note the influence of social class on TV viewing. Middle-class youngsters watch less television than do working-class youngsters. But in early adulthood (perhaps because as students they lack the money necessary for other enjoyments), they seem to watch *more* television than do young working-class adults, who, on the other hand, are more inclined to enter into TV relations. In general, however, TV relations are less strongly influenced by background variables than is TV consumption, possibly because they may be related to one personality variable or other (see section 4.2).

The intricacies of such causal relationships between aspects of media use and background variables are interesting, but in this connection we are more interested in discussing the causal relationships *within aspects of media use itself.* It is striking to note how, even after statistical controls for the influence of the two powerful background variables of gender and social class, the so-called stability coefficients for TV consumption are quite strong. The really striking thing, however, is that this applies not only to *amount of viewing* but also to the much more subtle and presumably fleeting variable of *TV relations.* Indeed, unexpectedly, the coefficients for the relations are at least

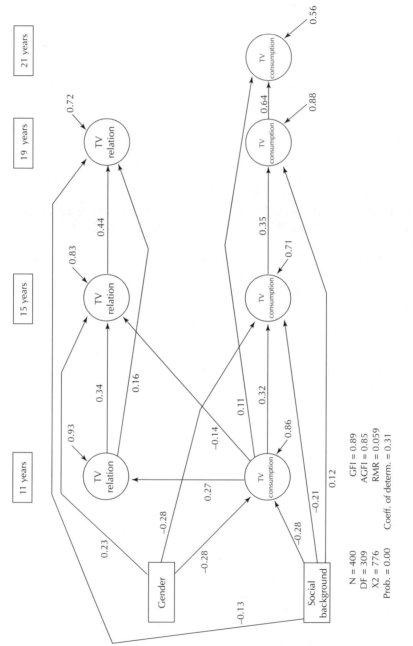

Figure 6.5 TV viewing and TV relations, ages 11–21 (*source*: Rosengren et al., 1994)

as strong as are those pertaining to the amount of viewing (0.34 and 0.44 versus 0.32 and 0.35, respectively). In causal terms this means that not only does TV viewing breed TV viewing; TV relationships also breed TV relationships.

More generally, what we see is the power of media habits. Once a TV fan, the chances are you will remain one, even after having passed that period of turmoil called adolescence. Expressed in stronger terms, what we see is not only the development and conservation of a habit, but a process of habituation, sometimes resulting in mild forms of media dependency, so-called 'TV addiction'.

On the other hand, when discussing phenomena such as those just presented, we should always remember that what our models show are statistical tendencies, not universal, general laws of nature. Not every child watching a lot of television later on becomes a TV addict. All the same, we cannot deny the fact that it is for good reasons that the consequences of heavy TV viewing among youngsters are the concern of not only parents and teachers but also other citizens. One good reason for such concern, we have just seen, may be that frequent and extended viewing tends to become a habit, so that it could be said that to some extent viewing itself causes and ensures continued viewing. Even if viewing only *tends to* and not *inevitably does* reduce other activities, even if effects and consequences of viewing are only *sometimes*, not *always* harmful, these are facts of life which should be (and often are) matters of some concern. (The terminology is not clear in this area, but it has been suggested that the term *effect* should be related to the *content* of mass media consumed; the term *consequence*, to the *amount of media use as such* (hours spent in front of the screen, etc.)).

Actually, the influence of viewing on the amount of viewing is not limited to one's own viewing. Parental viewing is a strong causal factor behind children's viewing, even after controls for background variables. More surprisingly, perhaps, is the finding that children's viewing may exert an influence on parental viewing, especially in mid-adolescence when many youngsters leave mainstream television for music coming to them through other media. As a consequence, their parents also tend to reduce their TV viewing, presumably as their adolescent children sometimes leave home for more interesting locations and activities. In cases where youngsters continue to watch, however, so do their parents.

It should be added, finally, that the influence of viewing on viewing is not limited to the *amount of viewing* and *relations established with TV content*. Also the *type of content preferred and consumed* at one time – say, sports, fiction and information programs – tends to influence the type of content preferred and consumed at a later point in time. Within the MPP, an attempt was made to untangle the longitudinal relationships between television content preferences in childhood and early adulthood. We thus took a long look at the long-term stability of preferences for

(a) sports, contests and competition programs;
(b) fiction programs; and
(c) information programs

as measured in grade 5 (age 12) and at age 21. The results obtained are shown in Figure 6.6.

As it turned out, the beta coefficients - again after controls for gender, social class, town and TV viewing – were statistically significant and not negligible in strength: 0.15 and 0.19 for preferences for information programs and fiction, respectively, and 0.43 for competition and sports programs. Given the many variables controlled for, as well as the nine years' interval between the two sets of data collection, the coefficients are rather impressive – especially, of course, the one between competition programs and sports programs. What they show is that the foundations for television content preferences are laid at an early age, and that they tend to be pretty stable. Again we see that the child TV viewer may indeed be said to be the parent of the adult TV viewer.

Now let's summarize. Having once been initiated, media use tends to breed media use. As far as television is concerned, this goes for at least three central aspects of media use: amount, content preferences and relations established with the content used. It holds true also after controls for a number of basic background variables, and in a long-term perspective. The fact that this is so should not be forgotten when in the next section we turn to a discussion, not about consequences of media use for media use, but about effects and consequences of media use on other, and perhaps more important, characteristics and activities.

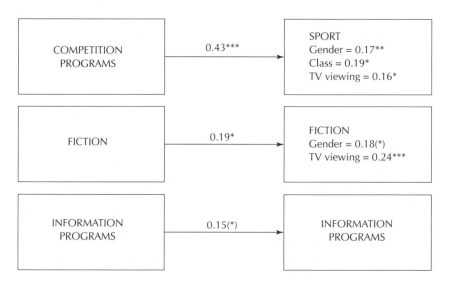

Figure 6.6 Long-term stability in media preferences (beta coefficients; ages 12 and 21) (*source*: Rosengren et al., 1994)

6.6.4   Effects of television viewing

What about the effects of all those hours of TV viewing during childhood, adolescence and young adulthood? Most basic among such effects are, perhaps, those which have to do with the youngsters themselves, and their views about the world surrounding them.

Figures 6.7 and 6.8 offer some examples of the effects which TV viewing may have on a quite central characteristic of young men and women: the way they regard themselves, that is, their *self-esteem*. Note that only variables exerting a statistically significant influence on other variables in a given figure have been included in Figure 6.7, although more variables were also included in the statistical analyses as such; therefore, the sets of variables included in the Figures 6.7 and 6.8 are not completely identical.

The figures offer simplified pictures of analyses undertaken by means of the LISREL program mentioned above. In this case, the analysis admits locating the individual's amount of TV viewing within a broad social context, covering such important aspects as the young people's social class and type of neighbourhood, school readiness at the age of seven, self-esteem at the age of 11, 15 and 21. As before, the coefficients vary between −1 and +1: negative coefficients indicate a negative influence; positive, a positive influence. (Note that the words 'positive' and 'negative' here are purely technical terms. Thus, in the case of a *positive* influence, when the causal variable is high, so the effect tends to be variable. In the case of a *negative* influence, on the other hand, when the independent variable is high, the dependent variable tends to be low.) It will be seen, for example, that school readiness as tested when school begins (in Sweden, at the age of seven) later on exerts a strong positive influence on the self-esteem of both girls and boys – although, it would seem, at somewhat different ages.

Actually, self-esteem is a central variable in the complex statistical analyses shown in Figures 6.6 and 6.7. Not only is TV viewing during childhood and adolescence related to self-esteem among both boys and girls, it also affects their self-esteem later on when they have grown up. This is an interesting finding *per se*.

Even more interesting, however, is the fact that the influence is radically different for young men and women: positive for the former; negative for the latter. High self-esteem during childhood thus tends to *increase* the TV viewing of teenage boys, while it tends to *reduce* that of teenage girls (co-efficients of 0.25 and -0.20, respectively). Later on, high TV viewing among teenage boys tends to *increase* their self-esteem as young men, while for teenage girls it tends to *reduce* their self-esteem as young women (co-efficients of 0.39 and -0.37, respectively). (Note that this relationship is comparatively strong – actually, about at the same level as is the influence of adolescents' self-esteem itself on the self-esteem of the young adult men or women.)

Thus, among boys and young men TV viewing and self-esteem are *positively* related in spirals of mutual influence and among girls and young women, *negatively* related. Television, then, seems to work in close alliance

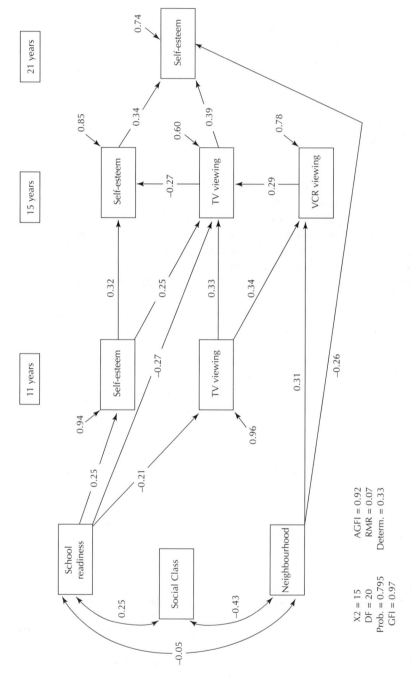

Figure 6.7 Self-esteem and TV viewing, boys aged 11–21 (beta coefficients) (*source*: Johnsson-Smaragdi and Jönsson, 1994)

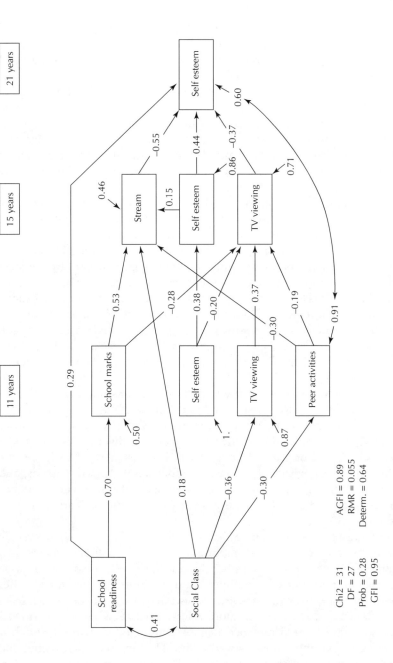

Figure 6.8 Self-esteem and TV viewing, girls aged 11–21 (beta coefficients) (*source*: Johnsson-Smaragdi and Jönsson, 1994)

with other agents of socialization (school, family, etc.) in relegating young women to that lower position, unfortunately still characterizing women in most societies, despite a number of efforts to oppose this tendency.

The type of influence exerted by television on boys and girls just discussed may be described in terms of what is sometimes called 'structural violence', that is, the strong negative influence exerted by some agents of socialization on some categories of individuals within the young generations seeking their place in societal structure. Television is a strong societal force indeed. We have just seen, for instance, that its 'structural violence' helps to locate young men and women at different positions within the societal structure surrounding them. It thus 'helps' them to live up to the so-called gender roles guiding their future lives, roles which – even after decades of concerted societal efforts in the opposite direction – are rather different for boys and girls, young women and young men.

An important element in gender roles is the tendency for men to be more aggressive, more prone to physical violence than women. There is small doubt that part of this tendency is biologically inherited. But it is also quite clear that other, equally important parts are transferred, not by our genes, but by way of socialization. Parts of this socialization are being carried out by the mass media – television, for instance, and not least television distributed by way of the VCR. Figures 6.9a and 6.9b show two concrete examples of this general tendency. As before, the coefficients attached to the causal arrows are so-called 'beta coefficients', expressing the strength of the relationships between two variables, after controls, for a number of relevant background variables. As before, the number of asterisks symbolize the statistical significance of the relationships.

It will be seen that we find the same tendency of spiralling interaction between individual characteristics and mass media use as previously found. As before, the patterns are rather different for boys and girls. Tendencies towards aggressiveness and violence against other individuals dominate the pattern for boys. For girls, although there is an element of violence, the pattern is more strongly characterized by tendencies towards restlessness and lack of concentration. In both cases, however, we find a significant influence from television and the VCR. This influence can hardly be characterized as a good one.

Similar results may be found in other areas of life. For adults, working life is one of the two or three most important areas of life. Among adolescents, working life may appear to be rather distant, but nevertheless they do have their dreams and plans, sometimes quite ambitious, sometimes rather modest. Such dreams and plans are not always realized, of course, but from time to time they do come true – more or less, at least. Young people's media use are sometimes said to influence their relations to the adult world, and their dreams and plans about their own adult life. The long-term perspective and the panel design characterizing the Media Panel Program allow us to follow the influence of TV viewing during childhood on the actual educational status of young adults. This was done in an interesting study undertaken by Professor Gunilla Jarlbro and Dr Ulf Dalquist.

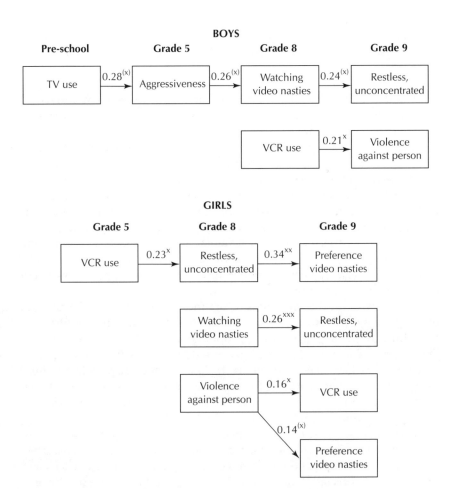

Figures 6.9a/b   TV and VCR, violence and restlessness
(*source*: Rosengren et al., 1994)

Comparing the social background of children at age 11 and their educational status at age 21, it was possible to classify them as either 'Climbers', 'Droppers', 'Stable working class' or 'Stable middle class'. TV viewing and other leisure habits among members of the four categories were then studied by means of a number of statistical techniques, with controls for gender, place of residence and, when applicable, other relevant variables. Here are some of the results that were obtained, complementing more traditional analyses showing that working-class children tend to watch more television, etc:

- Working-class children with low TV viewing at the age of 12 tended to be climbers at the age of 21.
- Middle-class children with high TV viewing at the age of 12 tended to be droppers at the age of 21.

- Droppers tended to have high TV viewing at the age of 21, to often visit restaurants, and to be heavy VCR users.
- Climbers and stable middle-class young adults tended often to visit libraries.

It is hardly high or low TV viewing as such which sends youngsters up or down the social ladder. What we see, rather, is youngsters starting to choose their future, more or less consciously and intentionally, more or less compelled by strong but often hidden forces within themselves and outside of them, in their surroundings. Starting to form their lives, they sometimes make a virtue out of necessity, choosing and liking whatever, under the circumstances, seems to be the thing to do given their ambition or lack of ambition. Sometimes they seem consciously, deliberately to choose patterns of living corresponding to their inner cravings and inherent capacities. What we see, then, are specific patterns of values, attitudes and actions emerging out of a common *form of life*, patterns which are partly determined by social position (*ways of life*), partly by individual choice (*lifestyles*) (for definition of these concepts, see section 3.4).

With or without the intentions of the individual actors, different ways of using mass media, whether consciously chosen by the actors or not, thus contribute to the shaping of young people's present and future lives. Young people often use mass media to express their basic values, their beliefs and opinions, their tastes and whims. In so doing they help society to fulfil the more or less subtle sorting procedures which its agents of socialization – in this case, primarily, family, school, mass media – have been applying for as long as the young people have been around.

It almost looks as if the young people themselves choose a pattern of media use which later on affects them in a way which, to the outsider, may sometimes seem tragic and sometimes cynical, sometimes conventional and sometimes unexpected. Quite naturally, they often do this, not one by one, but in groups of friends and aquaintances broadly sharing similar interests. Sometimes, such groups are specifically focusing on media use, specializing in enjoying and interpreting this or that type of media content. Such groups are called *interpretative communities*. Within those communities for better and for worse, the media content consumed and received is often the focus of sometimes lively discussions which help individuals create meaningful pictures not only of the media content consumed, but also of themselves and of the world surrounding them.

The empirical findings presented above stem from research undertaken within the Swedish Media Panel Program, from the late 1970s to the early 1990s. But the theoretical framework is international – common to the international community of scholars and researchers working in this field of studies. Also, empirical results similar to those presented here have been presented in other parts of the world, and in other periods of time. We know, then, that television and video do indeed exert a strong influence on the lives of young people. Already, the *consequences* of the simple fact that young people spend a lot of time in front of the TV screen are quite important. Television becomes a 'thief of time', depriving us of opportunities for other activities – say, physical activities. It has been shown, for instance, that a result of heavy TV viewing among young people is a tendency towards inadequate physical activity, accompanied by increasing body weight (see Box 6.4). These are results which cannot be said to be trivial or unimportant.

Even more important, however, may be the *effects* of the content consumed. The television screen is a powerful educator and it works in close alliance with another powerful agent of socialization: the individual's circle of friends and acquaintances. It is thus a formidable rival to those more traditional agents of socialization, the family and the school, not to mention the church which, in most countries, long ago abdicated the strong position it once held.

Many other examples could be offered of the influence of television upon generations of young and old people. It should be remembered, however, that while much research has been dedicated to the consequences and effects of television on its viewers, that influence is continuously varying over time, as both television and society develop in various ways. The results just presented refer to Sweden from the 1970s to the early 1990s. It is a fair guess, though, that they would not have changed much had they covered also the latter half of the 1990s. Indeed, the tendencies just discussed may be supposed to have grown even stronger in the wake of the so-called new media which had their breakthrough during the late 1990s.

BOX 6.4 FATTENING TELEVISION

'The prevalence of overweight continues to increase in the US adult population. . . . Similarly, the prevalence of obesity in England has doubled in the past decade, yet daily energy intake and fat consumption have actually been reduced in that country during this time period. . . . Increasingly, leisure time activities are more sedentary, with television watching, video games, and personal computing among the most popular pastimes. . . . Next to sleeping, television watching occupies the greatest amount of leisure time during childhood. . . . We found that skinfold thicknesses increased in both boys and girls as the amount of television watched increased. This finding is consistent with an earlier study that found a significant relationship between television watching and the prevalence of obesity in children. . . . Children who watched more television and were less likely to participate in vigorous activity tended to have higher BMIs (Body Mass Index). . . . One quarter of all US children watch four or more hours of television each day. . . . Hours of television watching is related to both BMI and skinfold thickness.'

From: R.E. Andersen et al. (1998) 'Relationship of physical activity and television watching with body weight and level of fatness among children', *Journal of the American Medical Association*, 279 (12): 938–42.

7

International and Intercultural
Communication

7.1 International and intercultural
communication: an introduction

In section 2.5 above we discussed some basic levels of human communication: communication within and between individuals, groups, organizations, communities and societies, as well as coalitions and other international organizations of sovereign states. In section 2.7 we presented a two-dimensional typology of within and between levels of communication, 'intra- and inter-level communication' (Figure 2.4). That two-dimensional figure must now be expanded into a three-dimensional one by adding the dimension of 'arena': the different types of geo-political space within which communication between agents active at identical or different levels may take place. We thus get the cube presented in Figure 7.1. The figure shows the important fact that all levels of communication, and all combinations of levels of communication may be located within at least four different types of 'arena', located at different levels of geographical and/or geo-political space: the *local, regional, national* and *international* levels. At local, regional, national and international arenas, then, communication may be carried out within and between

- individuals;
- small groups;
- local, regional, national and international organizations;
- communities, towns, cities;
- societies (nations, states);
- coalitions and other international organizations of sovereign states.

Although at first sight Figure 7.1 may appear to be self-explanatory, it does raise some questions. Some readers may wonder, for instance, how international and/or intercultural communication may indeed be carried out even *within individuals*. The reason why this is so is that, due to the many large intra- and inter-national conflicts having raged during the last century, generally increasing international co-operation, and generally increasing international trade, transportation and individual mobility, increasingly many people have for considerable periods of their lives been living and working outside their home country, thus acquiring familiarity with more than one national culture.

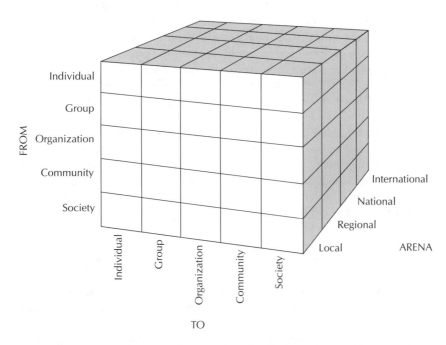

Figure 7.1 Levels and arenas of communication

Indeed, so great is this familiarity that they may feel at home in more than one country or culture. Such individuals may then experience that, say, the Danish part of their individual personality finds itself in conflict with, say, the German, Algerian, Chinese (or whatever) part of their individual personality (see section 4.2). This has been going on, of course, for as long as there has been individual mobility between different national cultures. Indeed, a similar phenomenon may turn up without any international mobility at all – for instance, within people who, having spent their childhood and adolescence in the countryside, have moved to a nearby town, or even to a large city. The farm-girl of decades ago may thus, more or less explicitly of course, discuss with today's middle-aged shop assistant or director general, considering how, according to her two different backgrounds, she should deal with the important and difficult moral problem right now facing her. In so doing, she may communicate also with her brother, who took over the farm from their father. In this sense, not only national and international mobility, but also *social* mobility, may give rise to what is actually *intercultural communication*.

Yet another complication is that within some states there are regions predominantly inhabited by people belonging to a different nationality from the one dominating the state. In addition, people of that same different nationality are also found on the other side of the political border. Here are three examples although more could be given.

The Sami people in northern Scandinavia and north-western Russia (the Kola peninsula) (the Laps as they are often called by outsiders) by now are partly integrated into the national cultures and, as a rule, have permanent residence at one geographical location. But they still graze their herds of reindeer within, and sometimes between, northern Sweden, Norway, Finland, much as their forefathers did more than a thousand years ago. They may be Swedish, Norwegian or Finnish citizens, but their common nationality is Sami.

The Basques, inhabiting the border area between Spain and France, are another example of this type of phenomenum. They are the descendants of a proud people which, according to an old tradition, in 778, at Roncevalles in the Pyrenees, conquered an army commanded by Roland, a leading general of the emperor Charlemagne. Today, they have got a limited measure of independence, but conflicts are still smouldering. The Kurds have the unhappy fate of living in four countries in a conflict-ridden region of the world: Iran, Iraq, Syria and Turkey. Cruel civil strife and guerilla warfare are not uncommon in the region, and various Kurd groupings often play important roles in those conflicts, a fact mirroring their nationally exposed situation. A related but different phenomenon is represented by the Romans (Gypsies) who a thousand years ago migrated from India and have since been moving about, within and between countries in Europe and Asia. Only in the last few decades have substantial groupings of Romans become more settled.

In most cases, however, when discussing international and intercultural communication, what is meant is communication between units having politically different geographical location or place of origin, and thus also – as a rule, at least – different cultural background. This chapter is primarily dedicated to the field of international and intercultural communication studies in that sense. It is dedicated, that is, to *the study of communication physically or mentally crossing one or more borders between the type of societies called states.*

International communication has been with humanity for millennia – more precisely, since the first states were created in various parts of the world. For millennia, it was limited by the fact that messages could not travel faster than a galloping horse or a fast-sailing ship (see section 5.5.5). Following the technological advances in communication technology during the nineteenth and twentieth centuries (see section 2.3.4), international communication and transportation received a tremendous impetus. In addition, due to the facts that since the Second World War a number of former colonies have become independent states, and relatively recently, some states have been divided into a number of new states, international communication has, by definition, increased. As the twenty-first century approaches, international communication is more widespread than ever and is more important than ever. Consequently, the study of international communication is more important than ever.

7.2 Ways and means of international communication

7.2.1 The origins

We have already noted that processes of communication and transportation often run in parallel. Sometimes, they are very closely intertwined indeed. That was the case when, some 200,000 years ago, our ancestors, small groups of individuals belonging to the species *homo sapiens*, started to replenish the world (see section 2.1). Drawing on their unique communicational capacity, which offered immense advantages in all manner of both peaceful and conflictual activities, they multiplied, and finally, after several millennia, they actually conquered the world. Starting off from somewhere in Africa, they reached the Middle East some 90,000 years ago. From there they could go directly into Asia. It is estimated that Europe was colonized quite some time later on – about 40,000 years ago, which was about the same time as other groups of *homo sapiens* took the leap from Asia to Australia by way of New Guinea. (That it took so relatively long time to go from the Middle East into Europe may have been at least partly due to resistance from the Neanderthals.) From Asia, *homo sapiens* could also reach North America by crossing the Bering Strait (some 12,000 years ago). After yet another 3,000 years or so they had arrived at the southern tip of South America. The globe belonged to *homo sapiens*.

The globe belonged to *homo sapiens* but to what specific groupings of *homo sapiens*? As they were wandering around the globe, they changed. As 200 millennia passed away, as thousands of generations lived and died, *homo sapiens* evolved into the variants briefly described in section 2.1 above. So did their gradually emerging cultures, their systems of ideas, manifesting themselves in actions and artefacts (see section 3.1), traces of which may still be found by archeologists and geologists. Such remnants demonstrate the existence of prehistoric cultures now long ago completely extinguished.

7.2.2 Migration in an historical perspective

Over the millennia, *homo sapiens* continued to be on the move. Many such movements were left uncharted, but some are relatively well known. Obviously, the best-known routes are those taking place in relatively recent periods of time, for instance, the so-called 'Völkerwanderung Period' (the 'Period of Wandering Peoples') in Europe, stretching from about AD 350 to about AD 600. During this period, the East Roman Empire, having for centuries survived the West Roman Empire, finally fell to pieces. This opened the way for a number of Germanic tribes in Eastern Europe to move westward, and then southward into Northern Africa by way of what is today Portugal and Spain.

The movement of whole peoples and their belongings was accompanied by corresponding flows of ideas, flows of culture. Also, the invaders were quick to appropriate not only the *material* riches to be found in the remnants of the disentagrating Roman Empire, but also the *cultural* riches of their conquered enemies: their ideas, artefacts and patterns of action (see section 3.1 above). In the long run, however, the fact that the invaders were much fewer than the invaded caused not only the *cultural* heritage of the invaders, but also their *genetical* heritage gradually to dissipitate. In addition, core elements of the original Mediterranean culture survived, partly because of the Catholic Church, which used its spiritual message to familiarize the invaders with other aspects of the Mediterranean and Central European culture. In its turn European culture later on conquered large parts of the world – symbolically, that is. Similar processes of assimilation occurred when, between the eighth and eleventh centuries, parts of Europe were repeatedly raided by the Vikings from what is now Scandinavia. At about the same time missionaries, primarily from what is now Germany and Great Britain, started converting Scandinavia (see Box 3.1 on p. 69).

Much the same types of process took place about 1500 when the so-called 'New World' was discovered by the Europeans, offering seemingly boundless opportunities to enterprizing individuals, groups of individuals, organizations, nations and countries. (Even Sweden for a short time had a colony of her own on what is now the East coast of the USA.) After a slow and hesitant start, a new *Völkerwanderung* took place, in which millions of Europeans and Asians moved across the oceans to the two Americas (see Box 7.1). These processes culminated in the late nineteenth and early twentieth centuries. In the meantime, the millions of people moving from Europe and Asia into North and South America were ruthlessly pushing the original inhabitants, today as a rule only to be found in the most inaccessible and/or barren regions of the two Americas, further west. Much the same happened on the other side of the globe, in Australia.

Migration may be due to both push and pull factors, and these factors may be located in different sectors of the Great Wheel of Culture in Society, discussed in section 3.2 above. The sectors of economics, politics and religion are probably the most important ones in this respect. After the French Revolution in 1789, many members of the nobility had to flee their country to save their lives. During a famine in 1845, about a million Irish men and women left their country for the USA. In the 1840s, the Mormons moved westward in the USA, by horse and carriage, to what is now the state of Utah. Anticipating what was to happen, many Jews left Germany in the late 1930s. The Second World War (1939–45) as a whole caused immense waves of refugees, the total number of which has been estimated at about 40 million people. When shortly thereafter, in 1947, the then British colony of India was divided into two sovereign states – India and Pakistan – some 15 million people crossed the borders between the two states, in both directions. In today's Africa, millions of people have been and are on the move, for economic and political reasons, and often from sheer hunger.

BOX 7.1 'UNTO A GOOD LAND'

'Karl Oskar Nilsson walked alone through the wilderness. . . . In spite of the many obstacles hindering his progress, he felt in high spirits. . . . He was in high spirits because he was the first one here, because he knew a freedom which none of those would have who came after him. He walked through the forest as if he had a claim to everything around him, as if he now were taking possession and would rule a whole kingdom. Here he would soon feel at home and know his way.

'Now he was searching for Ki-Chi-Saga; the name was like a magic formula, like a word from an old tale about an ancient, primeval, moss-grown, troll-inhabited forest. . . . At first glimpse he was disappointed: this was only a small lake, it was not the right one. But as he approached he discovered that it was only an arm of a lake. . . . All that he saw agreed with what he had heard – this lake must be Ki-Chi-Saga. . . .

'A vast field opened to the north between the lake and the forests's edge – open, fertile ground covered with grass. . . . The lake shores were low and easily accessible everywhere. Birds played on the surface of the water – splashing, swimming in lines, wriggling about like immense feathered water snakes, and there were ripples and rings from whirling, swirling fins.

'Karl Oskar measured the sloping meadow with his eyes. It must be about fifty acres. He supposed a great deal of this ground once had been under water, the lake had at one time been larger. The soil was the fattest mold on clay bottom, the finest earth in existence. He stuck his shovel into the ground – everywhere the topsoil was deep, and in one place he did not find the red clay bottom until he had dug almost three feet down.

'Earlier in the day he had seen the next best; he had gone on a little farther, and now he had found the best. He had arrived.'

From: Vilhelm Moberg (1959) *Unto a Good Land.* Stockholm: Bonniers.

Whatever the cause of such migrations, it is obvious that they create enormous *needs*, as well as enormous *problems* for international communication, problems which can be solved only by way of international co-operation.

7.3 High politics and international communication: a brave new world?

7.3.1 Peace and conflict

Towards the end of the Second World War and afterwards there was widespread agreement that the time had come to build an international organization of states, with a view to prevent future international armed conflicts – a new attempt after the failure of the League of Nations which was established after the First World War. To this end, the United Nations (UN) was formally created in 1944. It now encompasses practically all the states of the world (Switzerland, for constitutional reasons, being an exception). Its primary aim was not reached, however. International and intercultural conflicts have been going on all the time. In the early 1950s, the Korean War raged between North and South Korea, supported by, respectively, China together with the Soviet Union, and the USA. Since then, many other international and national armed conflicts have occurred, and some are going on right now. But it should not be forgotten that, sometimes thanks to the UN, a number of international conflicts have been solved more or less peacefully. And it is a fact that, in spite of many local and regional conflicts around the world, there has been no third world war. With the downfall of communism in the late 1980s and early 1990s preceded by decades of uprisings in Eastern Europe and finally epitomized by the collapse of the Soviet Union – the main international political rift disappeared, making the economic rift between what is called the developed and developing parts of the globe stand out even more starkly.

There is still no shortage of local and regional armed conflicts – in parts of the former Soviet Union, or in the Balkans, the Middle East, Africa and South America – but on the large international scene what might be called a *Pax Americana* has been established. In communicative terms, the vision behind this state of affairs was eloquently expressed in the title of a UNESCO report published in 1984 – *Many Voices, One World: Communication and Society Today and Tomorrow* (the MacBride Report). There is a vision, then. But it should be remembered that, for better and for worse, reality has a tendency to neglect visions. International diplomats still have difficult problems to solve. They have to rely on their three main activities: observing, reporting, negotiating, all of which are communicatively oriented. In performing such tasks on the international scene, they still get indirect support from home by way of more or less subtle forms of what used to be called propaganda – now an increasingly seldom used term, although no doubt the phenomenon as such lives on.

7.3.2 International propaganda

The word 'propaganda' roughly means 'more or less biased information issued by a government or other powerful organization to further the interests of the initiator of that information'. The origin of the term is a papal 'bull' (a formal document issued by the pope) entitled *Sacra Congegratio de Propaganda Fide* ('A Holy Meeting about the Furthering of the Faith'). The bull was issued in 1633 as part of the 'Counter-Reformation' then being carried out by the the Holy See. The Counter-Reformation, of course, was directed against the various Protestant movements which, during the sixteenth century, had emerged in Europe. Today, the term 'propaganda' has rather

BOX 7.2 PROPAGANDA

Propaganda has often been directly and indirectly criticized, not least in literary science fiction. An example of such criticism is offered in the following extract from that vision of a dark future presented in the now classic novel by George Orwell, *Nineteen Eighty Four*:

'It was nearly eleven hundred, and in the Records Department, where Winston worked, they were dragging the chairs out of the cubicles and grouping them in the centre of the hall, opposite the big telescreen, in preparation for the Two Minutes Hate. . . .

'The next moment a hideous, grinding screech, as of some monstrous machine running without oil, burst from the big telescreen at the end of the room. It was a noise that set one's teeth on edge and bristled the hair at the back of one's neck. The Hate had started.

'As usual, the face of Emmanuel Goldstein, the Enemy of the People, had flashed onto the screen. There were hisses here and there among the audience. . . . Goldstein was the renegade and backslider who once, long ago (how long ago, nobody quite remembered), had been one of the leading figures of the Party, almost on a level with Big Brother himself, and then had engaged in counter-revolutionary activities, had been condemned to death and had mysteriously escaped and disappeared. . . . Somewhere or other he was still alive and hatching his conspiracies. . . .

'Before the Hate had proceeded for thirty seconds, uncontrollable exclamations of rage were breaking out from half the people in the room. . . . In its second minute the Hate rose to a frenzy. People were leaping up and down in their places and shouting at the tops of their voices in an effort to drown the maddening bleating voice that came from the screen. . . . In a lucid moment Winston found that he was shouting with the others and kicking his heels violently against the rung of his chair. . . .

'The Hate rose to its climax. The voice of Goldstein had become an actual sheep's bleat, and for an instant the face changed into that of a sheep. Then the sheep-face melted into the figure of a Eurasian soldier who seemed to be advancing, huge and terrible, his sub-machine-gun roaring, and seeming to spring out of the surface of the screen, so that some of the people in the front row actually flinched backwards in their seats. But in the same moment . . . the hostile figure melted into the face of Big Brother. . . . Then the face of Big Brother faded away again and instead the three slogans of the Party stood out in bold capitals:

WAR IS PEACE
FREEDOM IS SLAVERY
IGNORANCE IS STRENGTH.'

From: G. Orwell (1949) *Nineteen Eighty Four*. London: Martin Secker & Warburg. (Quoted from the Penguin edition, London, 1990, pp. 11ff.)

negative connotations, but it was regarded in a positive light by three authoritarian regimes: Nazi Germany under Hitler (1933–45), Communist Soviet Union under Stalin (1922–53) and Communist China under Mao (1949–76). During the Cold War between the USA and the Soviet Union international propaganda was a widespread phenomenon (see Box 7.2). As a phenomenon, propaganda is still widespread, but it often turns up under other names such as, for instance, 'international information', or the US 'Voice of America', a well-known radio channel broadcasting in approximately 40 languages.

The term 'indoctrination' is sometimes also used to denote various forms of more subtle, indirect 'propaganda' in economic, political and religious matters. It can be found in informational mass media contents of all countries around the globe, not only in political or economic contexts, but also in fiction and entertainment, and in all systems of education. In more general terms, both propaganda and indoctrination may be regarded as special types of socialization and re-socialization (see section 3.3).

7.4 Levels of international and intercultural communication

Figure 7.1 visualizes the fact that, just as national communication does, international and intercultural communication may take place at the levels of interpersonal, organizational and societal communication. In this section, international communication taking place at each one of the three levels will be briefly discussed. Let's start, however, with a general discussion of the role of personality in international communication.

7.4.1 On time, space and personality

An important characteristic common to most communication in large international organizations is that it is rather time consuming. As a rule, of course, every international organization has a (more or less well-developed, more or less well-run) central administration active through the year: a 'secretariat' that takes care of running routine business, often headed by a Secretary General. But the main and formal decisions are often taken only once a year (or perhaps less frequently than that) at the annual (or bi-annual) *general assemblies*, for instance, the annual UN General Assembly. Communication during the long periods between those general assemblies is often sporadic and, as a rule, it is not direct, but mediated – one way or the other.

For natural reasons, on the other hand, communication in large inter-national business organizations often has to be very rapid. Not only the Chairman of the Board and the Director General, therefore, but also local decision-makers tend to have broad and yet relatively clearly-defined competences as to which types of decision may be taken at each level, by which incumbent of this or that position, in this or that situation.

In addition, however, the individual characteristics of the incumbent of a given organizational position inevitably affect the activities carried out at that position, in spite of even the most rigidly formal organization. This is so not least in international organizations where not only individual talents and other characteristics of the incumbents affect their activities, but also national backgrounds (sometimes characterized by what to the outsider, may seem quaint habits and mores) can influence the way in which business is done. For example, in Scandinavia the general habit of always communicating on a first-name basis is widespread (see Box 7.3).

BOX 7.3   THE 'DU REFORM'

In Sweden, cleverly riding on the general tendency towards equality that predominated in the late 1960s and early 1970s, a new Director General of the otherwise rather conservative National Board of Medicine in 1967 introduced by decree the informal pronoun 'du' as the general interpersonal address within the Board (cf. German 'du', French 'tu'), instead of the formal 'ni' or the then frequent habit of addressing each other in the third person, using the title of one's interlocutor ('Has the Director General received my new statement of accounts?' 'No, I have not, Senior Accountant.'). At first publicly derided, the decision gradually became popular, and indeed it may have contributed to the tendency then beginning and now prevailing in Sweden to address even complete strangers with the second person, informal pronoun '*du*' accompanied by communication on a first-name basis. This tendency, in its turn, has often surprised and sometimes amused or irritated foreign visitors to Sweden. It should be remembered, however, that this method of an address is actually the original one. It is still common in all five Nordic countries. In Iceland, the old way of addressing everybody with 'du' and the first name, was never really abandoned.

Striking examples of the influence of both individual personality and national culture on high-level international communication may be found among the various Secretaries General of the UN. Some have tried – more or less successfully, of course – to widen the scope of activity available to the Secretary General. The best-known example is, perhaps, Dag Hammarskjöld (UN Secretary General, 1953–61) who died in office. Others seem to have been content to operate within the narrower brief for this type of international organization.

7.4.2   International communication at the interpersonal level

International communication at the interpersonal level must have much the same basic characteristics, of course, as has interpersonal communication between individuals from one and the same national community. Some of these basic characteristics were discussed in Chapter 4 where we also saw that on top of such general characteristics of interpersonal communication may be found sometimes quite striking differences rooted in the culture of the communicator's home country (see Box 4.4 on p. 81). Such similarities and differences form the main theme of this section.

There are a number of different dimensions along which individual human communication may vary between societies in different parts of the world. A basic dimension is the way in which, consciously and unconsciously, we use our faces when trying to express (or hide) our thoughts and emotions. No doubt there are a number of ways in which such expressions may differ between people from different countries and cultures. In a series of ingenious experiments carried out by an international group of leading psychologists, however, it has been shown that facial expressions of emotion are indeed recognizable between widely different cultures around the globe (see Box 7.4).

BOX 7.4   YOUR FACE SHOWS YOUR EMOTIONS – EVEN TO PEOPLE FROM OTHER PARTS OF THE WORLD!

'Face-to-face communication between people of different nationalities is the most direct form of international communication. An important element in all forms of face-to-face communication is, of course, our faces themselves – what they look like and how they express and mirror our thoughts, feelings and emotions while we communicate. A basic question in this connection is whether during interpersonal communication the facial expressions of thoughts and emotions vary between people from different cultures in different parts of the world to such an extent that we do not recognize the emotions facially expressed by people from other cultures than our own.

An international team of psychologists used an ingenious experimental research design to study this problem. Photos of people from different parts of the world expressing a number of different emotions were shown to people from six different European, Asian and American countries. The subjects were then asked to identify the emotions. As it turned out, the scientists in this way were able to demonstrate that there is indeed high agreement between people from different parts of the world in interpreting emotions facially expressed by people from other parts of the world than their own.

There were some differences, however, when it came to estimating the exact level of intensity of the emotions expressed. These differences may be attributed to variation in either the *facial expressions of feeling* or the *interpretations* of those facial expressions of feelings.'

From: M. Biehl et al. (1997) 'Matsumoto and Ekman's Japanese and Caucasian Facial Expressions of Emotion (JACFEE): reliability data and cross-national differences', *Journal of Nonverbal Behavior*, 21 (1): 3–21.

A somewhat more abstract, but very important dimension differentiating between processes of interpersonal communication taking place in different cultures is the dimension called 'Individualism/Collectivism'. In most cultures, and especially in cultures characterized by a high degree of *individualism*, an individual's capacity to realize the various potentials inherent in his or her personality is held to be very important. To do so, the individual must show considerable capacity for personal initiative and a strong will to constantly stand up for his or her personal opinions even in controversial matters. He or she must also be able to operate more or less inpendently of his or her various membership groups, although, of course, such groups may offer important resources, and also impose heavy restrictions, both of which possibilities must not be neglected.

In *collectivistically-oriented* cultures, on the other hand, the individuals tend to be subordinated to their main 'ingroups'. Although they may rank order their various ingroups differently, collectivistically-oriented cultures tend to have quite a number of such ingroups. In most societies, however, the three most important ingroups are the same ones: the extended family, the neighbourhood, and the company, community or social organization within which the individual is doing his or her main work and leading his or her daily life. Between them, these three ingroups define the social status of the individual in a rather complex way. For people coming from cultures in which the status system is relatively simple, its main dimensions being the individual's economic, educational and vocational position (see the causal model shown in Figure 3.3 on p. 62), these complex status systems can be quite difficult to understand.

Obviously, interpersonal communication crossing boundaries between societies characterized by different degrees of individualism and/or collectivism may become quite complicated; the risks for misunderstanding, quite frequent. In order to understand these basic characteristics better, we can relate them to the fundamental values of *freedom* and *equality* discussed in section 3.5.2 above (see Figure 3.6). In strongly collectivistically-oriented societies, individual freedom tends to be rather low. In addition, although equality *within* a given stratum of the population may be high, equality *between* strata also tends to be low. (Extreme examples of such societies are Nazi Germany under Adolf Hitler and the Soviet Union under V.S. Lenin or Joseph Stalin.) In strongly individualistically-oriented societies, individual freedom quite naturally tends to be relatively high, while equality between strata may be variable. Modern capitalist democracies are examples of this type of society.

In communicative contexts, tendencies towards one or the other of these types of society are sometimes expressed in terms of personal address:

- the use or non-use of titles in interpersonal communication;
- the different or similar pronouns of address used to people of different status;
- the tendency to quickly or only slowly and rarely turn to communication on a first-name basis, etc.

In French and English, for instance, social distance is often marked by the insertion of 'Madame', 'Mademoiselle', 'Monsieur', and 'Sir', 'Miss' or 'Madam' at the beginning or end of a sentence, a convention sometimes also used as a marker of a shift in conversational turn-taking (see section 4.3.4). In some languages, French and German, for instance, the pronouns of address are different between, on the one hand, family members and intimate friends, and on the other, more distant acquaintances or colleagues, not to speak of your superiors at work, or complete strangers. In other national languages, conditions are different (as shown in Box 7.3 above).

Another communicatively important dimension in this connection is represented by the concept of *context* – the extent to which actions and utterances are embedded in a given context provided by societal culture. In so-called 'high-context cultures', important parts of a given message are provided by the context; it is already embedded in the minds of the communicators. In 'low-context cultures', on the other hand, the significant content of a given message tends to be made explicit in the message itself. Low-context communication tends to predominate in individualistic cultures; high-context communication in collectivistic cultures. Especially in meetings between individuals coming from different cultures and not being aware of the different patterns of communication, such differences may, of course, give rise to surprise, amusement and sometimes considerable irritation on both sides.

Finally, in addition to the difficulties and problems of communication which may be caused by intercultural differences in individual communication of the types just presented, it must also be mentioned that ever-increasing international mobility not only creates problems in interpersonal communication but also widens our horizons. It makes us realize that there is indeed 'a world outside Verona', in spite of Romeo's assertion to the contrary in William Shakespeare's drama, *Romeo and Juliet* (1594/95). By trying to understand the strangers – men and women from 'outside Verona' – we may come to understand ourselves.

7.4.3   *International communication at the organizational level*

There are two main types of international communication at the organizational level. Quite naturally, local, regional and national organizations located in a given country communicate with similar local, regional and national organizations in another country. In each one of the five Nordic countries, for instance, there is a national academic organization for Media and Communication Studies, and those five national organizations regularly meet their sister organizations every second year (at the same time making one international meeting into five national ones).

Very often, however, international communication at the organizational level is carried out by organizations especially designed for that purpose: international organizations (see section 5.1). As a matter of fact there are a large number of international organizations, two examples being the

International Communication Association (ICA) and the International Association for Media and Communication Research (IAMCR) (see section 1.10).

Two main types of international organization are international *governmental* organizations (so-called IGOs) and international *non-governmental* organizations (so-called INGOs). In addition, there are mixed types of organization having both governmental and non-governmental members. Two well known IGOs are, for example, the United Nations and the European Community. The two international organizations, the ICA and the IAMCR, are INGOs, of course. A well-known mixed type of international organization is the International Labour Organization (ILO) which has both governmental and non-governmental components (see also Box 7.5).

BOX 7.5   SOME GOVERNMENTAL (G) AND NON-GOVERNMENTAL (NG) INTERNATIONAL ORGANIZATIONS

EC	European Community (G)
FAO	Food and Agriculture Organization (G)
FIFA	Fédération Internationale de Football Associations (NG)
IAMCR	International Association for Media and Communication Research (NG)
ICA	International Communication Association (NG)
ICS	International Chamber of Shipping (NG)
IMF	International Monetary Fund (G)
IOC	International Olympic Committee (NG)
NC	Nordic Council ('Nordiska rådet') (G)
OPEC	Organization of Petroleum Exporting Countries (G)
SA	Salvation Army (NG)
UN	United Nations (G)
WHO	World Health Organization (G)
WWF	World Wildlife Fund (NG)

A very old but increasingly important type of international organization is made up of so-called BINGOs: business international non-governmental organizations. These are often large multinational or international companies, huge conglomerates operating in all parts of the world, often through national subsidiaries, sometimes locating their main office in a part of the world especially favourable from the point of view of taxation. The Hanse, briefly discussed in section 5.2, is an historically interesting example of an early, relatively loosely organized BINGO. An example of a recent BINGO is the furniture and home decoration company, IKEA, active on three continents, founded by Ingvar Kamprad (b. 1926) from Eketorp in Agunnaryd, Sweden.

For some reason, the acronym for 'business international governmental organizations', BIGO, has not been used very much, but an example might be the Organization for Economic Cooperation and Development (OECD), an organization of 20 states set up in 1961 to further economic growth and international trade. Also, the Organization of Petroleum Exporting Countries (OPEC) might be called a BIGO. Other important international business organizations cover various lines of commerce and industry, the most general one being the International Chamber of Commerce – the world organization of business.

Finally, it should be mentioned that behind the discussions and decisions of many formally non-business international organizations may often be found very important business concerns – witness, for instance, the discussions carried on, and the decisions taken, within the International Olympic Committee. The IOC, of course, is an international non-business organization dealing with the really big business related to the Olympic Games (which is, in addition, politically delicate business).

7.4.4   International communication at the mass media level

In order to communicate successfully, the parties to communication must have some basic knowledge about each other. Two very basic conditions for successful and efficient international communication, therefore, are that important news be, first, efficiently *distributed* around the globe, and secondly, relatively quickly *diffused* among the various populations of the globe. Let us start by discussing the diffusion of news.

The study of the diffusion of national and international news is a research tradition in its own right. Figure 7.2 offers one example of the types of result which can be gained within this tradition. It shows how, in 1986, news about the assassination of Swedish Prime Minister Olof Palme spread within a number of national populations around the globe. It will be seen that the diffusion was very rapid, but also that, quite naturally, there were considerable differences between the diffusion processes within different countries. It was shown by multivariate statistics that no less than 50% of this variation could be explained in terms of effects from only three basic variables:

- geographical distance from the location of the event;
- the extent of trade relations between Sweden and the other countries under study;
- the amount of already existing communicative relations between Sweden and the countries under study (mail, telephone, etc.).

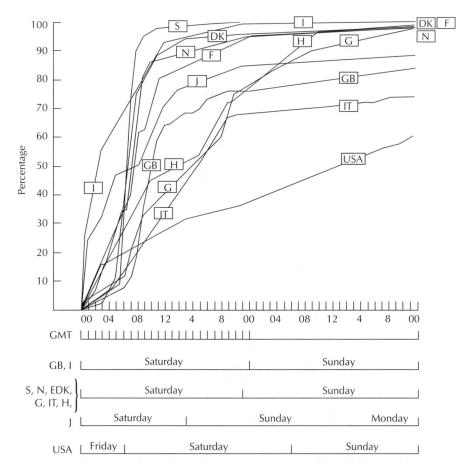

Figure 7.2 International diffusion of news: the assassination of Swedish
Prime Minister Olof Palme in 1986 (*source*: Rosengren, 1987)

The fact that a piece of international news can be diffused among the
different populations of the globe as quickly as is sometimes the case is due,
of course, to the relative efficiency of the international mass media system.
In their capacities as collectors and distributors of 'hard news' (basic news
about important events) the various components of the international mass
media system are efficient, although somewhat lopsided. Most of us get most
of our knowledge about the world outside our home country from the mass
media – and not only by way of news programs, but also by other types of
content, not least fictional programs imported from other parts of the world.
We thus get a somewhat distorted picture about what human life looks like
in other parts of the world – and in our own.

Indeed, we may get a lopsided and distorted picture not only about what
human life looks like in other parts of the world, but also about *what the world*

itself looks like. What has been called our 'mental maps' are clearly affected by our media habits, and not always positively so.

A crude but quite instructive measure of individuals' mental maps can be obtained by asking people where they would go, if they had to leave their home country for one reason or another. On the basis of people's answers, one can draw maps in which the size of the different parts of the world are made proportionate to their representation in the answers obtained. Highly preferred parts of the world are thus made bigger; less preferred parts, smaller. This technique was used in the Media Panel Program referred to in section 6.6 above. As expected, we found that the amount of TV viewing strongly influenced the mental maps of the youngsters under study. Obviously, other variables – primarily, age and gender – also exerted an influence on the mental maps of the viewers. When combined, the effects from age, gender and TV viewing were strong indeed, as can be seen from Figures 7.3a and 7.3b. As a comparison, the corresponding map of the world, as reported in Swedish television news and measured in a governmental report published at about the same time (the late 1980s), is also shown (Figure 7.3c).

It will be seen that while the world at the time reported in Swedish television news (Figure 7.3c) certainly was somewhat distorted, it was not grotesquely so. The mental map of girls aged 11 and with a low TV viewing rating (Figure 7.3a) is not exactly grotesque either, but it may perhaps be called rather narrow. The mental map of Swedish boys aged 15 and with a high TV viewing rating (Figure 7.3b), however, deserves to be called grotesque. Their own part of the world, Western Europe, is not over-distorted *per se*, perhaps, but Eastern Europe is completely missing, and Asia stands out as an isolated little island. North America, on the other hand, is much larger than the rest of the world taken together. South America is as invisible as Eastern Europe. This is a fictitious world: the world created by US fiction and entertainment which dominates even a vital public service media system such as that of Sweden in the 1980s, and which is strongly favoured by young people in particular. Sadly, there is little hope that the mental maps cultivated by the television contents that are available to youngsters around the globe today will be any better than they were in the late 1980s. Indeed, it is pretty safe to guess that they are not better at all but rather the reverse. Only the production of new models of mental maps will substantiate this guess, however.

Individual mental maps, then, are highly dependent on individual mass media habits. The greater the television use, the more lopsided the mental maps. The reason why this is so is obvious as we have already seen that even the 'international maps' offered by the media may be rather lopsided. Indeed, the amount of news reaching us from various parts of the world is strongly dependent on a few basic variables, the most important ones being the economic relations prevailing between countries.

In order to study such relationships systematically, we need other types of data than the ones discussed so far. That problematic will be shortly discussed in the following section.

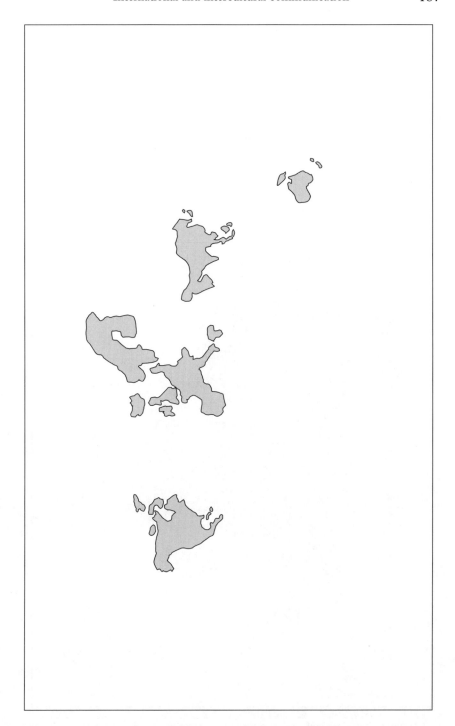

Figure 7.3a   Media maps, mental maps and real maps: girls aged 11,
          low TV (*source*: Rosengren and Windahl, 1989)

Figure 7.3b   Media maps, mental maps and real maps: boys aged 15,
          high TV (*source*: Rosengren and Windahl, 1989)

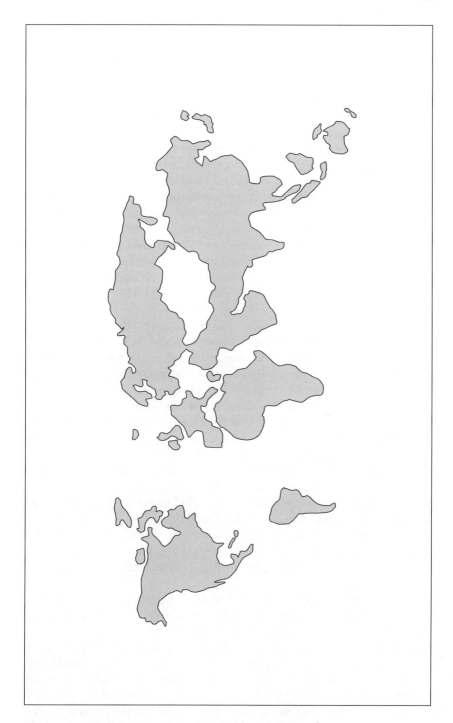

Figure 7.3c   Media maps, mental maps and real maps: media map of
             Swedish TV (*source*: Rosengren and Windahl, 1989)

7.5 International news: intra and extra media data

National and international mass media offer all of us a never-ending flow of pictures of the world surrounding us. Some of these pictures are obviously fictitious – indeed, the value of those types of picture resides precisely in the fact that they *are* fictitious. Abdicating from the ambition of offering detailed truths about these or those events, processes or structures, the ambition of fictional programming is to arrive at another type of truth: a type of more general truth, perhaps, or truth grossly and obviously exaggerated and distorted, so that we may really come to know what it is all about. Other types of programming have the ambition to offer what may be considered virtually true pictures of the world or, at least, as true and trustworthy as possible. This type of picture of the world is found in news programs, of course, and also in the kinds of programs that are based on news programs: programs offering comments to, views about, and discussions of the world as more or less truthfully mirrored in the content of news programs. How could we study these types of programs?

In order systematically to study mass media news about the world, we need two sets of data. We need *data about news*, and we need *data about the world*. The two sets of data should be as independent as possible in the sense that they should ideally stem from two different types of source. Obviously, data about media news must come from within the media; they must be what has been called *intra media data*. Data about the world, then, should stem from somewhere other than from within the media. They should be what has been called *extra media data*. By combining intra and extra media data we arrive at two types of new knowledge.

In the first place, we may use the two sets of data to *evaluate the news*: how true, reliable, representative, trustworthy, relevant, etc. are media stories about the world when compared to reality as defined in terms of extra media data? Intra media data about the world as rendered in Swedish television were graphically presented in Figure 7.3c above. The world as pictured in television news was found to be somewhat lopsided when (implicitly) compared to corresponding extra media data: the world as pictured in traditional maps of the world.

Secondly, we may use the two sets of data to *explain*, and thus better to *understand*, certain characteristics of the pictures of the world offered by mass media. Studies based on the intra/extra media data methodology have used extra media data regarding as different phenomena as, for instance, parliamentary elections and earthquakes in different parts of the world, with a view to examine the relative strength of the factors presumably explaining international news flow. In such studies it has been shown that considerable portions (30%) of existing variations in international news coverage are due to simple factors such as the size of population in the country of the event, and the geographical distance between the location of the event and the reporting mass medium. (For further information on the intra/extra media data approach, see Box 7.6.)

BOX 7.6 ON INTRA AND EXTRA MEDIA DATA

A. The basic idea

'The search for the truth of a matter requires a comparison to be made between the contents of a news report and a set of independent, external criteria related to that same matter. There are numerous potential avenues open. . . . All the same, there are cases where no ready-made external-to-media data are at hand. Then another solution must be utilised. The researcher must establish a list of relevant events and condition, and make this list the starting point of any investigation. . . . Comparisons can be made between different media or media channels or publications and broadcasts. . . . In this case, of course, one is making a comparison between different media versions of "reality", none of which, on its own, may represent actual reality.'

From: B. Gunter (1997) *Measuring Bias on Television*. Luton: University of Luton Press, p. 31.

B. Some intra/extra media data studies

Lippmann, W. and Merz, C. (1920) 'A test of the news', *The New Republic*, 4 August.

Rosengren, K.E. (1970) 'International news: intra and extra media data', *Acta Sociologica*, 13: 96–109.

Smith, R.F. (1971) 'US news and Sino-Indian relations: an extra media study', *Journalism Quarterly*, 48: 447–58, 501.

Hicks, R.G. and Gordon, A. (1974) 'Foreign news content in Israeli and US newspapers', *Journalism Quarterly*, 51: 639–44.

Rosengren, K.E. (1980) 'Bias in news: methods and concepts', *Mass Communication Review Yearbook* (vol. 1). pp. 249–63.

Adams, W. (1986) 'Whose lives count? Coverage of natural disasters', *Journal of Communication*, 36: 113–22.

7.6 International popular culture

7.6.1 *Popular culture as innovation*

In Chapter 5 we discussed five societal systems for the production of innovations, as well as the different reward systems prevailing in those various systems (see Figure 5.5). We noted that the most independent system for the production of innovations is basic science; the least independent is mass media culture. International popular culture – mass mediated popular art and fiction – is certainly part of the international mass media system. Regarded as a system for the production of innovations, it thus occupies a somewhat precarious position.

In terms of the 'Great Wheel of Culture in Society' (Figure 3.1) many innovations produced in the mass media system are located within the two broad spheres of art and literature. But most producers of those mass-mediated innovations are artistically less independent than are the producers of elite art, music and literature. Most of the innovations produced in the international popular culture system are not very original – rather, they might be regarded as clone-like variations of a few, general cultural patterns. This is true not least for popular fiction, regardless of the medium of publication (television, radio, weeklies, magazines, books, etc.). Only too often what we meet are standardized patterns of, say, the 'boy-meets-girl' or 'bad guy–good guy' types. Virtually endless sequels of series and serials reproduce and repeat the deeds of more or less standardized heroes and heroines in more or less standardized ways. It is a special kind of industry in which economists and communication experts work closely together with technicians and artists. In principle, the same pattern holds true also for popular music – today, in more ways than one, the most important sector of popular culture.

7.6.2   Popular music

Internationally, popular music is an economically important type of goods. For decades, the methods of its production, distribution and sales have to a large extent been controlled by a few international conglomerates, the so-called 'Majors', based in the USA, Japan and Germany: Time-Warner, Sony, Bertelsmann, Philips-Polygram. Popular music is produced, distributed and sold in much the same way as many other types of goods are produced, distributed and sold by other internationally more or less integrated industries: clothes, hobby articles, sports equipment, etc. It is subject to the same cycles of good and bad business. The most typical example of international popular culture is perhaps MTV (see Box 7.7). In a few cases, however, popular music has to some extent deviated from this general pattern of dependency on the economic system of society.

In the former German Democratic Republic, for example, those rock artists who were considered to be the best actually enjoyed high societal status. Indeed, some were relatively high-ranked civil servants. Instead of being integrated into the economic system, they were thus integrated into the political system. The leaders of the then Soviet satellite states actually used US-inspired popular music as a means to keep the masses quiet and happy. (Also on the other side of the Iron Curtain, of course, popular music was used for direct or indirect political purposes. For instance, the US radio propaganda station *Voice of America*, which was created during the Cold War, besides its 40 or so different languages also relied heavily on the language of popular music.)

BOX 7.7   THE DEVELOPMENT AND EXPLOITATION OF AN INTERNATIONAL YOUTH CULTURE

'MTV's most far-reaching strategy for its program services is the attempt to develop and exploit an international youth culture. MTV claims that young people from disparate countries are part of an emerging international youth culture that transcends any national cultural identity. MTV sees pop music as a key element in this culture, constituting a common denominator of youth in all countries. . . . "Music is the global language", proclaimed the channel's Sara Levinson. "We want to be the global rock 'n' roll village where we can talk to the youth worldwide. . . . This is the first international generation. They wear Levi's, shop at Benetton, wear Swatch watches and drink Coca-Cola. This is not to say there aren't cultural differences, that the French aren't different from the Germans. But a French teenager and a German teenager are much more similar to each other than they are to their parents. . . .

MTV encourages young people around the world to embrace a consumerist way of life, rejecting alternative values, traits or traditions as a part of their self-identity. . . . A program service successfully targeting youth throughout the world would be much sought after by advertisers seeking to expand their share of the world market for specific consumer goods of interest to youth, including jeans, designer clothes, watches and soft drinks. Moreover, such a program service could benefit these advertisers and itself by attempting to subtly define this transnational youth culture – and one's inclusion within it – in terms of the acquistion of fashionable consumer products advertised on the service. . . .

MTV exemplifies the growing globalization for popular culture and moreover is a key agent forstering this trend. Large cultural producers of various media (theatrical film, television and recorded music) seek global audiences for their offerings. MTV's worldwide network of services encourages the emergence of this global market both through its program content and advertising. In terms of programming, music video clips presented on MTV are a hybrid of film, television and music, so that the clips themselves can promote these cultural products globally. For instance, music videos often feature songs from film soundtracks including short clips from the film in the video. The film-related video played concurrently on MTV's services shapes and nurtures audience interest in the film everywhere MTV is shown. For record companies, MTV's play of certain genres of Western popular music helps create a global audience for this music. Music video is at its core a type of advertisement for cultural products: films, film sound-tracks, recorded music, live concerts, fashion apparel depicted in the clip and even the music clip itself as a home video retail product. Omnipresent play of music videos on MTV (and elsewhere) helps shape global demand for this array of products. Certainly, globalization strategies did not originate with MTV – film studios, television producers and record labels have been pursuing global markets for some time – but MTV clearly advances such trends.'

From: Jack Banks (1997) 'MTV and the globalization of popular culture', *Gazette*, 59 (1): 43–60.

The leading US creators and performers of Afro-American blues, spirituals and jazz reached some measure of artistic independence decades ago. More recently, much the same has happened to leading creators and performers of rock music. In these types of popular music, the leading artists may be compared to leading artists in more traditional forms of art. Although integrated in the economic system, they have a degree of artistic integrity, and their main frame of reference is built in complex interaction with a relatively limited group of artist colleagues. What may differentiate them from other types of artist is the complexity of the technical machinery necessary to produce their works of art, machinery with which they work competently but which, as a rule, they do not own (see Box 7.8).

BOX 7.8 THE RECORDER AS 'SKETCHPAD AND CANVAS, MODEL AND PAINTING'

'Inspiration is often regarded as a *sine qua non* for creating good art, be it visual or oral. Regardless of its precise definition, inspiration is by no means diminished by use of modern recording technology. Creation requires imagination, and a successful musician and producer will be able to, if not create 'original' music, to recombine melody, rhythm and sound in a unique way. The performance of a piece of music occurs via a creative process that has been compared to other arts, notably painting. Colour corresponds to sound; brushes, to instruments; the canvas, to the recorder. Modern recording technology, though, allows more than creation – it allows *design*. To further the painting–music analogy, the recorder machinery is both sketchpad and canvas, model and painting – as shown by the following quotation from the recording process of a piece of popular rock music.

Drummer:	Is that 'popping' like it should?
Producer:	What do you mean 'popping'?
Drummer:	It sounds weak.
Producer:	What do you mean 'weak'? We got terminology problems here.
Drummer:	It doesn't sound 'thick' enough.
Producer:	Oh, thick (still not sure, turns to assistant producer). How does it sound to you?
Assistant Producer:	On the lean side of thick.
Producer: [makes an adjustment]	How does it sound now?
Drummer:	Yeah! What'd ya do?
Producer:	We thickened it. What else? Once we know what you're talking about, we can fix it.'

From: S. Jones (1992) *Rock Formation. Music, Technology, and Mass Communication*. Newbury Park, CA: Sage, pp. 162, 186. (The drummer/producer dialogue originally appeared in E. Kealy (1982) 'The Real Rock Revolution'. Unpublished doctoral thesis, Northwestern University, Evanston, IL.)

The general solution to the problem of the heavy dependency of popular culture on the economic system of society is, of course, *professionalization* – in principle the same solution which long ago was found by a number of practitioners of various skills and arts, ranging from philosophers and scientists to mid-wives and barber-surgeons. An important step in the professionalization process is the creation of an award system unique to the activities in hand. This problem was solved long ago in many other sectors of society than that of popular music, the best-known professional awards probably being the Nobel prizes (see Box 7.9). An attempt to raise the status of artists working within the popular music system is the Polar Music Prize, since 1992 awarded by the Swedish Academy of Music and originally donated by Stikkan Andersson, the very successful manager of the Swedish pop group ABBA, which was internationally well-known in the 1970s and early 1980s.

**BOX 7.9 ON THE VALUE OF PROFESSIONAL
INNOVATORS' AWARDS**

The Guttman scale for innovators' reward systems presented in Figure 5.5 (p. 134) offers what is called an 'ideal model' of various reward systems. As is the case with all formal models, its value lies in the simplified way it models reality. In reality, things are not quite as simple as the models, however. One problem with some innovators' reward systems is that there may be a more or less widespread feeling among the innovators that the *material* awards (salaries, pensions, etc.) do not really correspond to the great value inherent in the innovations produced by them. This may be the case not least, perhaps, in esoteric and more or less independent systems: among scientific and scholarly professions, for instance. Another problem may be that the *symbolic* awards may be felt to be less than adequate. This may be the case not least, perhaps, among sub-cultural and hetero-cultural systems – often mass-mediated systems of innovation: television, movies, etc.

One solution to the problem of balance between material and symbolic awards is offered by various systems of professional awards and prizes gradually having been established. These are, as a rule, distributed by the professional innovators themselves, by their own academies, by universities, professional organizations, etc. The ideal type of such professional awards and prizes is represented, of course, by the annual Nobel prizes in literature, physics, chemistry, physiology and medicine (see section 5.2). (In 1969, the Bank of Sweden inaugurated an 'Economic Prize in Memory of Alfred Nobel', awarded in accordance with the principles of the original Nobel prizes.)

The Nobel prizes were originally donated by the Swede, Alfred Nobel, the inventor of dynamite. Since 1901 they have been awarded by the Swedish Academy of Sciences, the Karolinska Institute of Medicine in Stockholm, the Swedish Academy of Literature and by the Norwegian Parliament. The decisions are always preceded by a long, complex and carefully monitored process of international nominations and peer evaluations, not infrequently covering many years.

continued

Each Nobel prize represents a considerable amount of money (in 1998 corresponding to about a million US dollars). In addition, the indirect economic effects of the drastically heightened professional standing brought about by the prize are considerable. Nevertheless, the status conferred on the receiver of a Nobel prize may well be more important than the money. Status becomes even more important, perhaps, when it comes to the awards and prizes distributed in mass-mediated, popular culture, the great stars of which make much more money than even an outstanding university professor does. There are numerous such awards and prizes, the internationally best known ones probably being the Oscars, the film awards which, since 1929, have been awarded by the US Academy of Motion Pictures, Arts and Sciences, and the television equivalent, the Emmy, which since 1949 has been awarded by the US Academy of Television Arts and Sciences. These awards are not directly accompanied with money.

Thus, as a rule, an internationally leading cinema star does make much more money than an internationally leading university professor, but the awards granted to both categories by their professional systems take note of this discrepancy. The direct monetary value of the Nobel prizes is much higher than that of the Oscars and the Emmys and similar prizes in popular culture. So is their general prestige.

7.7 Computerized international communication: the global village green?

Today, any serious discussion of international communications cannot refrain from dealing with *computerized international communication* (CIC). In addition to the professional communities which use CIC on a regular basis in their work, there are three types of CIC that are widely used: electronic email ('email'), the Internet and the World Wide Web (WWW) (see sections 2.3.4, 4.7.3 and 7.3).

The Internet, it will be remembered, is a large international network of computers. The WWW is a 'hypertext program' distributing text, sound and moving pictures over the Internet. Electronic mail travels on the Internet from one computer to another one, yet other computers act as various types of interface. Between them, the Internet, the WWW and electronic mail have revolutionized commercial, scientific and scholarly systems of communication in particular.

From her desk at home or in the office, the owner of the fashionable milliner's shop in Zürich can follow discussions of recent developments carried out at this or that discussion list serving a more or less widely defined business area; from the WWW she can download illustrated catalogues from the leading fashion magazines published anywhere in the world; and she can send her orders by email directly to the producing companies or to the wholesale business firms. If using a so-called putting-out system of manufacture (created during the early days of transition to industrialism, see page 103), she can use email to tell her homeworkers what to do the following week.

From his desk on the top floor of the Company Tower in Tokyo, the Director-General can send out his weekly electronic newsletter to the directors of the regional headquarters in the capital cities of countries on five continents, warning them that not only production figures but also sales figures must be increased. From her desk at the Department of Bio-chemistry, the Scandinavian university professor can carry on day-to-day contacts with colleagues in her international research group operating on two or more continents. Between them, drawing on the time differences between various zones of the globe, they may actually work 24 hours a day, for a week. Using a search engine (Box 7.10), the undergraduate student can find data pertinent to his college paper due next Wednesday and his teacher can check that the student hasn't plagiarized copy.

On the other hand, most, if not all, innovations have both positive and negative consequences. It has been shown, for instance, that use of the Internet has been associated with a decline in social involvement and an increase in feelings of loneliness. More generally, it should be mentioned that when an innovation is gradually being introduced within a system, it tends to widen the knowledge gaps between the haves and the have-nots (see sections 2.3.4 and 6.2). But it is also the case that knowledge gaps have a tendency gradually to close (although the closing time may vary substantially

---

BOX 7.10   THE BIG SIX SEARCH ENGINES

'Of all the search sites available today, these are especially impressive: Alta Vista, Excite, Hotbot, Infoseek, Lycos, and Yahoo. The Big Six have all been around for two or more years. Their creators know the Net and the Web and originally designed their sites and the underlying software with the primary goal of making searching as easy and painless as possible.

'The Big Six carry advertising . . . that's how they finance their operations and avoid having to charge subscription fees for the use of their services. . . .

'The Current buzzword is portal. The Big Six want to be thought of not just as search sites but as your portal to the Internet, the first place you visit whenever you go online. . . . Here's where to find them.

Alta Vista	www.altavista.com
Excite	www.excite.com
HotBot	www.hotbot.com
Infoseek	www.infoseek.com
Lycos	www.lycos.com
Yahoo	www.yahoo.com'.

From: A. and E. Glossbrenner (1999) *Search Engines for the World Wide Web* (2nd edn). Berkeley, CA: Peachpit Press.

from case to case). When internationally launched in the 1950s, the computer caused large knowledge gaps between the haves and the have-nots, both between and within countries, as did various systems of communication based on the computer. So did the Internet when launched some years ago. These knowledge gaps now seem to be closing, both nationally and internationally. As information and communication technologies continue to develop, new gaps of information and knowledge will no doubt arise in the future. But they, too, will be closed. Right now, a 'global village' is being created.

PART FOUR

THE FUTURE OF COMMUNICATION

8

The Future of Communication and Communication Research

'It's always difficult to make predictions. And especially about the future.'

Unknown philosopher

8.1 Some general tendencies

Forecasting is as much an art as a scholarly or scientific undertaking. Yet there is an easy way out. If asked about what things will be like tomorrow or the next year, the best way of answering often is, 'Much the same as today or this year.' Actually, this a criterion which is not all that easy to beat. Thus, it seems that future human communication will be much the same as today's communication. Another way of answering the question is, 'Much the same, only more of it.' When it comes to human communication, that's not a bad answer at all. 'Human communication will remain much the same, but there will be more of it.'

There will be more of it for at least two reasons. In the first place, there will be many more human beings around (since, in spite of massive efforts for birth control, etc., world population is still growing far too fast; see section 2.3.3). Talking is a favourite pastime of humankind, and chatting on the Internet offers increased possibilities for new and interesting ways of talking. Very probably there will also be more communication facilities available, and more powerful ones, adding new ways and means of making talking still more interesting. The MUDs discussed in section 4.7.3 offer telling examples of what, for better and for worse, may be waiting around the corner, even for rather private, individual communication. For organizational communication, such facilities will, of course, be more powerful, and more numerous.

In addition, increasing internationalization in all sectors of the Great Wheel of Culture in Society (see Figure 3.1 on p. 55) will continue to call for more, better and quicker means of international communication. Such developments have already been foreshadowed by communications in the economic sector, in which not only company stocks and shares but also money in all viable currencies are traded 24 hours a day, the trade moving from continent to continent, continually following the sun. Similar developments may be found in other areas, too.

Generally, it could be said that computerized business-to-business is growing very fast, especially so in areas such as banking and ticketing. In Sweden, for instance, Internet banking grew from a marginal phenomenon to a mass phenomenon within the space of a year. The banking world is now looking forward to personal advice being requested, supplied and received over the Internet. Banking will always be necessary, of course, but personal visits to the bank will be reduced to a minimum.

Not surprisingly, the very fabric of the Internet itself is to a large extent being marketed and sold over the Internet. A successful provider of Internet switches and routers allows buyers to decide which options to include in their products before placing the order, and the entire process is completed over the Internet. But also individual electronic shopping over the Internet is continually increasing, especially in areas such as books and other standardized goods. Some computerized markets are growing incredibly fast. The computerized bookshop, Amazon.com, for instance, became the third largest bookshop in the world within three years, and there are thousands like it.

Such computerized bookshops can have catalogues covering millions of books, so therefore are almost regarded as book-*brokers* rather than book-*sellers*. They can display their enormous book catalogues on the Internet and even send some book reviews to potential buyers. But as a rule they have no book stocks of their own. They just relay their order to centralized stores run by other business organizations. Their prices are not generally lower than those of the traditional bookshops. In spite of the rapid success of computerized book shopping, it has been estimated that perhaps as much as 90% of the total book market will remain in its present, traditional shape, although the total book market may be growing as a result of the computerization attempts. Plans for 'printing on demand' of rather special types of book have also been discussed and realized, and this approach may well be the shape of things to come. Daily shopping of groceries, etc. can also be carried by computer.

In other cases, too, the computerized 'shop' will act primarily as a broker between customers and wholesale trade organizations which distribute the goods directly to the customer. This type of shopping may draw on price differences between countries, the brokers forwarding the buyers' orders to a trader in a neighbouring country delivering the goods once a week – say, from Germany to Sweden, or *vice versa*. Complaints may turn out to be tricky things to handle in this type of business, of course. Also, impulsive orders may become an increasing problem – not least to the buyers, perhaps.

Cars represent another type of standardized product which is being sold over the Internet, especially new cars, of course. Large, computerized companies have contacts with hundreds of retail sellers in a given country. The customers shop over the Internet and finalize the purchase with the dealer closest to them to have the type of car in stock, at the best price. Even cars customized to the special preferences of a specific buyer may be sold that way, by companies such as, say, Volvo. These tendencies mean, of course, that the need for retail sellers is being reduced.

While the examples above represent highly standardized types of general consumer goods, very special types of goods are also about to find their niches on the Internet, for instance, highly specialized scientific or medical instruments or equipment for specialized activities, often carried out in relatively close-knit, international networks of professionals. As a rule, payment is made by traditional credit cards, of course.

Not surprisingly, the very fabric of the Internet itself is to a large extent being marketed and sold over the Internet. A successful provider of Internet switches and routers allows buyers to decide which options to include in their products before placing the order, and the entire process is completed over the Internet.

Then again, the amount of Internet shopping should not be exaggerated. It has been estimated, for instance, that 20% of Swedes have access to the Internet (1998). Around 20% of the Internet users are also Internet shoppers. Even information-related products, such as books, will rarely be sold over the Internet to more than a small percentage of the total book market. Even so, however, electronic shopping is an internationally important phenomenon. What is missing though, is an internationally recognized legal code for users of and buyers on the Internet, much like the maritime laws that regulate international shipping. Many international political and economic organizations, ranging from the United Nations to the European Union to international banking, to say, Consumers International are now active in finding ways and means to build and implement such a system of regulation.

The computer is the central element, of course, both *behind* and *in* these developments, just as it is in many of the new communication facilities. One way or the other, an increasing portion of human communication already has the computer as an integral element. This fact has created the enormous, ongoing process of change over the last couple of decades, sometimes called the 'communication revolution'. The communications revolution will no doubt strongly affect the future of all human communication. Consequently, it will also affect the future of *communication research*.

8.2 Scholarship and research in the area of computerized communication

Quite naturally, the future of communication research is closely related to the future of our general means of communication, including the new means of communication which have been provided by the Internet and the World Wide Web. These and related phenomena are products of advanced communication science and engineering. Very probably, computerized content analysis of computerized communication contents produced by a number of different organizations and individuals will form a growing portion of international communication research and scholarship.

All technological progress has both positive and negative effects on social and cultural phenomena in the surroundings, and that is true for technological progress in communication, too. Recent research, exemplified by some results presented in Box 8.1, suggests that although electronic communication systems of different size and complexity have no doubt increased the rate and amount of communication world-wide, they may also in the long run have some negative effects at the individual level, for instance, reducing face-to-face communication and increasing feelings of loneliness and isolation. Such tendencies have indeed already been observed in the type of research referred to, and in other types of research as well.

Also, all innovations when first introduced cause increasing 'knowledge gaps' between the haves and the have-nots – a necessary price, perhaps, for progress, but in many individual cases a rather high price to pay (see section 2.3.4). This type of argument is valid on the societal and international levels, too. It is sometimes expressed in terms of what has been called 'cultural lag'. For natural reasons, rich societies are quicker to use new communication developments to increase their wealth, thus widening the gaps between them and less wealthy societies, which have to lag behind in those initial phases of expensive development.

On the other hand, it could be argued that electronic communication may contribute to the maintenance and even expansion of what US social scientist Robert D. Putnam has called 'social capital': mutual trust between individuals and groups of individuals. Such social capital necessarily exists in all human societies, but to rather different extents. It is regarded as an important precondition not only for the development of societal wealth, but also for social welfare and individual well-being (see section 3.5.2 on social indicators). Hopefully, continually increasing world-wide individual, group, organizational and mass communication by way of the World Wide Web will increase mutual trust between and within individuals, groups, organizations and societies. It may thus increase social capital not only at the individual level, but also at the international societal level.

Obviously, the ongoing technological developments briefly discussed above will also affect science and scholarship, not least communication science and scholarship. A basic way in which communication science and scholarship will be affected is by the availability of vast amounts of computerized data on individual, group, organizational and societal communication and information which are continually being stored in computers around the world. Obviously, the fact that these vast amounts of communicatively-oriented information are computerized makes it far easier to study them, although it will call for new techniques of research, and much creative

BOX 8.1   INTERNET – FOR BETTER AND FOR WORSE

The Internet Paradox

'The Internet could change the lives of average citizens as much as did the telephone in the early part of the 20th century and television in the 1950s and 1960s. Researchers and social critics are debating whether the Internet is improving or harming participation in community life and social relationships. This research examined the social and psychological impact of the Internet on 169 people in 73 households during their first 1 to 2 years on-line. We used longitudinal data to examine the effects of the Internet on social involvement and psychological well-being. In this sample, the Internet was used extensively for communication. Nonetheless, greater use of the Internet was associated with declines in participants' communication with family members in the household, declines in the size of their social circle, and increases in their depression and loneliness. These findings have implications for research, for public policy, and for the design of technology.'

From: R. Kraut et al. (1998) 'Internet paradox: a social technology that reduces social involvement and psychological well-being?', *American Psychologist*, 53 (9): 1017–31.

A nation of strangers?

'Every new technology finds dour critics (as well as ebullient proponents). Communication technologies in particular can be seen as opening the doors to all varieties of social ills. When the telegraph, telephone and the automobile were in their infancy, each of these three earlier 'communication' technologies found vitriolic critics who said these 'instruments of the devil' would drastically alter society (which they did), with disastrous consequences for the quality of life and the moral order (readers may judge for themselves about this point). . . .

'The Internet is no exception to this rule. Indeed, it has stimulated so many commentators that not even the most indefatigable reader can stay abreast of the flood of speculation and opinion. Yet, as might be expected . . . one area in particular has been singled out for comment: the way the Internet affects social relationships generally and participation in community life in particular. . . . By contrast, optimists argue that genuinely meaningful communities can be established in cyberspace, and indeed even fostered via online communications. . . .

'In late 1995 we carried out a national random telephone survey which had among its objectives to: compare 'real-world' participation for Internet users and non-users, and to examine friendship creation via the Internet. . . .

'Based on our national snapshot, we found no support for the pessimistic theories of the effects of cyberspace on community involvement. When controlling for demographic differences between users and non-users, we found no statistical differences in participation rates in religious, leisure, and community organizations.

continued

'Moreover, the Internet appeared to augment existing traditional social connectivity. . . . Further, our survey suggests that the Internet is emerging as a medium for cultivating friendships which, in a majority of cases, lead to meetings in the real world. . . .

'In sum, although the "Jeffersonian ideal" may not be realized, a high proportion of Internet users are engaging in lots of social contact and communication with friends and family. . . .Far from creating a nation of strangers, the Internet is creating a nation richer in friendships and social relationships.'

From: J.E. Katz and P. Aspden (1997) 'A nation of strangers?', *Communications of the ACM*, 40 (12): 81–6.

First the TV, now computer Muds! What next?

'On any given evening, nearly eighty million people in the United States are watching television. The average American household has a television turned on more than six hours a day, reducing eye contact and conversation. Computers and the virtual worlds they provide are adding another dimension of mediated experience. Perhaps computers feel so natural because of their similarity to watching TV our dominant social experience for the past forty years. . . .

'In the postwar atomization of American social life, the rise of middle-class suburbs created communities of neighbors who often remained strangers. Meanwhile, as the industrial and economic base of urban life declined, downtown social spaces such as the neighborhood theater or diner were replaced by malls and cinema complexes in the outlying suburbs. In the recent past, we left our communities to commute to these distant entertainments; increasingly, we want entertainment that commutes right into our homes. In both cases, the neighborhood is bypassed. We seem to be in the process of retreating further into our homes, shopping for merchandise in catalogues or on television channels for companionship in personal ads.

'Technological optimists think that computers will reverse some of this social atomization; they tout virtual experience and virtual community as ways for people to widen their horizons. But is it really sensible to suggest that the way to revitalize community is to sit alone in our rooms, typing at our networked computers and filling our lives with virtual friends? . . .

'Josh is a 23-year-old College graduate who lives in a small studio apartment in Chicago. . . . Josh has had to settle for a job working on the inventory records at a large discount store. He considers this a dead end. When a friend told him about MUDs, he gave them a try and within a week stepped into a new life.

'Now, eight months later, Josh spends as much time on MUDs as he can. He belongs to a class of players who sometimes call themselves Internet Hobos. . . . His programming on MUDs is far more intellectually challenging than his day job. . . . Within MUDs, Josh serves as a programming consultant to many less experienced players and has even become something of an entrepreneur. . . .

continued

'MUDs play a similar role for Thomas, 24 . . . : "MUDs make me more what I really am. Off the MUD, I am not as much me." . . .

'The stories of these MUDders point to a whole set of issues about the political and social dimension of virtual community. These young people feel they have no political voice, and they look to cyberspace to help find them one.'

From: S. Turkle (1996) 'Virtuality and its discontents', *The American Prospect*, 24 (Winter): 50–7. (Based on Turkle, S. (1995) *Life on the Screen*. New York: Simon & Schuster.)

thinking about the best ways to go about it all. Some examples of such research are offered in Box 8.1. Many more could be given. And in a few years' time this type of research will have formed new, dynamic traditions of research, often themselves developing on the Internet. Future textbooks will present, discuss and criticize such research. Some of these books will come to their readership, perhaps, directly out of the computer. But the book will live on. So will the primeval forms of individual, group, organizational and societal communication.

References

In the list of references and sources below, the reader will find references to books and other publications which have been quoted, referred to or otherwise used as more or less direct sources of knowledge in the running text of this book. In the list of recommended reading, some general suggestions for further reading are presented. The communications literature is immense, and no individual has it all at his or her fingertips. All such lists therefore must, of necessity, be limited by the horizons of their authors.

References and Sources

Ahrne, G. (1994) *Social Organizations*. London: Sage.

Andersen, R.E., Crespo, C.J., Bartlett, S.J., Cheskin, L.J. and Pratt, M. (1998) 'Relationship of physical activity and television watching with body weight and level of fatness among children', *Journal of the American Medical Association*, 279 (12): 938–42.

Bales, Robert F. (1976) *Interaction Process Analysis. A Method for the Study of Small Groups*. Chicago: University of Chicago Press.

Banks, J. (1997) 'MTV and the globalization of popular culture', *Gazette*, 59 (1): 43–60.

Bible, The Revised English (1990) Cambridge: Cambridge University Press.

Biehl, M. et al. (1997) 'Matsumoto and Ekman's Japanese and Caucasian Facial Expressions of Emotion (JACFEE): reliability data and cross-national differences', *Journal of Nonverbal Behavior*, 21 (1): 3–21.

Blumler, J.G. (1989) 'Pressure group', in E. Barnouw, G. Gerbner and N. Schramm (eds), *International Encyclopedia of Communications*. New York and Oxford: Oxford University Press. 3: 350–1.

Bok, S. (1978) *Lying: Moral Choice in Public and Private Life*. New York: Pantheon Books.

Borgatta, E.F. and Borgatta, M.L. (eds) (1992) *Encyclopedia of Sociology*. New York: Macmillan.

Borgman, C.L. (ed.) (1990) *Scholarly Communication and Bibliometrics*. London: Sage.

Brown, R. (1986) *Social Psychology* (2nd edn). New York and London: The Free Press.

Buller, D.B. and Burgoon, J.K. (1996) 'Interpersonal deception theory', *Communication Theory*, 6 (3): 203–42.

Burrell, G. and Morgan, G. (1979) *Sociological Paradigms and Organisational Analysis*. London: Heineman.

Cavalli-Sforza, L.L. and Cavalli-Sforza, F. (1995) *The Great Human Diasporas. The History of Diversity and Evolution*. Reading, MA: Addison-Wesley.

Chaffee, S.H., McLeod, J.M. and Wackman, D.B. (1971) 'Parental influences on adolescent media use', *American Behavioral Scientist*, 14: 323–40.

Curtis, P. (1996) 'Mudding: social phenomena in text-based virtual realities', in M. Stefik (ed.), *Internet Dreams. Archetypes, Myths and Metaphors*. Cambridge, MA, and London: The MIT Press. pp. 265–92.

Forester, C.S. (1937/1975) *The Happy Return*. London: Penguin.

Gillet, S.E. and Kapor, M. (1997) 'The self-governing Internet: coordination by design', in B. Kahin and J.H. Keller (eds), *Coordinating the Internet*. Cambridge, MA: The MIT Press. pp. 4–38.

Glossbrenner, A. and Glossbrenner, E. (1999) *Search Engines for the World Wide Web* (2nd edn). Berkeley, CA: Peachpit Press.

Golding, W. (1955) *The Inheritors*. London: Faber & Faber.

Gunter, B. (1997) *Measuring Bias on Television*. Luton: University of Luton Press.

Hadenius, S. and Weibull, L. (1997) *Massmedier. En bok om press, radio och TV* (6th edn). Stockholm: Bonnier Alba.

Hellman, H. (1999) *From Companies to Competitors. The Changing Broadcasting Markets and Television Programming in Finland*. Tampere: University of Tampere Press.

Hillve, P., Majanen, P. and Rosengren, K.E. (1998) 'Quality in Programming', *European Journal of Communication*, 12(3): 291–318.

Hofstede, G. (1991) *Cultures and Organizations: Software of the Mind*. London: McGraw-Hill.

Horwath, C.W. (1995) 'Biological origins of communicator style', *Communication Quarterly*, 43 (4): 394–407.

Ishikawa, S. (1996) *Quality Assessment of Television*. Luton: Luton University Press.

Johanson, D.C. and Edey, M.A. (1982) *Lucy. The Beginnings of Humankind*. London: Granada Publishing.

Johnsson-Smaragdi, U. (1994) 'Models of change and stability in adolescents' media use', in K.E. Rosengren (ed.), *Media Effects and Beyond: Culture, Socialization and Lifestyles*. London and New York: Routledge. pp. 97–130.

Johnsson-Smaragdi, U. and Jönsson, A. (1994) 'Self-evaluation in ecological perspective: neighbourhood, family and peers, schooling and media use', in K.E. Rosengren (ed.), *Media Effects and Beyond: Culture, Socialization and Lifestyles*. London and New York: Routledge. pp. 150–82.

Jones, S. (1992) *Rock Formation. Music, Technology, and Mass Communication*. Newbury Park, CA: Sage.

Joyce, J. (1922/1986) *Ulysses* (The Corrected Text). London: Penguin Books.

Katz, J.E. and Aspden, P. (1997) 'A nation of strangers?', *Communications of the ACM*, 40 (12): 81–6.

Kealy, E. (1982) 'The real rock revolution', unpublished doctoral thesis. Evanston, IL: Northwestern University.

Kiewitz, C., Weaver, J.B., Brosius, H.B. and Weimann, G. (1997) 'Cultural differences in listening style preferences', *International Journal of Public Opinion Research*, 9 (3): 233–47.

Kraut, R. et al. (1998) 'Internet paradox: a social technology that reduces social involvement and psychological well-being?', *American Psychologist*, 53 (9): 1017–31.

Lauristin, M. and Vihalemm, P. (1997) 'Recent historical developments in Estonia: three stages of transition (1987–1997)', in M. Lauristin and P. Vihalemm with K.E. Rosengren and L. Weibull (eds), *Return to the Western World. Cultural and Political Perspectives on the Estonian Post-Communist Transition*. Tartu: Tartu Universtiy Press. pp. 73–126.

Leaves, L.J., Eysenck, H.J. and Martin, N.G. (1989) *Genes, Culture and Personality*. London: Academic Press.

Liska, Jo (1953) 'Bee Dances', *Western Journal of Communication*, 57: 1–26.

Luft, J. (1984) *Group Processes. An Introduction to Group Dynamics*. Mountain View, CA: Mayfield Publishing Co.

Mintzberg, H. (1993) *Structure in Fives. Designing Effective Organizations*. Englewood Cliffs, NJ: Prentice-Hall.

Moberg, V. (1959) *Unto a Good Land*. Stockholm, Bonniers.

Ogden, C.K. and Richards, I.A. (1923/1994) *The Meaning of Meaning*. London: Routledge.

Osgood, C.E. (1975) *Cross-Cultural Universals of Affective Meaning*. Urbana, IL: University of Illinois Press.

Osgood, C.E., Suci, G.J. and Tannenbaum, P.H. (1957) *The Measurement of Meaning*. Urbana, IL: University of Illinois Press.

Orwell, G. (1999) *Nineteen Eighty Four*. London: Martin Secker & Warburg.

Peters, T.J. and Waterman, R.H., Jr (1984) *In Search of Excellence*. New York: Harper & Row.

Reid, E. (1995) 'Virtual worlds: culture and imagination', in S.G. Jones (ed.), *Cybersociety. Computer-mediated Communication and Community*. Thousand Oaks, CA: Sage. pp. 164–83.

Rogers, E.M. (1995) *Diffusion of Innovations*. New York: The Free Press.

Rokeach, M. (1973) *The Nature of Human Values*. New York: The Free Press.

Rosengren, K.E. (1984) 'Cultural indicators for the comparative study of culture', in G. Melischek, K.E. Rosengren and J. Stappers (eds), *Cultural Indicators: An International Symposium*. Vienna: Akademie der Wissenschaften. pp. 11–32.

Rosengren, K.E. (1987) 'News diffusions. A special issue', *European Journal of Communication*, 2: 2.

Rosengren, K.E. (ed.) (1994a) *Media Effects and Beyond. Culture, Socialization and Lifestyles*. London and New York: Routledge.

Rosengren, K.E. (1994b) 'Culture, media and society', in K.E. Rosengren (ed.), *Media Effects and Beyond. Culture, Socialization and Lifestyles*. London and New York: Routledge. pp. 3–28.

Rosengren, K.E. (1994c) 'Media use under structural change', in *Media Effects and Beyond. Culture, Socialization and Lifestyles*. London and New York: Routledge. pp. 49–75.

Rosengren, K.E. (1995) 'Three perspectives on media and communication studies in Europe', in P. Winterhoff-Spurk (ed.), *Psychology of Media in Europe. The State of the Art – Perspectives for the Future*. Opladen: Westdeutscher Verlag. pp. 15–29.

Rosengren, K.E. (1997) 'Different sides of the same coin. Access and gatekeeping', *Nordicom Review*, 18 (2): 3–12.

Rosengren, K.E. (1998) 'The climate of literature: a sea change?', *Poetics*, 25: 311–26.

Rosengren, K.E. and Arvidson, P. (1997) *Sociologisk Metodik* (4edn). Stockholm: Almqvist and Wiskell.

Rosengren, K.E. and Windahl, S. (1989) *Media Matter: TV Use in Childhood and Adolescence*. Norwood, NJ: Ablex.

Rosengren, K.E., Arvidson, P. and Sturesson, D. (1978) 'The Barsebäck Panic', in C. Winick (ed.), *Deviance and Mass Media*. Beverly Hills, CA: Sage. pp. 131–49.

Rosengren, K.E., Johnsson-Smaragdi, U. and Sonesson, I. (1994) 'For better and for worse: effects studies and beyond', in K.E. Rosengren (ed.), *Media Effects and Beyond. Culture, Socialization and Lifestyles*. London and New York: Routledge. pp. 133–49.

Rosengren, K.E., Gustafsson, G., Pettersson, T., Dahlgren, C. and Linderman, A. (1999) *Från Text Till Data*. Lund: Universitetstryckeriet.

Shakespeare, W. (1599/1968) *As You Like It*, Act 2, Scene 7, l. 139. Harmondsworth: Penguin.

Smith, A. (1776/1976) *The Wealth of Nations*. London: Penguin Books.

Taylor, F.W. (1998) *The Principles of Scientific Management* (2nd edn). Rochester, NY: Institute of Industrial Engineers.

Toffler, A. (1985) *The Adaptive Corporation*. Aldershot: Gower.

Turkle, S. (1995) *Life on the Screen*. New York: Simon & Schuster.

Turkle, S. (1996) 'Virtuality and its discontents', *The American Prospect*, 24 (Winter): 50–7. Based on Turkle (1995).

Twain, Mark and Neider, Charles (ed.) (1959) *The Autobiography of Mark Twain*. New York: HarperPerennial Library.

Whyte, W.H., Jr (1956) *The Organization Man*. Harmondsworth: Penguin.

Recommended reading

Dictionaries, encyclopedias, handbooks, yearbooks

Barnouw, E., Gerbner, G. and Schramm, W. et al. (eds) (1989) *International Encyclopedia of Communications* (4 vols). New York and Oxford: Oxford University Press.

Berger, C.R. and Chaffee. S.H. (eds) (1987) *Handbook of Communication Science*. Newbury Park, CA: Sage.

Communication Yearbook (1977–)(published annually for the International Communication Association). Newbury Park, CA, and London: Sage.

Goldhaber, G.M. and Barnett, G.A. (eds) (1988) *Handbook of Organizational Communication*. Norwood, NJ.: Ablex.

Knapp, M.L. and Miller, G.R. (eds) (1994) *Handbook of Interpersonal Communication* (2nd edn). Thousand Oaks, CA, and London: Sage.

Watson, J. and Hill, A. (1993) *A Dictionary of Communication and Media Studies*. London: Edward Arnold.

Human communication in general

Burgoon, M., Hunsaker, F. and Dawson, E.J. (1994) *Human Communication* (3rd edn). Thousands Oaks, CA: Sage.

Cobley, P. (ed.) (1996) *The Communication Theory Reader*. London: Routledge.

Crowley, D.Y. and Mitchell, D. (eds) (1994) *Communication Theory Today*. Oxford: Polity Press.

Fang, I. (1997) *A History of Mass Communication. Six Information Revolutions*. Boston, MA: Focal Press.

Littlejohn, S.W. (1996) *Theories of Human Communication* (5th edn). Belmont, CA: Wadsworth.

Mattelart, A. and Mattelart, M. (1998) *Theories of Communication. A Short Introduction*. Thousand Oaks, CA, and London: Sage.

Severin, W.J. and Tankard, J.W. (1992) *Communication Theories: Origins, Methods, and Uses*. New York: Longman.

Tubbs, S.L. and Moss, S. (1994) *Human Communication* (7th edn). New York: McGraw-Hill.

Interpersonal and group communication

Frey, L.R. and Barge, J.K. (eds) (1997) *Communication in Decision-Making Groups*. Boston and New York: Houghton Mifflin Company.

Gudykunst, W.B. (1998) *Bridging Differences. Effective Intergroup Communication* (3rd edn). Thousand Oaks, CA, and London: Sage.

Hartley, P. (1997) *Group Communication*. London: Routledge.

Hirokawa, R.Y. and Poole, M.S. (eds) (1996) *Communication and Group Decision Making*. Thousand Oaks, CA: Sage.

Knapp, M.L. and Miller, G.R. (eds) (1994) *Handbook of Interpersonal Communication* (2nd edn). Thousand Oaks, CA, and London: Sage.

Nussbaum, J.F. and Coupland, J. (eds) (1995) *Handbook of Communication and Aging Research*. Mahwah, NJ: Erlbaum Associates.

O'Keefe, D.J. (1990) *Persuasion Theory and Research*. Newbury Park, CA: Sage.

Strate, L., Jacobson, R. and Gibson, S.B. (eds) (1996) *Communication and Cyberspace. Social Interaction in an Electronic Environment*. Cresskill, NJ: Hampton Press.

Trenholm, S. and Jensen, A. (1992) *Interpersonal Communication* (2nd edn). Belmont, CA: Wadsworth.

Organizational communication

Beairsto, J.A.B. (1997) *Leadership in the Quest for Adhocracy: New Directions for a Postmodern World*. Tampere, Finland: University of Tampere Press.

Deetz, S. (1995) *Transforming Communication – Transforming Business. Building Responsive and Responsible Workplaces*. Cresskill, NJ: Hampton Press.

Goldhaber, G.M. and Barnett, G.A. (eds) (1988) *Handbook of Organizational Communication*. Norwood, NJ: Ablex.

Grunig, J.E. (1992) *Excellence in Public Relations and Communication Management*. Hillsdale, NJ: Erlbaum Associates.

Kreps, G.L. (1990) *Organizational Communication: Theory and Practice* (2nd edn). New York: Longman.

Miller, K. (1995) *Organizational Communication. Approaches and Processes*. Belmont, CA, and London: Wadsworth.

Stohl, C. (1995) *Organizational Communication. Connectedness in Action*. Thousand Oaks, CA, and London: Sage.

Windahl, S., Signitzer, B.H. and Olson, J.T. (1992) *Using Communication Theory. An Introduction to Planned Communication*. London: Sage.

Mass communication

Barker, M. and Petely, J. (eds) (1997) *Ill Effects. The Media/Violence Debate*. London: Routledge.

Bryant, J. and Zillmann, D. (eds) (1994) *Media Effects: Advances in Theory and Research*. Hillsdale, NJ: Erlbaum Associates.

Carter, C., Branston, G. and Allan, S. (eds) (1998) *News, Gender and Power*. London and New York: Routledge.

Ettema, J.S. and Whitney, D.C. (eds) (1994) *Audiencemaking. How the Media Create the Audience*. London: Sage.

Glasser, T.L. and Salmon, C.T. (eds) (1995) *Public Opinion and the Communication of Consent*. New York: Guilford Press.

Lowery, S. and DeFleur, M.L. (eds) (1995) *Milestones in Mass Communication Research: Media Effects* (3rd edn). White Plains, NY: Longman.

McCombs, M., Shaw, D.L. and Weaver, D. (eds) (1997) *Communication and Democracy. Exploring the Intellectual Frontiers in Agenda Setting Theory*. Mahwah, NJ: Erlbaum Associates.

McQuail, D. (1992) *Media Performance. Mass Communication and the Public Interest*. Newbury Park, CA, and London: Sage.

McQuail, D. and Windahl, S. (1995) *Communication Models for the Study of Mass Communication*. London: Longman.

O'Sullivan, T., Dutton, B. and Rainer, Ph. (1998) *Studying the Media. An Introduction* (2nd edn). London: Edward Arnold.

Severin, W.J. and Tankard, J.W. (eds) (1997) *Communication Theories. Origins, Methods, and Uses in the Mass Media* (4th edn). New York: Longman.

International communication

Archer, C. (1992) *International Organizations* (2nd edn). London and New York: Routledge.

Archer, C., Asante, M.K. and Gudykunst, W.B. (eds) (1989) *Handbook of International and Intercultural Communication*. Newbury Park, CA: Sage.

Blumler, J.G., McLeod, J.M. and Rosengren, K.E. (eds) (1992) *Comparatively Speaking: Communication and Culture across Space and Time* (*Sage Annual Reviews of Communication Research*, 19). Newbury Park, CA, and London: Sage.

Boyd-Barrett, O. and Rantanen, T. (1998) *The Globalisation of News*. London: Sage.

Burnett, R. (1996) *The Global Jukebox. The International Music Industry*. London: Routledge.

Golding, P. and Harris, P. (1997) *Beyond Cultural Imperialism. Globalization, Communication and the New International Order*. London: Sage.

Gudykunst, W.B. and Kim, Y.Y. (1997) *Communicating with Strangers. An Approach to Intercultural Communication* (3rd edn). Boston, MA: McGraw-Hill.

Hamelink, C.J. (1994) *The Politics of World Communication. A Human Rights Perspective*. London: Sage.

Herman, E.S. and McChesney, R.W. (1997) *The Global Media. The New Missionaries of Corporate Capitalism*. London: Cassell.

Lull, J. (1995) *Media, Communication, Culture. A Global Approach*. Oxford: Polity Press.

Mowlana, H., Gerbner, G. and Schiller, H.I. (1992) *Triumph of the Image. The Media's War in the Persian Gulf – A Global Perspective*. Boulder, CO: Westview Press.

The future of communication

Barrett, D.J. (1997) *Net Research: Finding Information Online*. Sebastopol, CA: Songline Studios.

Bradley, Ph. (1997) *Going Online, CD-ROM and the Internet*. London: Aslib.

Glossbrenner, A. and Glossbrenner, E. (1999) *Search Engines for the World Wide Web* (2nd edn). Berkeley, CA: Peachpit Press.

Jones, S.G. (ed.) (1997) *Virtual Culture: Identity and Communication in Cybersociety*. London: Sage.

Kahin, B. and Keller, J.H. (eds) (1997) *Coordinating the Internet*. Cambridge, MA, and London: The MIT Press.

Lynch, D.C. and Lundquist, L. (1996) *Digital Money. The New Era of Internet Commerce*. New York: John Wiley & Sons.

Porter, D. (ed.) (1997) *Internet Culture*. New York and London: Routledge.

Stefik, M. (ed.) (1996) *Internet Dreams*. Cambridge, MA, and London: The MIT Press.

Name Index

Adler, A., 21
Adorno, T.W., 24
Ahrne, G., 106
Annan, Kofi, 71
Arvidson, P., 89
Aristotle, 3

Bales, R.F., 93ff.
Banks, J., 193
Biehl, M., 180
Bildt, C., 71
Blair, T., 113
Blumler, J.G., 136
Bok, S., 34
Borgman, C.L., 148
Brown, R., 39
Buller, D.B., 34
Burgoon, J.K., 34

Cantril H., 24
Cavalli-Sforza, L.L. and F., 68
Chaplin, Sir Charles, 115, 142

Darwin, C., 39
Dickson, W.J., 115
Dietrich, M., 142

Eysenck, H.J., 77

Fayol, H., 113
Forester, C.S., 118

Garbo, G., 142
Gerbner, G., 145
Glossbrenner, A. & E., 197
Goebbels, J., 73
Granovetter, M., 95
Grice, H.P., 35
Gutenberg, J., 43, 139
Guttman, L., 80, 195

Habermas, J., 145
Hammarskjöld, D., 71, 179
Hertz, H., 141

Hitler, A., 73, 178, 181
Hofstede, G., 126ff.
Hovland, C., 24
Huxley, A., 115

Johnsson-Smaragdi, U., 153
Jones, S., 194
Joyce, J., 75

Kealy, E., 194.

Lasswell, H.D., 24
Lazarsfeld, P.F., 24
Leaves, L.J., 77
Lenin, 181
Levinson, S., 193
Linnæus, C., 3

Mao-Tse-Tung, 178
Marconi, G., 141
Martin, N.G., 77
Marx, K., 9, 56ff., 113
Maxwell, J., 141
Mayo, E., 115
McCombs, M.E., 145
Milgram, S., 96
Mintzberg, H., 122
Moberg, V., 175
Moreno, J.L., 88
Morse, S., 141
Moses, 109

Neider, C., 34
Nobel, A., 195
Noelle-Neumann, E., 145

Orwell, G., 115, 178
Osgood, C.R., 59

Park, R., 24
Peters, T.J., 123
Plato, 42, 110

Reath, Sir John, 141

Roethlisberger, W.J., 115
Roosevelt, F.D., 71, 145

Schiller, F., 55
Shakespeare, W., 79, 182
Shaw, D., 145
Simmel, G., 22
Smith, A., 112
Socrates, 42

Taylor, F.W., 113
Toffler, A., 123
Twain, M., 34

Waterman, R.H., 123
Weber, M., 20, 22, 113ff.
Whyte, W.H., 108
Windahl, S., 153

Subject Index

Académie Francaise, 11
access, 51, 148ff.
action, 36 f., 56
adhocracy, 121 ff.
adoption of innovations, 131, 133, 135
advertisements, 193
advertizing, 131, 135
Africa, 174, 176
agenda setting, 144ff.
advertisement, 193
advertising, 35, 131
age, 78
agency, 61ff.
agenda setting, 20
alphabet, 41
   binary, 43
apes, 30
AR (administrative rationalization), 111
art, 55, 57
articulation, double, 31
awards, material and symbolic, 195ff.

Balkans, the, 176
Basques, the, 172
behaviour, 36ff.
BBC, 141
Bible, the, 4, 76, 109, 149
   Gutenberg, 139
BIGO (Business International
      Governmental Organization), 184
BINGO (Business International
      Non-governmental Organization), 110,
      183ff.
biology, 15
blues, 194
bonobos apes, 30
book media, 139
brain, human, 6, 27ff., 59ff., 75ff., 121, 139
bureaucracy, 41

Chamber of Commerce, International, 184
Cheka, the, 111
chimpanzees, 28, 30

China, 176
Church, Roman Catholic, 107, 113
circumplex, 55
cinema film, 142
citation analysis, 148
cities, 47, 170
class, social, 1, 79
classification, 3
clique, 89
code, 30ff.
coalitions, international, 170
collectivism, 126, 181
common sense, 1
communication
   apprehension, 77
   arenas of, 171
   computerized, 196
   defining factor, 48
   direction of, 48
   dyad, 84
   face-to-face, 56, 180
   formalized, 40
   functions of, 45
   group, 86ff., 170
   human, definition of, 38
   individual, 70ff., 170
   intercultural, 170ff.
   international, 56, 71, 170ff.
   interpersonal, 56, 70ff., 170, 179ff.
   'interpersonal mass', 73
   intra-individual, 46, 70, 170
   levels of, 171
   mass, 56, 138ff.
   mediated, 40ff., 56
   national, 56
   non-verbal, 38ff.
   oral, 140
   organizational, 56, 105ff.
   patterns of, 48ff.
   political, 18
   satellites, 143
   social psychology of, 18
   societal, 47
   sociology of, 18

communication *cont.*
  style of, 81
  verbal, 38ff.
communication studies, 16
communicative structure, 72
community, 47, 170, 181
  virtual, 47
computer, 5, 43, 87, 139ff.
  science, 13
computerization, 5
concept, 3
conceptual space, 3
conceptualize, conceptualization, 3
confession, 84
conflict, 5, 9
  international, 170
connotation, 59
consciousness, 33, 36
  stream of, 74
consensus, 5, 9
consultation, 49
consumer research, 131
context, 182
conversation, 49
country/ies, 1
cube of humanities and social sciences,
    10ff., 25
cultivation research, 144ff.
culture, 25, 56, 65, 170ff., 180
  climate of, 117, 129
  cuneiforms, 41
  Great Wheel of, 55ff., 109, 130, 146
  heritage of, 174
  high-context, 182
  international popular, 191ff.
  low-context, 182
  youth, 193
cybernetics, 13

data, 18ff., 22
  intra and extra media, 190ff.
deception, 34ff.
democracies, capitalist, 181
denotation, 59
diffusion, 131ff., 142
  of news, 20, 184ff.
disciplines
  empirical, 15
  formal, 15
displacement of goals, 125
display rules, 83
diversity in TV programming, 150ff.
dolphins, 33
dreams, 76
'Du Reform', the, 179

dyad, 84, 87

ecology, 15ff.
economics, 16
economy, 55
education, 79
electro-magnetic waves, 1
elephants, 33
Emmy (TV award), 196
epidemics, 133
equality, 101
espionage, 111
ethos, 11, 55
evolution, 27ff.
exclamation, 49
explanation, 4
extraversion, 76

family, 13, 90–1, 106ff., 181
family communication climate, 91–3, 126
family therapy, 85
fax machine, 100
femininity, 126
FIFA (Fédération Internationale de Football
    Associations), 107
forms of life, 62
freedom, 181

gaps of information, 44
gaps of knowledge, 198
gatekeeper, gatekeeping, 14, 51, 95, 130,
    146, 148ff.
gender, 79
generalization, 19
genotype, 29
Germany, 181, 192
Gestapo, 111
global village, 198
globalization, 193
God, 4
graffiti, 104
grapevine, 96, 116ff.
group, 53, 86ff., 170, 181
group communication, functions of, 93ff.
group leadership, 91
group structure, 88
Guttman scale, 80, 195
Gypsies, the, 172

Hanse, the 110, 125, 183
heritage, genetical and cultural, 174
hieroglyphics, 41
Hollywood, 142
hominids, 27ff., 31
homo, 27ff., 31,

homo neanderthalensis, 27ff.
homo sapiens, 1, 27ff., 33, 173
HTTP, 102
Human Relations School, 115ff.
humanism, radical, 9

IAMCR (International Association of
    Communication Research), 24
ICA (International Communication
    Association), 24ff.
icon, 30, 33, 40
idealism, 57
IGO (International Governmental
    Organization), 183
illocution, 45
ILO (International Labor Organization),
    107
incidence, 132
index, 30ff.
India, 174
indicators, societal, 66ff.
    cultural, 66ff.
    economic, 66
    social, 66
individual, human, 5, 70
individualism, 126ff., 181
individualization, 25, 46, 78
individuation, 25, 46, 74, 78
indoctrination, 177
industrialization, 112, 140
information, 30
    concept of, 43
    science, 30
INGO (International Non-Governmental
    Organization), 183
ingroup, 181
inhibition, 83
innovation, 64ff., 131ff., 191ff.
innovativeness, 68
insects, 33
institution, 12
interaction, 36
Internet, 101ff., 131ff., 196ff.
intersubjectivity, 36
intraversion, 76ff.
irony, 33
ITU (International Telegraphic Union),
    107

Japan, 192
Johari Window, the, 83, 85
journalistics, 13

kilobyte, 43
Korean War, 176

Kurds, the, 172

lack of knowledge, specified, 84
language, 30ff.
language human, 33ff.
law, 13
    Faculty of, 17
League of Nations, 176
Leninism, 9
Liberalism, 113
lies, lying, 33ff.
lifestyle
    definition of, 62
    research, 21ff.
linguistics, 5, 13
literacy, general, 140ff., 149
literary traditions, growth and decline,
    147ff.
literature, 55
    climate of, 147ff.
lobbying, 135ff.
logic, 15
logos, 11, 55
long-term/short-term orientation, 126

MacBride Report, the, 176
mafia, 111
mammals, 27
maps, mental, 186ff.
marriage, 90
Marxism, 9, 113
masculinity, 126
masking, 83
Masonic Order, the, 111
materialism, 57
mathematics, 15
meaning, 32, 58ff.
    meaning of, 59
media and communication studies, 13
media economy, chairs of, 18
medicine, 15
    faculty of, 17
media, book, 139
media, mass, 138ff.
    individual use of, 152ff.
        among young people, 153ff.
    ownership concentration, 150
    ownership integration, 150
Media Panel Program, 153ff.
media, periodic, 139
megabyte, 43
megalomania, 117ff.
Middle East, the, 176
migration, 173ff.
Minitel, 100

mobility, individual, 170
model(s), 5, 18ff., 22ff.
    ideal, 113, 195
    of organization, 118ff.
    verbal, 113ff.
modem, 44, 100
moral choice, 34
Mormons, the, 174
morphem, 31
motivation research, 131
movements, social, 13
MTV, 193
MUDs (multi-user dungeons), 103
municipality, 47
music
    jazz, 194
    popular, 192ff.
    rock, 194
musical, 142

nation, 1, 47
nationality, 79ff., 171
Neanderthals, 31ff.
neighbourhood, 181
networks, 46, 108
network analysis, 86, 89
neuroticism, 76
New Guinea, 42
news
    hard, 185
    diffusion of, 144ff., 184ff.
    international, 190ff.
newspaper studies, 24
newspapers, 21
Nobel Prizes, 110, 195

object, 37
objectivism, 9
occupation, 79
Öffentlichkeit, 145ff.
'omnivore' of media content, 150
ontogeny, 78
operetta, 142
order, 49
organization, 13, 54, 105–137
    divisions of, 121
    formal/informal, 114
    governmental, 183
    international, 170, 177, 182
    line, 120
    matrix, 120
    models of, 118ff.
    non-governmental, 183
    product, 120
    social, 181

'organization man', 108
organizational communication, 116ff., 170
Oscars, 196
Osgood scale, 59ff.

Pakistan, 174
panics, moral, 24
Papal Bull, 176
parchment, 1, 138
pathetic fallacy, 36
pathos, 11, 55
pedagogy, 13
peer group, 13, 68
periodic media, 139
personality, 72, 76, 79, 177
phenotype, 29
philology, 13
philosophy, faculty of, 17
phoneme, 31
phonology, 31
phylogeny, 78
physiology, 38
pictograms, 41
pilgrims, 99
political science, 16ff.
politics, 56
power, 55
power distance, 126
pragmatics, 31
praxis, 11, 55
pressure groups, 136
prevalence, 132
primates, 27
printing, invention of, 43, 138ff.
propaganda, 35, 178
    international, 176ff.
psychology, 16
    of organizations, 116
public relations, 130ff.
publicity, 35
putting-out system, 103, 196

quartet, 87
quintet, 87

race, 29
radio, 1ff., 141
rationality, limited, 116
readability, 140
reception analysis, 21ff.
reciprocity norms, 86
recording technology, 194
refugees, 174
registration, 49
religion, 13, 56

report, 49
re-socialization, 177
reward systems, 133ff.
rhetorics, 23
rites of passage, 143
roles, social, 78
Roman Catholic Church, 107, 113
Romani ('Gypsies'), 172
rumours, 96ff., 117

Salvation Army, the, 113
Sami people, the, 172
samples, representative, 23
schizophrenia, 77
scholarship, 1, 3ff., 9, 55ff.
schooling, compulsory, 139, 141
science, 1, 3ff., 15, 56
   behavioural, 5, 9
   social, 2, 5, 9
scrolls, 138
S-curve, 132
search engines, 102, 197
self-deception, 33
self-reflection, 35
semantic differential, 59
semantic space, 59
semantics, 31
Shi Huangdi, 10
sign, 1, 29ff.
signal, 30ff.
Singing Revolution, the, 73
sleep, REM, 76
small world problem, 96
social, 1, 72
socialization, 12ff., 16, 25, 58ff., 68, 91ff.,
   177
   agents of, 12ff., 48, 57, 60ff., 68, 144
   animal, 58
   types of, 64
socialization research, approaches in, 64
social movements, 13
sociology, 16
societal, 72
society, 47,
   pre-historic, 72
sociogram, 88ff., 108, 114
sociology, 16
sociometry, 53, 88ff., 108
South America, 176
Soviet Union, the, 176, 181, 192
space, 14, 177
speech acts, 45ff., 49, 93ff.
spiral of silence, 20, 144ff.
Stalinism, 9
states, 47

statistics, 15
structuralism, radical, 9
structure, 61ff.
structure, communicative, 72
subject, 37
subjectivism, 9
symbol, 1, 29ff., 40
symptom, 29ff.
syntax, 31
system, 11, 53
   cultural, 54
   social, 54
   material, 54

technology, 15, 56
telegraph, 99
telephone conference, 99
telephone visit, 100
television, 1, 42
temperaments, four classic, 76
term, 3,
terminology, 3
theology, 16
   faculty of, 17
theory, theories, 18ff.
   substantive, 19, 22ff.
time, 14, 177
time shifting, 142, 143
towns, 47
trade, international, 170
transportation, 1, 71, 125, 170, 173
triad, 87
turn-taking, 85
TV program preferences, stability of,
   162
TV relations, 159ff.
TV/VCR viewing
   effects of, on self esteem, 163ff.
   gender roles and aggressiveness, 166ff.
   and listening to music, 156ff.
   and obesity, 169
   and social mobility, 167ff.
typology, 3ff., 9, 15

uncertainty avoidance, 126
understanding, 4
UNESCO, 24, 176
United Nations, 48, 117, 176, 177ff.
United States, 176, 192
universities, 110
uses and gratifications, 20ff.

value orientation, 54
value system, 53, 57
Verfremdung, 116

vertebrates, 27
video, 142
   camera, 142
   cassette recorder, 142ff.
   clips, 193
   conference, 100
Vikings, the, 174
Voice of America, 192
Völkerwanderung, 174
   period of, 173

Wall, Chinese, 110
Watergate, 111
way of life, 62

weak tie, 96, 98
working group, 13
World Bank, 107
World System, 11
Word War, the First, 176
Word War, the Second, 174ff.
World Wide Web (WWW), 44, 102, 140,
   143, 196ff.
writing, 42

youth culture, 193

zero, concept of, 43